Other books in The New Explorer series:

Red Salmon, Brown Bear by Theodore J. Walker

The Armies of the Ant by Charles L. Hogue

The Blue Reef by Walter Starck

ABOVE TIMBERLINE

ABOVE TIMBERLINE

A Wildlife Biologist's Rocky Mountain Journal

by DWIGHT SMITH

Edited by ALAN ANDERSON, JR.

Alfred A. Knopf   New York   1981

THIS IS A BORZOI BOOK
PUBLISHED BY ALFRED A. KNOPF, INC.

Copyright © 1980 by Alan Landsburg Productions, Inc.

Created by Alan Landsburg Productions, Inc.

Grateful acknowledgment is made to several friends of Dwight Smith for the use of their photographs in the picture section. They are: Bruce Johnson for his shots of the bighorn sheep, the pika, and alpine forget-me-nots; Stephen Torbit for the elk; William Alldredge for the pine marten; Clait Braun for the ptarmigan.

Library of Congress Cataloging in Publication Data

Smith, Dwight R   Above timberline.

(New explorer series)
Includes index.
1. Natural history—Rocky Mountains.   2. Smith, Dwight R.
3. Biologists—United States—Biography.
I. Anderson, Alan, [date]   II. Title.   III. Series.
QH104.5.R6S64   591.978   80-7618
ISBN 0-394-40037-2

Manufactured in the United States of America

FIRST EDITION

The following acknowledgments of sources were omitted from the copyright page:

For descriptions of the pika (p. 16) and of the adaptation and pollination of plants in the alpine (pp. 52, 53, 103): *Land Above the Trees*, by Ann Zwinger and Beatrice Willard (1972). By permission of Harper & Row Publishers.

For the discussion of "red snow" (pp. 217-19): "What Colors the Mountain Snow," by Robert Pollock (*Sierra Club Bulletin* 55, 4 [April 1970]: 18–20). By permission of the Sierra Club.

For descriptions of many of the mammals—in particular those of the elk, montane vole, snowshoe hare, beaver, coyote, red squirrel, and red fox (pp. 29–30, 67–8, 101, 106–7, 157, 188): *Rocky Mountain Mammals*, by David M. Armstrong (1975). By permission of the publisher, The Rocky Mountain Nature Association.

CONTENTS

Eight pages of illustrations
will be found following page 138.

INTRODUCTION

Above Timberline is the fourth volume of The New Explorer series, a project initiated by Alan Landsburg Productions of Los Angeles. The idea of the series: to immerse a biologist in a natural environment for an extended period, alone, far from any laboratory or highway. Each biologist was asked to observe his environment and the organisms sharing it with him, and to record those observations on tape at the end of each day. The goal of the series: to understand not only the creatures and rhythms of that natural place, but also the ties between those creatures and rhythms and the human life of the biologist himself.

For the first three volumes, Dr. Theodore J. Walker studied a remote Alaskan lake (*Red Salmon, Brown Bear*); Dr. Charles L. Hogue the Costa Rican rain forest (*The Armies of the Ant*); and Dr. Walter Starck the remote Pacific atoll of Enewetak (*The Blue Reef*). For this one, Dr. Dwight Smith, a wildlife biologist at Colorado State University, spent four and a half months just below the Continental Divide in Colorado's Rocky Mountains, living in an eighty-five-year-old cabin that had been the center of a gold-mining operation. There he studied, ate, and kept his primitive house, alone except for occasional visitors. He came to know not only the hardy plants and animals of this region but also what it is like to live in such a high, cold, and windy place.

Dwight Smith's personal environment was complex. For much of the time he lived at Brown's Cabin his activities resembled those of the animals he studied. He, like them, braved the lightning storms, sudden blizzards, treacherous stream crossings, and bitter cold that characterize alpine ecosystems. And he lived, also, with the human frustrations of poor communications, imperfect technology, and the intrusion of civilization in the form of noisy, go-anywhere motorcycles that gullied the fragile tundra and shattered the tranquility of the mountains. Finally, he faced the loneliness of life far from family and friends, in a wilderness where the jays and marmots and chipmunks were his only companions.

Physically, Dwight Smith responded to his surroundings much as any organism would—he adapted. He became for part of a year a creature of his environment, breathing the thin air, drinking pure water from a spring, feeling the cold bite of the alpine wind. His body responded to it: His legs and lungs grew strong, his skin toughened against the cold. He found he could hike all day with a heavy pack at 12,000 feet; he learned to "navigate" the dense forests of spruce and fir without getting lost; he let his hair and beard grow long for the first time and enjoyed the feeling. He became, for four and a half months, a part of the natural world Above Timberline.

Smith's existence at Brown's Cabin, like that of the plants and animals he lived with, was shaped more than anything else by altitude. Brown's Cabin sits 11,740 feet above sea level—an elevation above which few trees can survive. It is 400 yards or so below a crossing in the Continental Divide called Brown's Pass. Both cabin and pass are named after Homer Brown, the miner who built the cabin and who crossed the pass countless times on his way to and from civilization.

The Continental Divide is America's great watershed, a dividing line between east and west. If we imagine a large raindrop falling on the topmost point of Brown's Pass and splitting in two, half would end up in the Gulf of Mexico, by way of the Mississippi River, and half in the Gulf of California, by way of the Colorado River. The western half of the raindrop would, after joining countless other raindrops, slide past Brown's Cabin on its way to fast-flowing Texas Creek, the Taylor and Gunnison rivers, and eventually the Colorado at Grand Junction. The eastern half would twist and trickle to become Denny Creek, then Cottonwood Creek, then the Arkansas River at Buena Vista, the small town some ten airline miles from the cabin, which was Smith's link with the outside world.

The Continental Divide lies like the spine of a vast dinosaur, reaching 3,000 miles from New Mexico to the Bering Strait. The reason this mountainous beast is so high and mighty is that it is so young. The Rockies are adolescents as mountains go, having buckled upward only at the end of the Cretaceous Period, some 65 million years ago. The Appalachians, by contrast, began to form 300 to 400 million years ago, and have been worn down since then by eons or erosion.

It was appropriate that Dwight Smith went to Brown's Cabin as a biologist specializing in large mammals. The birth of the Rockies coincided with the beginning of the age of mammals—and the two events were strongly related. Before the Rockies rose, North America was mostly a low-lying land of swamps in a warm climate. For some 250 million years, large reptiles, including dinosaurs, had ruled the continent, flourishing amid these swamps and their lush plant growth. The few mammals that lived during this, the Mesozoic Era, remained small and insignificant. The best they could do amid this landscape of giants was to bide their time, second-class citizens keeping out of the way and surviving on insects and seeds.

But as the Mesozoic Era drew to a close and the Cenozoic began, the face of the earth changed. The continent rose in a paroxysm of mountain building, and as it did so it became drier and colder. The broad lowland swamps became uplands and the dinosaurs disappeared. For the first time the cold-hardy mammal, with its insulating fur and ability to maintain a warm body temperature, emerged in spectacular fashion. Mammalian fauna exploded in what seemed like a fit of evolutionary exuberance, producing horselike herbivores with short hind legs, primitive deer with many antlers, the massive *Uintatherium* with long knobs on its head, the twelve-foot-long *Brontotherium*, a horned gopher with huge claws—flat-footed plant-eaters of every description. Most of these clumsy beasts lived in forests where they had no need for speed, relying on concealment to escape their predators. Nor had they a need for efficient, grinding teeth, since they simply swallowed the lush foliage that grew so abundantly.

The land continued to rise, and the Rockies rose fastest of all, great folds of old sediment bent upward by unspeakably great forces within the earth. The folds that formed the Front Range, west of Denver, are 10,000 to 20,000 feet thick; similar folds created the ridge above Brown's Cabin.

Even as these mighty folds rose, rainfall and streamflow began the inexorable process of wearing them down again, carving ditches, canyons, and finally broad valleys that carried eroded sediment toward the sea. Most of this sediment did not reach the sea, however. The young downcutting rivers gradually slowed, choked by their own tremendous sediment load. The valleys were filled; then the hills between the valleys were buried, until the whole vast region to the east was virtually level. That region today is known as the Great Plains. To the west, the sediment formed large alluvial fans in the geologically still-active Basin and Range Province between the Rockies and the Pacific coastal mountains.

The Rocky Mountains, then, were part of a process that gave mammals the evolutionary edge over reptiles and amphibians. Now conditions in the Rockies proceeded to change those same mammals. These towering mountains, higher 40 and 50 million years ago than they are today, blocked much of the moist air flowing eastward from the Pacific. Precipitation diminished in the "rain shadow" east of them, and the land grew drier. The woodlands gave way to grasslands and the browsers gave way to grazers, whose high-enamel teeth were tough enough to chew the dusty, silica-rich grasses, and a variety of rodents. Today, some 65 million years after the Rockies began to rise, the Great Plains are drier than ever. It is hard to imagine that dinosaurs once found comfort there.

At Brown's Cabin, of course, conditions are even more extreme, and mammals completely dominate the fauna. Only one cold-blooded animal lives above the tree line in that area—a boreal chorus frog—and Dwight Smith saw none of them during his entire stay. The chief handicap of cold-blooded animals—reptiles, fishes, amphibians—is that they cannot control their body temperature. When the outside temperature drops, they become sluggish and eventually cease to function. David Armstrong, in *Rocky Mountain Mammals*, writes that there are at most 11 species of reptiles and amphibians in all of Rocky Mountain National Park, less than one fifth the number of mammals. In Costa Rica, by contrast, where the climate is mild, there are 320 species of reptiles and amphibians and 200 species of mammals.

Winter, of course, is the worst of times above timberline, a time even the mammals try to avoid. The larger animals, like elk and mule deer, move to lower elevations. The smaller ones either hibernate, like the marmot; store food, like the pika; or feed on those that store food, like the weasel. Only one species of bird winters here—the ptarmigan, whose chunky body shape is well designed to retain heat.

Perhaps the most stressful feature of alpine living is the wind, which causes the rapid loss of both heat and water from organisms. To survive here during even the nonwinter months, most animals wear thick coatings of fat and fur. In addition, they find shelter to avoid strong winds. Large animals use the terrain, getting on the lee side of rocks and ridges, or they move down among the trees; small ones huddle beneath the grasses.

But the plants themselves, which cannot move, must endure the wind's full fury. Heavy ground winds can cause plants to droop and shrivel as though struck by drought. Wind is especially destructive if the soil is dry or frozen, which prevents the roots from absorbing moisture.

Wind also determines the shape of the plants that can live here. Alpine plants are characterized by their stunted form, which keeps them close to the ground and out of the wind. Stems are slender, short, and have few branches. Even so, flowers are the same size as their low-altitude counterparts, so that the wildflower season here is all the more startling for its beauty.

Alpine plants resist wind damage by a number of strategies. Most remain short, small, and compact (cushion plants like moss campion and phlox; mat plants like dwarf clover and sandwort). Still others are formed in flat rosettes, store water in thick stems or leaves, and have waxy surfaces to reduce water loss to the drying winds (stonecrops, saxifages).

Wind affects the whole environment, moving soil, tearing at alpine turf, carving outcrops of rock with blasts of sand and ice, abrading stems and branches. It rearranges the snow, scouring it from a windward slope and setting it down in the lee. The placement of snow, in turn, shapes plant communities, protecting the plants beneath it, exposing the others to the fury of the elements. Melting snowbanks nourish thirsty plants near them—and retard the emergence of plants beneath them.

Another consequence of high altitude is the intense solar radiation. High lands are not shielded by the thick air that cloaks the earth's surface at lower altitudes. Brown's Cabin receives twice as much ultraviolet radiation as it would at sea level, and 25 percent more total radiation. Plants must defend themselves against this searing sunlight with light-reducing mechanisms, like the furry hairs on the tiny alpine forget-me-not. These same hairs also serve to capture the sun's warmth and hold it close to vital plant parts.

Conversely, alpine plants benefit from the intense sunlight during a growing season which is extremely brief. Snow blankets many areas until July and begins to return as early as September. In those three months or less, every plant must both manufacture and store enough food to last the winter and produce the seeds that perpetuate the species. These plants have evolved a number of tricks that make this possible. They can, for example, photosynthesize at lower temperatures than low-altitude plants, and all their life processes are accelerated. Some of them can store food and produce seeds in just one month.

A related difficulty of life in the alpine is its thin air. There are fewer molecules of nitrogen, oxygen, water vapor, and so on at Brown's Cabin than there are at sea level. Because heat is a product of the movement of molecules, alpine air retains heat poorly. As soon as the sun goes down, the temperature follows; the summer nights are commonly 30 degrees cooler than the days. Even small shade has this effect. Plants found on the sunny side of a boulder cannnot survive on the shady, colder side, where different species grow. Thus, there are many "micro-climates" in the Rockies, which change as quickly as the land rises and falls, each having its own peculiar mixture of plant species.

Another effect of thin air, and its fewer molecules, is that water molecules evaporate faster into it. Plant and animal tissues lose water easily and rainfall evaporates quickly from the soil surface. Even snow evaporates, or sublimates, reducing the total amount of moisture accessible to plants.

Plant ecology is crucial, both in the alpine and elsewhere, because plants are the world's primary producers of food, capturing energy from sunlight to convert water and carbon dioxide into starch. A huge portion of the world's biomass is plant matter, and without plants no animals would survive. Because of this dependence, plant distribution generally determines whcre animals can live. When we know the kinds of plants that grow in an area, we know what animals to look for. We learn to expect squirrels in conifer trees, prairie chickens in grassland, and beavers in stream valleys.

In studying the distribution of plants, ecologists have found in the Rockies a marked vertical zonation. The effect of climbing in the mountains is similar to that of traveling northward. If we drive from the edge of the Great Plains to the Continental Divide, we experience roughly the same changes in plant communities we would by driving 2,000 miles north. Another way of putting this is to say that the average temperature drops 3° F. as we move 1,000 feet higher—or 600 miles northward. The maximum altitude trees can survive—the timberline—drops in Colorado by some 360 feet as we move northward one degree of latitude.

Biogeographers, those who study the distribution of organisms on the earth, describe the kinds of plants that grow at different altitudes by zones. The montane zone in Central Colorado extends from 7,500 to 9,000 feet; the subalpine zone from 9,000 to 11,500 feet; and the alpine or tundra above 11,500 feet. Brown's Cabin is located on the imaginary border between the last two.

The montane zone includes more species of trees, shrubs, and mammals than the other two; its climate is least extreme. The typical montane forest is a mixture of ponderosa pine and Douglas fir, with varying amounts of limber pine on rocky outcrops, dense stands of lodgepole pine in dry areas, and aspen in moist areas. Other common trees along stream bottoms are narrowleaf and balsam poplars, alders, water birches, and, most beautiful, the Colorado blue spruces. The typical pine-fir regions are inhabited by such animals as the snowshoe hare, Abert's squirrel, black bear, and a variety of rodents.

The subalpine zone is characterized by endless tracts of Engelmann spruce–subalpine fir forest. The ground beneath this forest is the wettest part of the zone because the trees hinder evaporation of the winter snowfall. As a result, moisture-loving flowers flourish here—fairy slippers, wood nymphs, twin flowers, dotted saxifrage. Voles, chickarees (red squirrels), snowshoe hares, porcupines, and other mammals move through the shadows. The trees are interrupted irregularly by rocks, bogs, ponds, and streamside stands of quaking aspen.

At the upper edge of this zone, tree growth is progressively more restricted by the cold winds. Finally the trees become dwarfed, their trunks low along the ground, their leaves joined in a canopy three or four feet high. This fringe of dwarf trees, called Krummholz (German for "elfin timber"), tends to be closed on the windward side by a dense shield of twigs and needles.

Above the Krummholz is timberline, the end of the trees, where the alpine zone begins. Timberline swings upward and downward with local conditions. On southern and sheltered slopes, trees creep up higher; on northern and windy slopes they are beaten back. The prevalent ground cover here is grassland and rock fields. The zone is often called tundra for its similarity to the great treeless reaches of the Arctic. Alpine tundra is considered to be the region above the timberline and below the line of perpetual snow.

This is the zone of the spectacular alpine flower displays in late June and early July. They come in all colors—brilliant rainbows of reds, yellows, pinks, blues, purples, and whites. Flowers of the rose, mustard, saxifrage, aster, and other families bloom here in a profusion seen in few other environments. Remarkably, wildflower season occurs at the same time throughout the Rockies, from New Mexico to Montana. Spring comes earlier in this zone than in the subalpine. There are no trees to anchor the snow against the wind, so there is usually no snow in late spring to retard plant growth.

Beneath the flowers is a complex tapestry of species, mats of low grasses, sedges, and forbs over thin soil. This tight turf provides food and cover for ground squirrels, pocket gophers, voles, and mice, and good grazing for the herds of elk, deer, and bighorn sheep that summer at high altitudes. Amid the many rock fields on the tundra are pikas, marmots, and pocket gophers, which find shelter there from weasels, foxes, hawks, and other predators.

Near Brown's Cabin the last flowering plants disappear at between 13,500 and 14,000 feet. Beyond the alpine zone only mosses, then liverworts, and finally lichens can survive. Above the line of perpetual snow, life in any form becomes accidental.

None of these zones is uniform, of course; all are frequently interrupted by other plant communities or geological formations. Perhaps the most pleasing irregularities are the montane and subalpine "parks," so named by early explorers who thought these open valleys, flowery meadows, and small groups of trees looked like cultivated European estates. Some of the largest even have formal names—Estes Park, Horseshoe Park, Taylor Park, among others.

Ecologists poorly understand why these parks become neither continuous forest nor continuous grassland. But it is certain that without them both the flora and fauna of the Rockies would be poorer. By breaking up forests, these areas produce interfaces, or ecotones, where species diversity is unusually rich. Along park margins we find great numbers of ground squirrels, voles, mice, marmots, cottontails, chipmunks, bobcats, and foxes. Elk and mule deer find these parks ideal for grazing; buffalo used to roam here. Animals seem to prefer such areas, where they can use two different habitats—especially where one offers abundant food and the other good shelter from predators and bad weather.

Another distinctive habitat is the dense lodgepole pine forests, which are almost impenetrable to humans. So little light reaches the forest floor that few herbaceous plants can grow there. Among the few animals found roaming amid the gloom are chickarees, which feed on pine nuts, and martens, which feed on chickarees.

Each of these habitats may be interrupted by streams, which invite a whole complex of willows, alders, and other moisture-loving plants, as well as the shrews, beavers, muskrats, long-tailed voles, jumping mice, and weasels that congregate in such an environment.

Every plant community is established by a process known as plant succession. This is simply a formal term for the gradual take-over of an area by the species or group of species best suited to that environment. Once that species or group is dominant, the community is said to be at the climax stage, or mature. The climax community for the montane zone is ponderosa pine–Douglas fir; for the subalpine zone, Engelmann spruce–subalpine fir; for alpine zones, grasses and other small plants.

When a climax community is destroyed, as by fire, insect infestation, or clearing for pasture, it may be slow to return. The intermediary steps may take many decades, or even centuries. If a stand of Douglas fir is burned, it may be replaced by a dense growth of lodgepole pine, which gives way only grudgingly to the return of the Douglas fir climax forest.

If trees and grasses are the common dominants in a climax community, lichens are the hardy pioneers that begin the process of plant succession. These are the colored patches often found on exposed rocks and trees, ranging in color from gray to grayish green, dull yellow, orange, and black. Lichens are not simple plants but partnerships of symbiotic algae and fungi. These primitive teams combine talents to eke a living out of the poorest situations, such as bare rock. The fungi provide structural stability and absorb moisture, while the algae convert sunlight into food. Tiny rootlike hairs secrete acids and pry into cracks in rock, speeding the process of rock disintegration known as weathering.

When a lichen dies, its own detritus drops to the ground, along with air-blown dust, bits of rock, and other fragments, gradually allowing mosses and larger plants to gain a root-hold. Eventually these hardy pioneers are crowded out by grasses and other invading species which then flourish in the conditions created for them. All of the Rocky Mountains was once bare rock, and each expanse of soil we see today, supporting flowery meadows or mighty forests, represents a triumph that took millions of years to achieve.

To be immersed in such a landscape is to be humbled. Dwight Smith noted almost daily the emotion he felt hiking those huge landscapes, and remarked on the smallness of a single man against the sweep of these mountains. Who is man to be here, to be spying on the proud elk, stepping on the lowly lichen? To study such a place is to know how awesome is creation, how immeasurable the tiny lives and deaths that converted the stark rock of early time to the richness of life we see today.

When I took the job of editing Dwight Smith's tapes—they came to nearly 1,200 manuscript pages when typed—I faced the quandary of anyone who presumes to edit someone else's words. I had to choose what to include and what to leave out. The effect of this choosing is to reshape the original speaker, producing a new creation, a hybrid human with a personality that may or may not be faithful to the original.

Yet despite this danger, which I found to be real, I had the fun of growing to know another person well, and the adventure of listening in as he exclaimed and meditated aloud in the privacy of Brown's Cabin. As I grew to know his moods and habits, I came to feel that he was speaking ultimately to me, through his tape recorder.

There was adventure, too, in listening to Dwight change. As the seasons went by, his solitude deepened. On the early tapes his concerns were vigorously practical—setting up his equipment, trying out his photography, getting acquainted with the tundra.

But as the weeks passed he began to make time for himself. His thoughts dwelled not only on what was before him—the plants, the animals, the mountains—but also on what lay behind and ahead—his job, his family, his career. As he reflected on his career and his personal history, he found himself saying things he had never said before. He was speaking in private, several hours' hard hiking from any other human, yet in the presence of tapes that were almost certain to find their way to the hands and ears of a typist, several editors, and perhaps thousands of readers. It almost seemed that the possibility of an audience was helping him call forth new thoughts and shape them into words.

His thinking went even further. It went not only ahead and behind himself, but also beyond himself—to the meaning of his life; to his mission, if any; to his creator. The tone of his remarks became profoundly confessional as he wrestled with those knotty "shoulds" and "oughts" that so few of us have time for back down here, off the mountain.

Dwight was no stranger to wilderness living. He was born in near-wilderness, in rural Idaho, and did much of his early research alone in remote regions of the west. It is likely that he had similar insights during other solitary adventures, studying bighorn sheep for his master's degree, working for the Forest Service. But we have no record of those thoughts. Indeed, we have few records of the thoughts of anyone living in conditions of prolonged isolation and natural splendor.

A project conceived for the purpose of knowing an environment has done that and more, bringing us also the interior environment of the scientist, the daily flow of his emotions and reflections.

For Dwight, his stay in the mountains had many of the qualities of a retreat—discipline, hardship, physical work, prolonged silence. His own frailty in the vast extent of nature became overwhelming—as did his own vast importance. It was a time when the scientist learned as much about himself as he did about the mountains.

Alan Anderson, Jr.

Mars Hill, N.C.
January 1980

Part I

SNOWMELT

June 15

Today is the first day at Brown's Cabin, which was named after Homer Brown, who prospected here for gold. I am about 12,000 feet above sea level, near the Continental Divide, ninety miles or so southwest of Denver. I'll be here for about five months.

It has been a busy day. An Army helicopter from Fort Carson, near Colorado Springs, has brought in nine loads of cargo and people, including me.

June 16

Well, I see that I didn't say much yesterday. By the time we had moved the cargo in and cleaned up the cabin a bit, we were all so exhausted there seemed little point in narrating at length. Now I'm sitting on a large rock two hundred yards above the cabin at our "heliport." It is the closest spot of bare ground we could find for a safe landing. Between here and the cabin the snow ranges from one to three and a half feet deep and it is melting rapidly. As I watch it go I want to get down some of my thoughts about starting this segment of The New Explorer series.

At 7 a.m. Monday I loaded myself, my wife Carol, my son Mark, and some of my gear into our Volkswagen and drove from Fort Collins, where we live, to Salida. There we met with Ross Moser, the district forest ranger, and Bill Nelson, his new assistant, who will be helping me this summer. We went over the list of supplies I would need and the schedules I would follow during the next five months.

Our farewells were not sorrowful; I have spent a good deal of time alone in the wilderness, and my family is accustomed to long absences. But we were a little concerned about our son Gary, who left home Friday

3

for Maine. There he is going into a partnership with Henry Briggs of Skowhegan, a nature photographer and lecturer. Gary has just graduated from high school and this is his first attempt at making a living on his own.

The trip in was very smooth, and Forest Service cooperation has been excellent. Two men from Pike National Forest came to help load cargo, two others from San Isabel National Forest brought two truckloads of equipment to the airport, and an electronics technician came to check out conditions for radio communication. I did get a bit of a jolt during a chat with one of the helicopter pilots. "You know," he said, "this is the first time I have ever flown heavy loads at such high elevations." I was glad he told me that on the ground. We had brought about 5,000 pounds of cargo, including twelve bottles of propane, fifteen boxes of firewood, photographic supplies, food, and other gear that I would need.

The electronics technician delivered an unfavorable verdict. He decided that I will not be able to communicate with the outside world with ordinary equipment. However, they are going to set up a repeater station on a mountain knob southeast of the cabin. If this system works, I will be able to contact Charlie Combs in Buena Vista and the Forest Service at Salida. Charlie holds the mining claims to the land Brown's Cabin's on.

Conditions at the cabin are depressing, though almost exactly what I had expected. A young man named Rodgers had used the place last fall as a hunting camp and failed utterly to clean it up. There were dirty dishes, garbage in pasteboard boxes and buckets, and filth everywhere. The shed at the end of the cabin is filled with rotten hay, three bags of grain, horse manure, and about two feet of ice.

Although the Colorado mountain men were the salt of the earth in many ways, they were not the neatest breed. I think it is fair to say that most of the junk brought to Brown's Cabin since it was built eighty-five years ago is still here. So one of my evening chores will be to put in a few minutes every day digging a huge hole, into which I am going to shovel all this trash.

Spring is arriving rapidly, almost visibly, moment by moment. We saw deer tracks in the snow and a red fox on the way in. A number of early-flowering plants are already in bloom; a week ago they were buried by snow. Just three days ago Charlie Combs cut a trench from the cabin to the springs, exposing some branches of willow. Now the catkins, or pussy willows, are already swelling with the promise of spring.

The alpine weather showed off its versatility yesterday evening. At about eight-thirty we had lightning and thunder, followed by severe hail, followed by sleet and snow, followed by a light rain. At eleven-thirty I looked out the window to see a sky of deep blue-black, filled with unimaginably brilliant stars.

I am surprised by a feeling of wanting all the crew to leave. While everyone has been tremendously helpful in getting me set up, I am anxious to have things exactly as I want them and to be alone here.

June 17

Two young men from Colorado State University, Kirk Berger and Jim Bolick, left at 7 a.m. today, before breakfast. They had completed some movie and still photography for the university, where I teach. Jim hopes to have a three- or four-minute special on a Denver television program. Although Kirk and Jim thought this alpine setting was terribly romantic, I think neither was sorry to be leaving. They helped bring three loads of propane down from the heliport and the high altitude seemed to be getting to them. Kirk in particular was complaining of nausea, headache, and excessive weariness. So far, luckily, I have not been bothered.

June 18

Charlie Combs left at 8 a.m., so Brown's Cabin is now my exclusive and private abode. I walked half a mile down to the head of Denny Creek with Charlie, then returned and did a little investigation of the basin I am living in. It is a bad time for foot travel. The snow is too deep for normal walking, and I must wear snowshoes although the snow is too wet for easy snowshoeing. In other places there are large bare areas where I have to take the snowshoes off.

Last night I had my first animal visitor. About midnight I heard some gnawing downstairs (there is an upstairs room in the cabin for sleeping). I went down to investigate. Something had found its way into one of the boxes of food and selected a piece of Canadian bacon to eat. The something, however, was unable to carry the bacon down through a hole in the floor and was attempting to enlarge the hole. It vanished just as I got down, so I put the bacon back in the box, and the box on the kitchen table. About forty-five minutes later I heard more gnawing and some thumping in the kitchen. This time the target was my bread supply. I improvised a heavy cover for the box and went back to bed. Charlie, meanwhile, slept soundly.

I assumed the culprit was a wood rat, also called a pack rat, but

Charlie told me this morning that in his thirty-five years at Brown's Cabin he had never seen a wood rat. He thought it was a pine marten. And it turns out he was right, because this afternoon when I was working in the kitchen I followed a noise into the other room to discover a marten walking slowly toward a hole we hadn't patched yet. The marten is a large, weasel-like animal, quite beautiful and relatively unafraid of humans. This one behaved coolly, ambling slowly to the hole, pausing at the entrance for a long glance at me, then slipping through.

Let me give a brief description of the marten, as I shall for the principal characters who share the mountainside with me, so that readers can visualize how they fit into this very special environment. The pine marten (*Martes americana*) belongs to the family Mustelidae, which includes weasels, badgers, skunks, and otters. It is medium-sized as mustelids go, weighing up to four pounds and resembling a huge brownish squirrel. This comparison is apt beyond looks: the marten leaps through trees with squirrel-like agility, and in this area it is often leaping *after* red squirrels, which are its primary food source.

Even when bounding along as pedestrians, making rippling three-foot leaps over the ground, martens are graceful animals as well as beautiful ones. They are also called American sables, and their fur is of such high quality that they have been overtrapped throughout much of their original range, which extended eastward to Illinois and Ohio. Today they are found mostly in Alaska, Canada, and the mountains of the American West. They are intelligent and curious, features that often lead them into traps set for bobcats and other animals.

Like other weasels, martens sleep soundly and awake in a great burst of activity. They hunt summer and winter, by day and night, racing after birds and squirrels in the trees; mice, chipmunks, and rabbits in the meadows; marmots and pikas in the rock piles. They prefer to hunt at night, but I've seen them out during the day as well; their habits, unlike those of many other creatures here, seem to be governed by their stomachs more than the hour.

After mating occurs during the summer, fetal development is extremely slow. By a feat of adaptation, the beginning of life for young martens is delayed, and it is not until about eight months later that the female produces her litter of one to five blind, one-ounce baby martens. Then, as the alpine summer begins, the young grow quickly. Their eyes are open by six weeks after birth, and they reach full size in about three months. This adaptational response to the brief summer is one we shall observe in both animals and plants around Brown's Cabin.

Later in the afternoon I had the door open and a Clark's nutcracker flew in, found the Profile wheat bread, and demolished three or four slices. Using the butcher knife, I carefully cut out the pecked area, salvaging the remainder of the loaf. This bird (Latin name *Nucifraga columbiana*) is unmistakable in the mountain landscape. It is about a foot long—very nearly as large as a crow—and very aggressive around humans. Its harsh, rattling call—*char-r-r char-r*—is so conspicuous that it became for me one of the biological landmarks of the Brown's Cabin area.

To complete my animal stories for the day, I was going out of the cabin to perform my final bodily functions for the evening when I almost tripped over a porcupine. I picked up a stick and heaved it at the porky, which ambled away a few feet, then turned and looked at me reproachfully. I felt disgusted with myself for having tried to drive away this little animal. In the past, when I worked in the woods logging, I had been trained to believe that the only good porcupine was a dead porcupine, because of their habit of feeding on certain desirable species of trees. But I have come to believe that we must think about the importance of each species in different ways; certainly I'm going to have to improve my attitude toward some of my new neighbors. And, to be honest, I must admit that this lumbering creature is one of the most astonishing animals. Any animal willing to carry, lifelong, a prickly armor of some 30,000 barbed quills so that it may peacefully eat tree bark deserves some respect.

Porcupines (*Erethizon dorsatum*) are adaptable enough to live nearly everywhere in these mountains, though they prefer the dense stands of willows. In the summer they feed on herbs, and in other seasons on bark, choosing the succulent inner bark of conifers when possible. This inner bark, or cambium, is rich in stored sugars and starches, providing a surprisingly robust diet. They may also eat the bark, leaves, and twigs of broad-leafed trees, and at times they gnaw the bark all the way around a trunk, usually near the top. It is this girdling that kills or deforms a tree, by interrupting the flow of food from leaves to roots, and earns the porky its low reputation among foresters.

Oh, and they do not shoot their quills. In fact, they never attack in any way. They will, it is true, swing their tails if chased closely, but that is the extent of this creature's aggressiveness. Passive resistance is usually adequate, because the merest touch will dislodge a quill, which has a painful tendency to work deeper into the tender tissue of a hand or nose the longer it remains. The best way to remove one is to give it a quick twist rather than drawing it straight out, which tends to rip the skin.

It is hard to believe, but even this forbidding quill-bearer is not without enemies. Coyotes, bobcats, and mountain lions are known to attack them when times are hard, flipping them onto their backs to get at the quill-less belly. Although there are none in Colorado, the most effective porcupine killer is the fisher, a large, aggressive relative of the marten that can weigh twelve pounds or more. In boreal forests where fishers are abundant, few porcupines are found. But most predators, at most times, will avoid porcupines; occasionally, dead or dying carnivores are found bearing a mouthful of quills as mute testimony to the difficulty of getting past the porky's defense.

This plodding creature, surprisingly, has a romantic streak. Its courtship behavior is elaborate. The male wanders in search of a female for great distances, relative to his ground speed, and as he goes, he "sings" in a falsettolike voice. Once he finds her, they rub noses and he may shower her with urine in a burst of passion. She often responds by squalling loudly; then copulation is accomplished, in more restrained fashion.

June 19

Last night, my first night alone, was quiet; all the other snorers and interesting noisemakers were gone. I had the first good night's sleep since coming up here.

In the morning I tried to start the generator, without success. Although the dealer in Salt Lake City knew the exact elevation here, I suspect the regulator is not the correct one for this altitude. Until it runs I have no electricity for lights; nor can I charge the batteries that power the movie cameras.

I spent much of the day battling the garbage and left-over equipment around the cabin. I can't get much of a feeling for the natural environment when the immediate surroundings resemble a junkyard.

I also spent a little time brushing up on identification of early spring plants and the songbirds.

June 20

The snow is reasonably firm until about 9 a.m., when it begins to soften. Then I have to put on snowshoes to get around, and even so I sink in a foot or two.

There is a predictable pattern to the weather. The mornings are splendors, calm and extremely clear; not a cloud. Then toward noon the wind begins to rise and the clouds come in. They may or may not produce a short storm. Today the clouds dropped some rain and sleet, but only for a few minutes at a time.

I was awakened again, about midnight, by a humming below my window. I went to the kitchen door to find that a porcupine was serenading. He was standing on the walkway where he would have to jump about ten feet to the ground to escape. He didn't, and I didn't want to force him, so I went back to bed. He woke me again at 2 a.m. and though he was far off key, even to my untrained ear, I did not intervene.

June 21

This morning I took the 16-mm. movie camera up to the Brown's Pass area and photographed a number of blue grouse snow-nesting sites. These big birds—the males are about twenty-two inches in length and two and a half to three pounds in weight—often come into an area such as this during the wintertime and allow themselves to be buried by falling snow. This helps insulate them from the cold; especially from the cutting mountain wind. They may emerge to feed, then return to the same nest at night.

Although I had been reading up in the instruction manual about the 16-mm. camera, I realized that I was confused about the filters, some of which were new to me. I decided to go to Buena Vista and call Los Angeles to find out about them.

I left the cabin at noon and was at the road around two o'clock. I was lucky to catch a ride into Buena Vista within a few minutes. I called Don Velasquez, chief of the communications section in the regional Forest Service office in Denver, and he was very encouraging about bringing me a battery-powered relay station for the two-way radio—a station that is now on a mountain in Wyoming. I may not be able to communicate with the Forest Service in Salida, but I will be able to talk with Charlie in Buena Vista, who can then relay messages by phone. This will be convenient because Charlie will be available in the evenings, whereas I would have to call the Forest Service between eight and five.

I reached the people in L.A. and learned about filters. Then, after picking up the mail and a few supplies I needed, I had dinner with Charlie and Mrs. Combs. He brought me back to the mouth of Denny Creek at a quarter to seven. It is considered a two-and-a-half-hour hike from there in to the cabin, so I was pleased to be able to make it with a fairly heavy pack in two hours and twenty-two minutes. It looks as if jogging three miles a day back home has a practical use, after all.

When I got to the cabin it was obvious that the marten had been busy during my absence. The chip bucket, wastepaper baskets, and wood box all had been overturned, and he'd helped himself to more bread. I've been covering holes with chicken wire, but obviously there is at least one more.

June 22

This morning I returned to the Brown's Pass area to photograph the blue grouse snow-nesting site. I was armed with my new information about filters and the operation went smoothly.

This bird, by the way, is usually found in the conifer forests, where its mottled plumage blends well with the environment. It belongs to the same family as the chicken, and has earned the nicknames of pine hen and fool hen. It may, when disturbed, jump onto a low branch and simply look around, offering an easy target for hunters.

To humans, and perhaps to the grouse themselves, the most interesting part of their behavior is the mating ritual. The male displays in spectacular fashion, perhaps mounting a fallen log to strut around with wings lowered and tail erect, his neck puffing and swelling. The feathers on his sides spread and turn outward, forming white rosettes, and a large red sac on its neck fills with air.

A female may watch this magnificent display from among nearby shrubbery. Eventually he struts toward her, his fiery comblike wattles distended above his eyes. He bows low and abruptly deflates the air sacs, expelling air with a deep booming sound which can be heard at great distances.

As for the female, her strong suit is modesty, being so inconspicuous when incubating eggs in her crude ground nest as to be nearly invisible. She is so confident of her invisibility that she may sit tight before an advancing human until almost stepped on.

There were no grouse here to step on, of course—just lots of snow. Since I still had some film left, I decided to photograph the snow-melting process, which is now well under way. Water is a crucial natural resource in the Rocky Mountain area. Up here, where it is produced, it is of high quality, coming crystal clear from the snowfields. As the water passes from the alpine zone into the spruce-fir forest, down through the Douglas fir and ponderosa pine regions, on down through the brushy foothills, and finally out to the plains, there are many opportunities for it to become polluted. Long before this water reaches the Colorado border it is a vastly changed product from what I see here.

While I was there, I took a look at the old ore mill, which has an interesting history. Apparently an 1876 steam engine was brought up here, in 1885, to power the mill, and even though it has not been used for a good many decades the boiler and much of the equipment are still intact. Most of the building that used to shelter it has fallen down around it, however, and Charlie Combs has proposed to the Forest Service that it be restored; he would like to see this whole area made into a historic site.

I view that idea with mixed emotions. I certainly agree that the old mill, which was put in and operated only by tremendous human effort, has great historical significance. But much of the value would be lost by trying to make it an attraction. There are more obvious historical artifacts in well-known communities, like Central City and Cripple Creek, where the average tourist has highway access to facilities. Although perhaps I am being overprotective of Brown's Cabin.

June 23

Today I filmed the results of pocket gopher activity. Their fresh spring mounds and "soil casts" from winter burrows contrast against the vegetation they lie on, last year's dull-colored plant remains. The activity of this rodent, the Northern pocket gopher (*Thomomys talpoides*), is important in the ecology of most wild areas in western United States and Canada. As it digs its burrow, the pocket gopher brings the soil, often mineral-rich, to the surface. Once the burrow is complete, the rodent hauls grasses and forbs belowground and stores them for winter consumption. (Forb is a catchall term used to describe all nonwoody flowering plants that are not grasses.) Seldom is all this vegetable matter eaten, so its organic content is added to the deeper levels of soil. This mixing of minerals upward and organic matter downward is critical in improving and even creating these alpine soils.

It would be difficult to overemphasize the role of these animals. David Armstrong, author of *Rocky Mountain Mammals,* calls their work a "biological excavation service." The two most important factors controlling alpine vegetation patterns are probably (1) the length of time snow remains on the ground and (2) the work of the pocket gophers. There are few situations in nature where an animal, rather than environmental forces, controls an ecosystem to the extent that this rodent does.

The pocket gopher is a creature known almost wholly by its works. It is rarely seen aboveground, where it would be as awkward as a seal on dry land. One writer calls them the "gnomes of the mammal world," and they are so perfectly adapted to digging that their movement through the earth has been likened to swimming. The eyes and ears are greatly reduced, and its front toes are greatly enlarged into digging claws. It is powerfully built, with a compact, thickset body some eight inches long and half a pound in weight. The body begins with a set of long, yellow-orange incisors. These teeth are always in view because the lips close behind them—an unusual arrangement that allows the animal to "swim" along carrying rocks and debris between the teeth without swallowing a flow of soil. For the same reason, it has exterior cheek pouches for transporting the variety of plant matter that serves as food. These pouches are fur-lined and reversible, so that the gopher can easily discharge their contents.

The output of this furry digging machine is prodigious. A single burrow system may be 500 feet long, ranging from four to eighteen inches below the surface. Twenty or more individuals may build tunnels in a single acre, and one researcher has estimated that a dense population can move between four and eight tons of soil per acre per year. In this entire maze, it is rare to find even one of the entrances, which are plugged with soil when not in use.

All this digging, of course, may undermine the soil so that the surface caves in when walked on. This earns the ire of stock owners, who blame gophers for an occasional sprained or broken leg among their cattle and horses. Pocket gopher populations are restrained somewhat by coyotes and badgers, and to a lesser extent by weasels and owls. But this small animal has a remarkably high rate of reproduction, and populations of the forty species of gophers flourish throughout its range, which covers most of North America except for the eastern seaboard. Both public agencies and private individuals try to eradicate these animals through the use of poison and other means, and I'll have more to say about that later.

In spring, when the pocket gophers' attention turns to procreation, conditions for digging are poor. The soil tends to be either frozen or saturated with snowmelt. So they carve nesting chambers within the snowpack itself. They also make snow tunnels, packed with soil, two to four inches in diameter and several feet in length. Long after the snow is gone, the molded soil, or "soil casts," from these tunnels remains a conspicuous feature of the mountain landscape.

By the time I returned this afternoon, the marten had been in the cabin again despite my work with chicken wire. Food and equipment were strewn around the kitchen floor, and one of the Forest Service radios had been turned on. I wonder if the marten was broadcasting the good news about the bread and Canadian bacon.

June 24

I took some footage of a yellow-bellied marmot to determine if the noise of the camera disturbs these small animals. It does. I tried shooting at a distance of about forty feet, and the marmot was clearly startled. This leads me to agree with my photographer friends, who warned me that I'd need some sort of device to muffle the noise. (I was later able to photograph a bee feeding on the pollen of a willow, but most of the animals I want are more self-conscious.)

I came across some of the strange-looking slush that forms almost daily on certain ponds at this time of year. In the mornings, at the base of some of the larger snowfields, there is a marshy area which warms up as the day progresses. As the snowmelt comes down, it swells this damp area into an icy pond covered with an inch or two of slush. I picked up a handful and found it to have the consistency of the orange crush you can buy at a drive-in.

These ponds are not only strange but also dangerous. Two men and a boy from Idaho Falls recently slid into one while climbing in the Tetons. They couldn't get back out and all three drowned. News of this disaster has been on the radio for the last two nights, and needless to say I've been very cautious when crossing a snowfield that has one of these ponds at its foot.

This morning shortly after breakfast I heard an ungodly squalling from a rocky promontory above the cabin. I ran out and a minute later saw a marmot hobbling painfully up through the rocks. It seemed to have lost a battle. Later, on the way to Brown's Pass, I was going past the same promontory when a second marmot, apparently the winner of that battle, came out on a rock to watch me. I decided to test the sound of the movie camera on a victorious marmot. It turned out that he was no braver than an ordinary marmot, immediately twitching his head from side to side as the sound began and soon vanishing among the rocks.

I have taken some footage of tire tracks made by all-terrain vehicles up here, to illustrate how damaging and long-lasting they are. There are no restrictions against these vehicles in national forests. The ones I filmed were in the San Isabel National Forest, on the other side of the Continental Divide from the cabin. I have some very strong feelings about this type of use. On steep slopes, easily erodable trails, and moist areas, even the most careful driver cannot avoid creating tracks that erode to substantial ditches. And most of these drivers are anything but careful. In addition, I feel that gasoline engines are simply incompatible with most other uses of this environment. I think we cannot afford the considerable soil erosion, the gullying, the resultant invasion by undesirable types of vegetation, and the noise caused by a relatively small number of users who find it convenient to travel in these vehicles.

Some people, including many of our public land managers, hold to the philosophy that everyone has the right to see every last niche in every wild region of the country. I challenge that notion. Our nation has thousands of local, county, state, and national parks. These areas are already laced with thousands of miles of roads, as are our national forests and other public lands. People who are tied to the internal-combustion engine have many, many places they can see without wandering all over our fragile and spectacular wilderness areas. I just can't buy the argument that it is unfair—a kind of "class legislation"—to restrict certain areas to nondestructive uses. In fact, instead of following our present policy of permitting mechanized travel everywhere in a national forest unless otherwise specified, I suggest that this policy—and the philosophy behind it—be reversed. Such travel should be prohibited unless specifically *approved* for an area.

Take the Brown's Cabin area, for example. There is an old corduroy road near here that was constructed in the late 1800s. It was traveled by horses and wagons hauling ore out and supplies in. Today the logs used to build the road are pretty far gone and should be left to rot in peace. But because there are no regulations about travel, the four-wheel-drivers and the trail bikers have been attempting to use this old corduroy road, even though you can hardly see where it goes. The drivers get partway up, discover the road is doing them no good, and then light out across the meadows, tearing the hell out of them.

The next time I talk to the Forest Service people I'm going to see if we can't get a sign placed by the Hartenstein Lake road barring motorized vehicles from this area. Otherwise I wouldn't be surprised to wake up one morning to the roar of a jeep or trail bike right outside my window. This would ruin my day, and my comments would probably earn me a punch in the nose, so I want to prevent that at all costs.

I saw elk tracks nearly everywhere I walked today, as well as fresh deer tracks. These animals are rarely seen except very early or very late in the day when they feed. But now that I know they are here I'll start watching carefully. I also saw over a dozen marmots and could hear their lively calls all around the rockslides. On the domestic wildlife front, my own household marten succeeded in getting in again, eating about a third of my last loaf of bread, and scattering papers on the floor. He walked across an unfinished letter to my wife, so she will soon know what the footprint of a marten looks like. Again I made chicken-wire repairs, in hopes of getting ahead of this fellow.

June 25

Today I made an attempt with the movie camera to pan from Brown's Pass to the cabin. I don't know very much about panning technique, except that "pan" is short for "panorama," but it seems very difficult without a tripod (which I am without!). I'm getting increasingly anxious to see the Landsburg crew in here with more equipment and advice about how to use it.

This morning I left the cabin at eight-fifteen and climbed eastward to the two mines over that way. I should mention that the cabin lies in a deep basin—so deep that on June 21, the longest day of the year, the sun didn't reach me until eight-thirty in the morning. So I put a premium on sunshine.

I almost got photos of two pikas that came out to sun on a rock. Pikas, which live on mountain slopes from Alberta to New Mexico, are also called conies or rock rabbits or, since they are more often heard than seen, whistling hares. Pika colonies emit night and day an eerie cacophony of whistles and peeps that seem to come from every direction.

Unfortunately these pikas were too quick for me. It is going to take camouflage and luck to get close enough for photographs, which I certainly want to get. Pikas (*Ochotona princeps*) are unlike any other mammals, not even their cousins the rabbits and hares. Their ears are short and the tail vestigial, virtually lost in fur. A pika probably resembles a guinea pig more than any other animal, though when it sits bunched up on a rock top it looks as much like a furry egg as an animal.

Their preferred habitat is rock piles, where they find shelter and passageways safe from predators. Their biology is poorly known; they are not easy to study because of their shyness. The pika's best-known habit is building hay piles near its den. These piles, each of which may contain about a bushel of cut grass, are assumed to provide food for winter.

Pikas begin building hay piles by mid-July and continue until the fall snows cover the vegetation. Their vegetarian diet is not high in calories, so pikas must fill their stomachs almost hourly to meet their energy needs. A meadow worked by a pika looks like a new-mown lawn.

To obtain maximum value from their food, pikas re-ingest their own fecal matter, which is high in protein and energy value. They preserve body moisture by depositing almost crystalline urine, which leaves the white nitrogenous salt deposits often seen by hikers on boulder surfaces.

Pikas are active during every month of the year (I have seen them in the alpine between Christmas and New Year's Day when the weather was warm), and there is no evidence that they hibernate. Since fresh vegetation is available here only for three months or less, they must rely on stored food for nine to ten months of the year. Therefore these animals must, like any farmer, guard against spoilage. To avoid mold, each pika builds its pile gradually, so that the stems of each layer become completely dry before more is added.

I continued on past the rock, over the Divide into Kroenke Basin, which has considerably more snow than my basin. Two or three snowfields appeared to be at least thirty feet deep, so it will be a while before they melt. There are several very large and active beaver dams adjacent to Kroenke Lake, but I saw no beaver. Walking along the Divide, which is at an elevation of about 12,600 feet at that point, I encountered very high winds. There were gusts of around 50 miles per hour and I had some difficulty keeping my balance.

I shall end this day's narration on a note of success. The marten did not get into the cabin today. My own reaction to this success was peculiar, however. I felt a little lonely when I discovered the cabin empty and in order.

June 26

I have been wanting to locate some typical alpine habitats and to record seasonal changes by photographing these habitats at regular intervals throughout the summer. This morning I finally selected several, near Brown's Pass: (1) a snowmelt pond surrounded by willows, (2) a willow bog, (3) the edge of a snowfield which will ultimately become a meadow, and (4) a Krummholz, or dwarf forest, near timberline. I spent a good deal of time just sitting on a rock, looking at these four different areas, thinking about the best way to depict the ecology of each through the seasons.

This is my twelfth day at Brown's Cabin and my laundry situation is nearing a crisis. So I gave in and did it. Just as I feared, it took three hours by the time the water was carried and heated in all kinds of pots, pans, and buckets on my little wood stove and all the different categories of laundry soaked in these same containers, rubbed clean on a washboard, rinsed, and hung up. I resent spending that much time on housework, but there seems to be no alternative.

I also prepared a plywood drying rack for the plant press that I will use to preserve vegetation. When we get the generator going I can put two 100-watt bulbs under the press, and heat from the lamps will cause air to circulate upward through it, drying the plants out.

I made today what I might call the "Outhouse Resolution." I'm getting pretty tired of carrying a shovel and digging kittycat holes every day. Charlie Combs has been able to get by without even that nicety; he has just used the ground wherever he happens to be. When I pointed out the undesirability of this situation, he said that down in the timber under the snow someplace is an old outhouse. This afternoon I was wandering down among the spruce trees, and sure enough, the form of an outhouse on its side is beginning to appear. Perhaps in a few days I can find enough material to reconstruct this artifact of civilization.

June 27

Today was my first long hike through the dense spruce-fir timber that lies to the north of the cabin. The shade there is heavy and I couldn't find the Forest Service trail except on rare occasions. Most of the area was 30 to 50 percent snow-covered, with most drifts from one to three feet deep. Travel is still difficult in the basin, but improving every day. I wore rubber shoe packs rather than leather climbing shoes. The way along Texas Creek, a mile below the cabin, was steep and narrow, brushy and heavily timbered. I followed the bank for a while until it began to open into broad willow meadows. The stream is swollen with snowmelt and, surprisingly, is crystal clear. This certainly reflects the present lack of mining, grazing, logging, or other civilized activity. In most areas of the country the water at this time of year would be murky, if not completely opaque.

I saw my first elk today. It apparently was bedded in brush and timber until I came along. I looked up barely in time to see the back half of the animal and its distinguishing yellow rump patch before it disappeared. From its size I would say it was either a cow or a young bull.

I'm going to have to start talking to myself during the day. I spend all day in silence, then in the evening when I get ready to narrate the day's activities my voice cracks and squeaks. Back at the university I was in much better form. There I probably averaged twenty to thirty phone calls a day, half a dozen to a dozen visitors, plus innumerable chats with my secretary and the students who drop in. I could dictate at the drop of a faculty memorandum. Now there is a break-in period of rasping and hacking and coughing.

Speaking of voices, I have acquired a talkative neighbor who seems to live underneath the cabin. A marmot has taken up residence, and for long periods it vocalizes without letup. I have read up on marmots in *Wild Mammals of Colorado*, and the author describes three patterns of vocalizing: the whistle, the scream, and the tooth-chatter. These calls are its means of expressing anger, pleasantries, alarm, passion. The author went on to say there are six variations of the whistle. This marmot uses the whistle but it hasn't learned any of the variations—or it prefers simplicity—and it gets pretty monotonous. Sometimes I answer, and we chat back and forth for a while. The problem is that I tend to tire of talking long before the marmot, which can persist for hours. If this marmot is playing by the book, courtship should be under way and mating could occur at any time. The gestation period is about thirty days, so I can expect some baby marmots toward the end of July.

Marmots include the so-called woodchucks or groundhogs and are best described as large, bushy-tailed squirrels that live in holes in the ground. There are three American species: the eastern woodchuck, the hoary marmot of Alaska and the Northwest, and this one, the yellow-bellied *Marmota flaviventris*. It is a mountain creature, preferring boulder fields that offer cover from enemies and some lush herbage nearby to eat. Most of the yellow-bellies have a capelike pattern of lighter fur over the rump and undersides washed with yellow. They are stocky and quite bowlegged, so that they waddle more than they run. It is the largest and heaviest of the squirrel family, measuring twenty to twenty-eight inches in length, plus a six-inch tail, and weighing as much as nine pounds. They are most abundant around rock piles in subalpine meadows, which is why there are so many of them around Brown's Cabin.

Unlike the rather impulsive marten, the marmot is a creature of habit when it comes to daily routine. It arises each day with the sun and spends several hours foraging along extensive, well-used trails. By midmorning, when the sun is warm, it stops for a basking session. After some more feeding it retires to its burrow at noon for a nap until midafternoon. Then it is time for basking again, usually atop a sun-warmed boulder with a good view of any approaching enemies. In late afternoon it feeds again until, belly full, it retires for the night promptly at sundown.

These marmots usually live in colonies that consist of a single adult male, a harem of females, and some yearlings and young. If a young male disputes the dominance of the leader, the two will posture and threaten each other with a peculiar whistling or loud clicking of incisors. The young upstart usually gives in by cringing or by leaving the colony outright, waddling off for a mile or more to live in a new area.

This dispersal of individuals is important in expanding the range of a species. At the same time, it is perilous for those who are dispersed. A single marmot is exposed to much greater danger from coyotes or badgers than a colonial marmot. The members of a colony are always alert for danger, even when basking, and any movement elicits a chorus of warning whistles. One has only to walk toward a colony of these animals to learn why one of their nicknames is whistle pigs.

Because marmots prefer lush vegetation, there is little for them to eat except in summer. They have learned to deal with this situation by sleeping for most of the year. Marmots go into hibernation in September or October and do not emerge until late April or May. Mating (which I suspect of my friend beneath the house) occurs soon after they awake, with each female producing two to five young. These offspring do not appear aboveground for about a month, whereupon they begin to grow very rapidly. There is, after all, little time for feeding and maturing until they must return to their burrows and the long hibernation of another Rocky Mountain winter.

I mentioned several days ago that two marmots seemed to be fighting on a rocky knoll about a hundred yards up-mountain from the cabin. Today I saw one of them chase the other all the way across the knoll, fifty yards or so. I certainly would like to film this fighting activity, but it is going to take much preparation, a lot of luck, and a longer lens than I currently have. Again I hurt for lack of technical guidance. I thought Charlie Combs might be in on foot today bringing the mail and some supplies, but he didn't make it. I have seen no humans since I went out to Buena Vista last Monday.

June 28

This morning I was convinced that the helicopter would be in with the Forest Service man to set up my radio communications, so I carried the Forest Service radios up to the so-called heliport. I also repaired the wooden cradles that were built to protect the propane bottles; they will be needed to take the empty bottles out. About the time I had finished the repair work a single-engine plane circled the basin. I didn't think anything about it until it started circling again, lower. Then I realized it might be a Forest Service patrol plane and that I might be able to contact the pilot with the ground-to-air radio. I ran back to the cabin to get it, and about halfway there the plane came right over my head, maybe seventy-five feet above me, then flew off down the basin. I have no doubt that the pilot saw me, but when I got to the radio there was no response, so I'll probably never know who it was or what he was up to.

I had already decided that if the helicopter was not in by nine-fifteen I would start climbing toward the Continental Divide and try to get high enough to call the Forest Service in Salida. So taking the Salida district radio in one hand and the ground-to-air radio in the other, I started upward, stopping about every hundred yards to call. At the third stop I was able to hear that someone was responding. It was a woman's voice and I'm sure it was Joanne, who is a secretary in the Salida ranger district. Her voice was garbled, however, so I told her I would move to another position and call back. Apparently she was able to understand this, for she answered with a very short transmission; then when I said "Brown's Cabin, out" there was no further transmission. I continued up the Divide, stopping every hundred yards to try the radio. And believe me, I was ready to stop each time. A hundred yards, in steep terrain, at an elevation of over 12,500 feet is a real workout with two heavy radios in hand. To make a short story long, I did this for about a mile without getting any response and then gave up. I assume that it was Salida who picked me up, however, and that they at least know I'm still alive and complaining.

It is frustrating to have one of Motorola's best shortwave products on the top of a mountain not more than thirty airline miles from Salida and not be able to contact them. After all, I have a little portable radio with a sixteen-inch antennna that my son bought me as a present, and it brings me news from places as far away as Vatican City and Munich. After staggering back to the cabin with my two radios I decided to hell with the outside world. I've got enough food to last about two months, so I'll just go about doing the things of greatest urgency and assume that one of these days somebody will check up on me.

My mood wasn't helped when I noticed, on the way down the Divide, a glistening spot about a mile away that my binoculars revealed to be two Jeeps and a third vehicle that looked like a Scout. They were in the upper reaches of a willow meadow that stretches downward from Brown's Pass. It was obvious even at that distance that they were having difficulty getting through the moist meadows. I shudder to think of the ditches they were digging. In the last few days, as the snow has been melting near the cabin, the track of a trail bike has emerged; it was probably made last summer. The bike seems to have come straight down, or up, the mountain, and in places this one track has eroded into a ditch about ten inches deep.

Spring must finally be here. Today I saw my first grasshopper and yesterday was the first day I had to use insect repellent for mosquitoes. Also today, for whatever interest it may be to anyone, I washed my hair and took a bath—events of substantial magnitude up here. It took over an hour to get enough water hauled and heated, using two pots, a washtub, and a tea kettle. I snuggled up so close to the kitchen stove, trying to stay warm in this drafty old cabin, that I nearly branded my butt on the oven door.

June 29

I had visitors today—the first since coming in on the fifteenth. At about ten-thirty Charlie arrived with some welcome fresh food and news from the outside. In the afternoon a young fellow and a girl, who said they were students at Berkeley, California, came by on their way to Texas Creek and, hopefully, on over the Divide to Silver King Lake. I'm not eager to have overnight guests.

We decided to take advantage of Charlie's presence by going over the history of the area. Charlie himself has played a leading role in that history, and to a large extent the story of Brown's Cabin is Charlie's story.

He graduated from the University of California in July 1934 and came up here for the first time soon after that. His brother-in-law was in the prospecting and mining business, working with Homer Brown, who then owned the cabin. Charlie had been a dairy industry major at college, but he liked prospecting and got started on an old claim owned by a man named Goldie Smith, over in Magdalene Basin. Goldie Smith's mine is the only one Charlie knows of that actually produced silver, despite a lot of promoting and sale of stock. In 1890 alone Goldie Smith took $75,000 worth of silver out of his mine.

The road up Denny Creek was constructed around 1885. Homer Brown told Charlie that twenty or thirty men had worked on it for a dollar and a half a day. To get through a big swamp, this crew constructed the corduroy log road which has lasted until today. It was built by laying two or three stringers first and then placing logs across the stringers. The Denny Creek corduroy road is a quarter of a mile long.

Brown's Cabin was built at the same time as the road, in 1885. Homer Brown was an engineer by profession, born in White Plains, New York, and married there before he came West. His wife died in childbirth, and then he came here and found this property. He never took out a claim; things were done informally then. But he spent thousands of dollars on buildings, mining equipment, ore cars, track, and other gear.

I told Charlie I remembered a description of five mining claims listed on our special-use permit, and he said that he took them out himself in 1967. Each one is about 500 by 1,500 feet.

He also told me that some of the equipment—an 1872 boiler and an 1876 steam engine, for example—is still in good condition. The boiler was built in Pennsylvania and the stamp mill in Denver, all hauled up the corduroy road by wagon. There is an old forge to the east of here, used for sharpening drill steel. The drills were needed to make holes in rock for dynamite charges. Each time Charlie and the others wanted to sharpen the drill steel they had to walk all the way over to the east side of the basin, then back across to the mill and mine on the west side—a lot of strenuous walking. Charlie said that no one thought this an unusual hardship. "It was just the times, I think."

He spent three seasons here—1934 to 1937. His sister Pearl spent the winter of 1934 at the cabin with her husband and Homer Brown. When she was up here she made a lot of quilts and they played three-handed bridge.

Charlie said the snow was about five or six feet deep during the winter, although lately it's been as high as eight or nine feet. They used to tunnel out to the spring under six feet of snow. He said that camp life was pretty tame and sober—Homer Brown's kind of camp. He was neither a drinker nor a party-er.

Food didn't cost much; it was the middle of the Depression. Eggs were $2.50 a crate, peanut butter two pounds for a quarter. Ham was cheap; bread was a nickel a loaf; flour was probably a penny a pound. They heated with logs cut to four-foot lengths and hauled up by burros.

The burros were used by Goldie Smith to bring his ore out. He kept nine of the animals at his place at Magdalene Basin, about five miles away. Goldie would pack his ore out past Brown's Cabin to the Cottonwood Road in the morning and come back in the evening, a round trip of eighteen miles a day. He worked his mine all winter. On one trip out in the 1890s he became exhausted with severe frostbite below the cabin. Homer Brown heard his cries and brought him up to the cabin, saving his life.

Charlie, too, had a brush with death. In January 1937 there was heavy snowfall throughout Colorado. Avalanches took out the mill at the Camp Bird mine; others came down around Leadville. Charlie remembers about seven people being killed in avalanches around mines and mills in the high mountains that month.

On January 13 he was at the West Texas mine when a snowslide came down on him. Homer was checking a marten trapline when it started. Charlie hollered to him that an avalanche was coming. Homer was out of its path, but it came down right where Charlie was. He jumped into the portal of the mine and about six feet of snow packed solid on top of him. He had a pack on his back holding a pick and shovel, but the snow held him so tightly that he couldn't get at either of them. He took out his knife to cut the pack away and lost his glove. He clawed at the snow to try to get air and nearly froze his hand.

Homer arrived and started digging, but he was slightly off target, uphill from where Charlie was trapped. They couldn't hear one another. Homer was digging a trench and Charlie was scrabbling with his hands. Homer had dug a ditch about four feet deep and ten feet long by the time Charlie punched a hole through the snow to reach fresh air. For what seemed to him half an hour, he had struggled within about a foot of Homer's trench.

I asked Charlie if he had thought about death at the time. He said, "Yeah, yeah, I thought that was the end of it there."

June 30

Early this morning Charlie and I tore down the old outhouse that is finally emerging from the snowbank. Then we packed the lumber over to the site of its reincarnation. I think this is the third or fourth outhouse for this lumber. Every time it is used again, some of the lumber breaks away, so that less is available and the structure gets smaller and smaller. This one is tall enough but not very deep or wide, and there isn't enough wood to build a door. One thing can be said for it, however; it has the most beautiful view of any bathroom in Colorado—maybe in the world.

Yesterday Charlie put windows in each of the cabin doors, which makes the cabin a great deal more cheerful and livable. It was so bright this morning when I came downstairs I thought the doors had been left open.

Charlie is still an enigma to me. In my judgment he is completely reliable and very knowledgeable about the high country, and I am fortunate to have him as my contact man with the "outside." However, as with many people who have lived in the mountains for years, his rationale for doing things is sometimes surprising, not to say unfathomable. He was so concerned about how I was doing here at the cabin, whether I had enough food and was comfortable, that it didn't occur to him to check on what information was available from Salida about the radio, or to see if I had any mail. He brought some fresh milk and vegetables, as well as a number of items I didn't need, but it was a little annoying to have him come all the way in without any of this essential information.

So I decided to hike out with Charlie and ride into town to make some phone calls. We left at one-thirty and arrived in Buena Vista a little before four. I called Bob Cermak, supervisor of the San Isabel National Forest. Bob said they had brought the relay station down from the mountain in Wyoming, but that two crystals were needed to complete the installation and they were just waiting for them to arrive. It was dark before I started hiking to the cabin, and I arrived about midnight.

Despite this moderately good news, I found that the experience of hiking out, of going to town for an hour or two of hurried activity and a few telephone calls, is not a desirable one. I ended up with a feeling of frustration and lack of accomplishment. When this communication system is established it is not going to be hard to convince me to stay put at Brown's Cabin.

July 1

Today began with a bang—hailstorm and thunder. The thunder has continued throughout the day. It is now evening and the skies are beginning to clear.

I went through two boxes of slides Charlie brought in. These are slides I took during the first day here at the cabin. I seem to have been fascinated mostly by the Army helicopter. I have more than a dozen shots of the helicopter coming in, landing, and taking off, from all conceivable angles.

Speaking of photography, Charlie said he thought there was some coverage of the project on the evening news on Channel 7 in Denver last Friday evening. He said there was footage of Jim Bolick, one of the young men from Colorado State who came up with us, interviewing me in front of the cabin. Charlie said they honored our request not to pinpoint the location, simply saying we are someplace in the Rocky Mountains. That ought to be vague enough.

After sorting out the slides I began to clean up around the cabin. This is not the type of project I like to spend time on, but there is a reason. About a hundred feet from the front door, in a large rockslide, is a marmot den. A huge boar marmot has been coming out of the entrance, a large opening among the boulders, where he stretches and rubs himself. I could be getting some excellent middle-distance shots of him—except for the eighty-five-year accumulation of human refuse and litter between me and him. There are cookstoves, heating stoves, old tools, old bedsprings, old windows and cans, tea kettles, chamber pots, whiskey bottles, beer cans, and a surprising number of soft-drink cans.

Well, I'm having the darndest time narrating this. Right now the funniest thing is happening. I'm sitting out here on the porch and this marmot . . . just a minute, well, my friend has disappeared again. He has really been going through antics. He'll jump off the rockslide and head up to the willows at a dead run for thirty or forty feet, generally in my direction. Then he lies on his belly and wiggles toward me. Finally he sits straight up and looks right at me. This has happened, let's see, I guess three times now and I've been trying to take movies of him while I'm narrating. But each time I start the camera he stops what he is doing, whirls, and runs back to the rockslide. Then he climbs on a rock, looking over his shoulder, and slowly works his way around until he's facing me, sometimes with part of his body behind a boulder. I can tell by his head movements that he hears me when I resume dictating; then he begins his antics again.

I have no idea what his behavior indicates. I have a feeling that he's trying to play with me; all of his moves are clearly related to me and the camera. He's watching me all the time. Just now he's worked his way around to some trees quite close to where I'm sitting . . . now I've lost him.

I'll have to watch myself or I'll have the animal behaviorists down on me. Attributing human behavior patterns to animals is taboo, and I seem to be flirting with just that. But these animals are effectively my only neighbors, and when it begins to seem they are also my only friends, it is difficult to remain scientifically aloof.

July 2

Again today I have been cleaning up, repairing a plank walkway from the cabin to the ground, and watching the antics of the marmot. He has been dashing out from the rockslide and back, just like yesterday, then flopping onto a rock in the sun, positioned so he can watch me all the time. This pleases me both for the feeling of wordless communication and because this animal should be easy to photograph, if I can only find a way to muffle the noise of the damned movie camera.

All the animals seem to have caught spring fever, including the gray jays. Gray jays (*Perisoreus canadensis*) are perhaps the most noticeable bird in these high mountain areas. Dark gray above and light below, with a white band around its neck and an almost white face, these noisy birds will join in picnics or other human activities where food is involved. They are popularly known as "whiskey jacks" or "camp robbers," and have been known to take food from a plate in use. They are hardy and nest early here, sometimes even before the snow is gone. They generally make bowl-shaped nests in evergreen trees, perhaps thirty feet off the ground and lay three to five greenish-gray spotted eggs. In the absence of scraps from campers and hikers, insects form the major portion of a diet that in the wild may include berries, small mammals, and young birds. When these birds are really uptight about something, their scolding becomes quite raucous. Before I had finished breakfast they were making a loud fuss. I went outside to investigate and found them chasing a chipmunk around. But it seemed to me that neither their pursuit nor their scolding was very serious. More remarkably, the chipmunk seemed to be making only a mild effort to escape. When I came upon the scene the jays flew directly toward my face, braking and turning about three feet away and flying off, all the while making a soft kind of *ch-r-r-r* sound. They seemed no more genuinely aggressive toward me than they were toward the chipmunk. Perhaps I am being at least tentatively accepted by new friends who are trying to include me in their play activities.

Last night was so miserable, damp, and cold with only the kitchen stove going that I built a fire in the heater as well. It rained, sleeted, and hailed until about seven o'clock, when the temperature dropped below 40 degrees. Then it cleared off but remained cold. I still do not have all the photos I want from the permanent photo points, so I hope it is sunny in the morning. For the past two days I have seen fresh snow on the 13,000-foot mountain peaks across Texas Creek.

July 3

Today offered only occasional periods of sunlight, but I decided that I would have to go ahead with photographing from the photo points regardless of the poor light. The snow is melting, and I need to record what's happening at the various stations.

At about ten-thirty a young fellow and girl came to the cabin area with backpacks. They were from Denver and said they were getting away from the Fourth of July crowds to do some fishing at a lake near Magdalene Basin. About an hour later two motorcyclists appeared on the crest of the hill, with all the attendant roaring caused by unnecessary use of the throttle. One fellow called to the other, hey, there's somebody down there, but they didn't come down the trail. Instead I heard them snarling around the bench above the cabin for a short time. Finally they faded over Brown's Pass and were heard no more.

The Forest Service has installed no restrictive signs yet. I'm going to bring this to the attention of regional forester Bill Lucas and hope that something can be done to prevent vehicular traffic around Brown's Pass this summer.

I'll be glad to have some warmer weather. For the past week it has been uncomfortably cold most of the time, ranging from 35 to 55 degrees most days. When the sun is out it is quite pleasant, but this happens rarely and briefly. The cabin is distinctly cold throughout the day and whenever I work inside my hands become stiff.

Tomorrow I'm going to leave early for Magdalene Basin in search of ptarmigan and blue grouse. I understand this is a good area, especially for ptarmigan. Ptarmigan (pronounced tarmigan) are grouselike birds that thrive in cold, high-altitude environments, such as the tundra and mountain slopes of Canada and Alaska. Of the three North American species, only one, the white-tailed ptarmigan (*Lagopus leucurus*), ventures this far south; the others prefer the boreal cold. Of course, you might consider the Brown's Cabin area to be a pinpoint of Arctic tundra, jutting up as it does into a zone of low temperatures and harsh winds.

Ptarmigan are perhaps best known for their ability to survive in a zone which affords little vegetative cover. Without some sort of protection, ptarmigan would be easy prey for foxes, hawks, and other predators, so they have evolved a seasonal camouflage that makes them nearly invisible year-round. The ground up here is a mottled brown in summer and white in winter, and so are the ptarmigan. They are so successful in blending with their environment, and so confident of their invisibility, that it is possible to step on a nesting bird without seeing it.

July 4

I have been doing very little filming recently, and there are several reasons for this. I've never done any TV photography before, very little movie photography, and I don't have any kind of an outline for this documentary, since the Landsburg people seem to favor a "let it happen" approach. Nor do I have any idea if the film that I've taken so far is of any value. I definitely do not like this kind of disorganized situation.

Well, it's Independence Day, and it was a delightful day even if I didn't get much filming done. I left the cabin at seven-thirty and reached Texas Creek at eight-fifteen, only to find it swollen with water. I tested one possible crossing place where there were large rocks, using a pole to test the first rock. It seemed to be stable and to offer good traction, so I jumped on it. I immediately lost my pole, my balance, and almost my butt before I was able to grab hold of the rock again. I imagine there are finger marks where I caught that rock. I don't know how I stayed on it, but I did. I suffered only a bruised shin and ankle, which I didn't notice for half a day, what with the excitement. Finally I was able to get off the rock and back to shore.

Please don't assume that I'm reckless when out alone in this backcountry. It just happened in this case that I came to the wrong conclusion: I decided the rock was safe and it was not. After that, I moved about two hundred yards upstream, found myself another pole, and this time took off my boots and socks and hung them around my neck, rolled my pants as high as I could, and set across on foot. Texas Creek was twenty-five feet wide there, two feet deep, and very, very swift, so it was kind of a hair-raiser even by this conservative technique. After about four steps my feet were so numb with the cold that I couldn't feel anything. On the other side I sat in a sunny spot with a feeling of great relief and let my feet dry. Then I put on the dry socks and boots and continued on my way.

The hike to Magdalene Basin is only about five miles, but all of it is either down or up, and steep. Just as I was coming into the basin I saw four elk feeding across a mountain slope about half a mile away. I noted the direction they were moving and decided to stalk them through the timber. Everything went exactly as planned, except that I never saw the elk again. I don't say it wasn't exhilarating fun to sneak up through the woods, conjuring visions of the wonderful movies I was going to take, but I had hoped for better.

I would add that even my long-distance glimpse of elk was worth a good deal, as it always is. The elk (*Cervus elaphus*) is one of nature's noblest creations; there are few animals anywhere that can rival the grandeur of an elk against the backdrop of the Rocky Mountains. Second in size among North American deer only to the moose, a bull elk stands about five feet high at the shoulder. He may weigh 750 pounds or more, and measure nine feet in length. A cow weighs about 500 pounds.

Unlike the mule deer, which I expect to see now at any time, elk are primarily grazers of grasses and forbs. Their diet changes with the season. When grass is scarce, particularly in winter, shrubs may make up a large portion of their food for short periods, especially the twigs and bark of aspen, where their lower incisors leave long, characteristic marks.

Elk are gregarious, often feeding in herds. They retreat to forested areas at night, however—a habit rare in herding animals. This custom may be a consequence of the expansion of civilization into their traditional grazing areas. They migrate each year by the season—to lower elevations in winter, back to mountain meadows in the summer, moving with the snow line. They'll probably be up here until November or so.

The antlers of the bull elk are as magnificent as the rest of the beast, spreading as wide as five feet and weighing up to twenty-five pounds. They are shed late in the winter. Once on the ground, shed antlers do not last long. To other animals, especially rodents, they represent a windfall of concentrated mineral matter, and are ultimately gnawed to bits and recycled into the ecosystem.

Antler replacement begins within two weeks. By early August a new set is nearly ready. During growth, the antlers are protected and nourished by a tender layer of "velvet" which is rich in blood vessels bringing minerals absorbed from the digestive system. When growth is complete this supply of minerals is cut off and the velvet is shed.

When fall begins, the behavior of the elk herd changes radically. The loud braying, or bugling, of the bulls is heard with greater frequency. The tension builds as mating time approaches. The neck and shoulders of the bulls swell and antlers are rubbed against trees to remove the velvet. Bugling reaches a peak in early October, when each bull tries to collect a harem of as many cows as he can keep together—perhaps a dozen or more. If another bull threatens his dominion, the two may lock antlers in battle. Although these fights can result in broken antlers and sometimes even death, the weaker of the two usually retires after some ritual sparring.

Calves are born about 250 days after mating, which will be next June. They weigh about 30 pounds at birth and can walk within a few hours. Inside of a week they will be able to run at a good pace. (When I was ear-tagging elk for the Idaho Fish and Game Department in 1955, I needed a good saddle horse to overtake a week-old calf.) At the end of six months they may weigh 250 pounds. But a bull calf will have to wait four or five years to qualify for a harem.

Cattle and sheep ranchers now own much of the elk's historical feeding range, or else it is occupied by mountain subdivisions, urban communities, and highways. Elk used to flourish throughout North America, coast to coast; today they are restricted mostly to mountainous areas in the West. Although at present the elk herds that remain are flourishing— there are more elk in the Colorado mountains than at any time in recorded history—an elk needs about twelve acres to graze during the winter, and overgrazing may become a problem.

The gray wolf that used to prey on calves is gone, and mountain lions are reduced in number, but the mighty elk is beset with a host of smaller enemies, especially flukes, tapeworms, roundworms, lice, botflies, and mites. This plague of parasitism may be aggravated by the overgrazing of the shrinking zones of winter ranges where these creatures are still free to roam.

Magdalene Basin is apparently good elk habitat in the summertime. There was abundant sign, including fresh tracks and spring droppings. These droppings can be distinguished from those made later in the season by their softness; biologists call them "agglutinated masses," and they resemble cow pies more than normal elk droppings. This is because the elk are on a succulent diet of grasses and forbs at this time of year.

I also saw many of the hard elk pellets of late summer and fall, so apparently the basin is occupied throughout the snow-free months. I shall plan to take a backpack trip into the area, after Landsburg's photographic crew has visited me, to spend some time just trying to get photographs of elk and deer.

I met and enjoyed talking to the two young people from Denver who had backpacked past Brown's Cabin the other day. They are now camped and fishing along Texas Creek. They were very well satisfied with having caught brown, cutthroat, and brook trout.

I got back to the cabin at six o'clock, very tired but pleased with the physical condition I'm getting into. I was gone ten and a half hours and, except for the few times I had the pack off, I was walking most of the time. I was a little concerned when I stopped for lunch and noticed that my ankle was beginning to swell and stiffen. After I'd eaten I was barely able to hobble. But by loosening the shoelace a little I could continue walking without too much pain.

Oh, yes, one final note on the day. While I was in Magdalene Basin I could hear the roaring of motors across the valley. I checked with the binoculars, and sure enough, just above my cabin two motorcycles were heading up toward Brown's Pass. Later I checked this on a map and found that I was three and a half to four airline miles away, yet still able to hear the motors crackling. It is easy to understand how a few trail bikers can disturb so many backpackers and others who like to be in the country to enjoy the wildlife, the scenery, and the isolation.

July 5

I woke up this morning feeling rather stiff and sore from yesterday's long hike. I decided that this day ought to be devoted to whatever I wanted to do. So although I carried the camera around a little I didn't take any photos. If I accomplished anything, it was to discover that my "do just what you want to do" philosophy fails to please. What I "wanted to do" turned out to be mostly cleaning up around the cabin, so at the end of this day I am not sure I feel any sense of accomplishment.

I truly believe this must be the dirtiest cabin in the Rocky Mountains. It's also probably the most difficult to keep clean. Chinking is continually falling out of the walls, and all kinds of dirt drifts down from above. I had to move some things around upstairs and decided to sweep the floor. Half the dirt came downstairs. So I had to clean down here, too. I also laid out forty-two feet of shelf paper. All these wooden shelves are so dirty and rough that it's impossible to get them anywhere near clean. And every object on the shelves was covered with dust, debris, and dead flies.

I did manage to shampoo my hair on the sunny porch this morning and bath water is now warming for my weekly bath. If this seems like a minute detail to narrate, just remember that carrying the water, heating it, and doing the bathing up here take the better part of an hour. Housekeeping in general is a major obstacle to spending time in the field.

My young friends came up from Texas Creek about nine o'clock this morning on their way back to civilization. I congratulated them for a sane way of spending their Fourth of July holiday. But this pleasantness was spoiled about two hours later when four motorcyclists roared over Brown's Pass and came to a halt beside my cabin. They were headed for Texas Creek and wanted to know how wet it was down there because they were

going to try to go across the valley to another trail that would lead them
out of the area. I hope that I treated them with the proper degree of hostility. Apparently they found another way out of the country, for it's 10
p.m. and they haven't come back past the cabin.

I celebrated part of the July Fourth holiday by beginning a modest
autobiography. I have no idea if any of this will be of the slightest interest
to anyone other than myself, or even to myself. But Landsburg asked me
to do it, and I offer it in the spirit of fair play to the reader. Perhaps something in my own history will shed light on my present antipathy toward
motorcycles, or my compulsive work habits, or any number of behavioral
quirks acquired over a period of fifty years. Also, I'm curious to know what
I shall come up with. I have never done this before, and I wonder what
has stuck in my mind through the years.

I guess the best time to start is when I was born. I was born to poor
parents at Sanders, Idaho, which was not a town or even a village. It was
only a general store, which included the post office and a gas pump out
front, operated by a family that included eight or nine children, and that
was it. Actually I was born in the "suburbs" about two miles from Sanders. My parents were living in a rented house on a dirt road, the third-
from-last place on the west side of West Dennis Mountain.

My parents tell me it was not much of a house. It was built of unpainted lumber, one of a series of rented houses we lived in. In fact, I
never lived in an "owned home" until I bought one myself after World
War II. We were thirty miles from the nearest town with a doctor, but he
made it in time for my birth.

There were two older half brothers in the family, but I was the only
child born to my mother and father for more than eleven years. Then a
sister arrived, who was so much younger that I never really got to know
her when we were young. I'm sure that my mother had a difficult time
being stepmother to two boys, the oldest of whom was only nine years
younger than she. Both had quit school at the end of eighth grade to go
into logging, and both were big rough men over six feet tall, weighing well
over 200 pounds. Dad himself was a rather rough-talking lumberjack who
spent nearly fifty years in the forests of the Northwest. When I was two
years old we moved to Eugene, Oregon, while Dad tried logging in the
Douglas fir country along the coast. But he didn't understand the huge
timber there and promptly went broke, so we returned to Idaho.

The first recollection of my own is of my fourth birthday. Dad was
working in a sawmill and Mother was cooking for the mill crew. I recall
standing on a floating plank walkway that went across the millpond, call-

ing out to the mill workers to tell them it was my fourth birthday and that Mother had baked a cake for my supper. I also recall getting a hatchet as a birthday present. After supper I went out and cut down a small tree with it. As soon as it was down I remembered that the lumberjacks always called out "Timber!!!" before the tree fell. So I went in to tell Mother that I'd forgotten to call out and asked if I could cut down another tree and do it right. It happened that she looked out the window and saw that the tree I had already cut was a favorite of hers that she watched as she did the cooking and dishwashing, so instead of getting permission to cut down a second tree I got a spanking.

I remember quite a bit about the summer of my sixth birthday and the one following that. We were living now in another unpainted house, up the side of West Dennis Mountain. I thought then it was a large house, but when I returned two years ago, the frame of the old place was still standing, and I was amazed at how small it really was. I guess it seemed big because it was the only two-story house we ever lived in.

A number of events seem important about the time we were there. One was that sheepmen brought their herds through from the winter ranges, heading for the mountains and summer forage. Dad would never charge them for driving their sheep through our place; he would say, well, if you have an injured lamb or sick ewe or something you can give it to the boy, meaning me. I remember one summer I had six sick sheep by the end of the spring drives. I was unhappy when Dad changed his policy and told them not to give me any more ready-to-die sheep.

That also was the summer I first saw a wild mountain lion. We were eating breakfast one morning when Mother looked up and said, "Look at that deer and fawn," and Dad looked out the window and said, "Well, it can't be a fawn because that deer is a buck." As they came closer we saw it was a mountain lion chasing a buck into a clearing above our house. When the lion heard our dog barking it jumped back into the forest and we never saw it again.

During that summer of 1927 my dad manned a fire lookout for the Forest Service on West Dennis Mountain. There was no fire tower then, so Dad lived in a tent and several times daily he would climb up a tree to scan the horizon for forest fires. I recall that at a prearranged time on sunny days Mother would go up the small hill behind our house. She would take a mirror, and Dad had a mirror, and they would signal each other to indicate that everything was all right.

For two or three years after I was four I had what the doctors then called spinal meningitis, now polio. In my first year of school I rode with the mailman, who was driving a brand-new 1928 Model A Ford. Mother would take me out to the road and lift me into the car. When we got to school the mailman would put me on the ground and I'd shuffle up to the schoolhouse. I had to learn to walk all over again.

One other memory involves the country dances we used to hold. Dad could play the violin, guitar, and harmonica, and Mother played the piano, so we used to have some really rousing good dances in an upstairs room of this old house. Dad had seen so much abuse of alcohol in the logging camps that he was extremely intolerant of drunks. I can recall him taking a man who had had too much by the nape of the neck and seat of the pants, literally carrying him to the front door, and pitching him outside in a belly flopper. I suppose it was due to this policy of Dad's that I don't recall a single fight at one of our country dances.

Some of the times during grade school that I remember best involved whippings I got from Mother, who was handy with Dad's razor strap. The first whipping I remember came after two other boys and I took a pack of cigarettes down by a millpond and smoked them all. In addition to getting sick, I got whipped. Another time I was coming home from school when I heard a meadowlark singing. This may have ignited my interest in wildlife more than any other single event. The meadowlark's song was so beautiful that I sat until after dark listening. I got home a good two hours late and received a sound thrashing for my newfound interest. Again, we boys were pushing an old horse-drawn road grader, the only kind they had in those days. We had been told not to touch this grader, of course. We were disobeying orders. Typically, I got a foot under the grader and the wheel ran over my toe. That night when I got home I lost a little skin off my butt, and about a week later I lost my big toenail, both because of the grader.

Another whipping was probably well deserved. The church in the community was the Free Methodist, a conservative, fundamentalist church. One Sunday afternoon the local preacher was baptizing adults in the local millpond. This church believed in total immersion as the only valid way to baptize. The preacher was standing in the middle of the millpond, and when the soon-to-be-christened women, in particular, waded into the icy water the air would fill with shrieks. When the minister pushed them completely under water there was a great flurry of activity as the women flapped their arms trying to push their voluminous skirts under too. Otherwise these old-fashioned skirts would float on top of the clear water, leaving the women's bodies visible underneath. Of course, we boys thought the intonations of the preacher and the shrieks and arm-flaying of the women were hilarious; in fact, I still get a chuckle thinking about it forty-two years later. Some other boys and I were hidden in nearby trees doing a good deal of giggling. Some darn stool pigeon told our mothers about it and I really got whacked.

I also remember a couple of head injuries that year. Perhaps if I reflected on some of the things I have done since then, I might find a connection. The first time was in school, and I was dipping the pigtails of the girl sitting ahead of me in my inkwell. The teacher caught me in the act and came back, lifted the ink bottle out of the inkwell, and hit me on the side of the head. I thought this was unfair but my mother, as usual, sided with the teacher. The next time I caught it in the head was during the winter. We used to make snowballs, then dip them in a pail of water to freeze. During a snowball fight, one of these ice-soakers, as we called them, hit me in the ear so hard I can recall bleeding from the nose and mouth.

When I was nine, a child specialist in Spokane found that I had tuberculosis, apparently caught from an adopted uncle who subsequently died of it. The doctors at the time recommended plenty of sunlight and a rubdown with olive oil every night. Dad was away from home cutting logs, so we went to where he was working in the timber, erected a tent, and lived there all summer. I dressed only in shorts and ran around the mountains most of the time. Perhaps this experience is partly responsible for the fact that I always feel at ease in the mountains. I was allowed to roam at will as long as I came back to the tent at mealtimes. I learned to be alone and to find my way even in heavily timbered mountain country. I did have one work assignment: sawing and splitting all our firewood. Dad made me a special small saw by cutting off a broken crosscut saw to a length of four and a half feet. I used that, a double-bitted ax, and a sledge to cut the wood.

The next summer, when I was ten, I joined a 4-H Club. Members of our group each purchased a guernsey heifer at a cost of five dollars each. That fall I took my heifer to the county fair at St. Maries, Idaho, population 2,000. This was a memorable event. It was not only my first stay in a "city" but also my first experience with running water, electricity, and indoor plumbing. Of course, my major memory is of winning several first and second prizes and finally the grand championship of the fair. The trophy was a silver cup; that year, 1931, was the first year this cup was given for the grand championship, and my name was the first one engraved on it. I went back to St. Maries a few years ago to see if it was still circulating, but it has vanished.

Two things that happened during my eleventh year stick in my mind. One might be called a first stab at philosophy. That summer a band of sheep grazed in the mountain meadows near our home for several weeks. A sheepherder living in a tent was taking care of them. I used to walk over and visit with him in the evening. He had a Bible and several books that appeared to me tremendously impressive works of philosophy. I no longer remember what they were. But he used to tell me his ideas about God and Life, and I was deeply impressed with his intelligence and insights.

I suppose it was this priming that led later that same year to my joining the Free Methodist Church that I had found so funny a few years earlier. We went to some of their services, which were filled with cries of "Hallelujah!" and "Amen, brother!" as well as some weeping and shouting. During one of these services I was caught up by the emotion and excitement and "went forward." I walked down the aisle to the front of the church and kneeled in front of the preacher, who said many grand things about receiving me in the name of Jesus Christ. Everyone in the congregation had a great time singing and shouting "Glory, hallelujah!" and "Praise the Lord!"

I don't recall that we ever had a Bible in our house. I know that no one read it if we did. However, in looking back I view my mother and dad as good God-fearing people. I remember no opposition from them to my being "saved," although I would be interested to know what they really thought about all that.

As for me, I pondered this new influence in my life for several weeks and went from heights of elation to depths of depression. Finally, after a few months, I decided that what I had experienced was mostly emotional and I felt rather ridiculous about it. But the experience did have an impact that initiated a search that has continued ever since.

The other lasting impression of that year, 1932, was that of the Great Depression. Those were hard times for my family, as they were for most others. I can remember Dad was cutting logs for thirty cents an hour. He was finally laid off, as were most of the other loggers. One day a lady from some organization came to our house and talked to Dad about something called "relief." It seemed that items of clothing and food were available free of charge for people who were out of work. I recall Dad's anger at the suggestion that he would accept something for nothing. He almost threw this lady out, telling her he wasn't going to take anything he hadn't worked for.

The next year Dad became seriously ill and nearly died. I don't even know what the cause was, although it was related to a hemorrhaging ulcer.

He almost bled to death. He was unable to work at all for the next three years. When at last he could, he was assigned to a crew of the WPA, the Works Progress Administration, which was, and still is, maligned by many people and ridiculed in newspaper cartoons. I know that having Dad on WPA had a great effect on my life, and I'm sure it was traumatic for him to have to accept what he considered a form of "relief." The Depression years were harsh ones, and many unkind things happened to people.

I also remember pulling a stunt that year so foolhardy that I'm probably lucky to have lived to tell about it. It happened on a Sunday. Apparently I had been out in the woods, probably daydreaming, which I did quite frequently. When I came back to the house there was a note telling me that my parents had gone to some relatives' for Sunday dinner and to fix my own lunch. Feeling sorry for myself, I decided to visit some newly acquired friends who were building trails for the Forest Service and lived in a tent camp about a mile from us. I started for the camp only to find a black bear sitting in the middle of the trail, blocking my way. I was determined to get to the camp, so I went back to the house and picked up a .410 shotgun and some slugs. I returned down the trail, which was now empty, and heard a bear on one side and saw two cubs on the other. The bear I was angry at was the mother. Fortunately she was out of sight and I went on down the trail. I didn't find out until later that a .410 slug would probably not have killed her. More likely, it would have infuriated her enough to end my wilderness career.

At the beginning of the summer of my thirteenth year we moved from Sanders to a large cattle ranch about four miles from St. Maries, the seat of Benewah County. I had just graduated from the eighth grade, in a class of three students. Our one-room country schoolhouse held grades one through eight. The largest enrollment the school ever had was seventeen, and these seventeen children, in eight grades, were all taught by one teacher. My uncle was manager of the ranch, and I drove a team of horses to haul hay and helped put it into the barn. Dad was now totally incapacitated, so I was charged with holding down a man's job.

Part II

EARLY SUMMER

July 6

Well, that does it for part of my life, I guess; my high school days will have to wait. I had to break off yesterday for some housekeeping chores and I never got back in the mood.

One of those chores, incidentally, might be considered symbolic of the end of the cold-weather season. I finally had to move my perishable food from the snowbank that has served for about three weeks as my refrigerator. What was once a beautiful snowfield six feet or more deep and hundreds of feet across has dwindled to a two-inch crust five feet wide. I took a camera out to photograph my food supplies sitting forlornly in the middle of this vanishing patch of snow. Then I moved the food to another snowbank, knowing that it, too, has but a few days to live.

It was not a good day for photography, so I spent the morning collecting, identifying, and pressing some of the spring plants that have emerged and are beginning to bloom. By noon it was so cold that I built a fire in the stove and made hot soup for lunch. This was a welcome change from the cold lunches I usually eat.

My wood supply is shrinking alarmingly. We brought in only half a cord with the helicopter, due to time and weight limitations, and it has been colder than I expected. So I went out and began looking around for a good dead tree. I found one about a hundred yards down the mountain. The Forest Service had loaned me a one-man bucking saw—I didn't want the noise of a chain saw—and with that and an ax I cut down the tree. The work was good therapy for getting rid of some of the frustrations I'm beginning to feel at not getting this motion-picture project under way as I would like. It also brought back memories of Idaho some thirty years ago where I worked one summer as a logger in the white pine forests for the Weyerhaeuser logging company. I was pleased still to be able to swing the tree away from the direction it was leaning and drop it precisely on the spot I wanted.

Unfortunately about twenty-five feet of the top broke and hung up between two live spruce trees directly over the trail. At first I thought, well, ain't this a helluva note, then I thought maybe a trail biker will come down the trail and it will fall on him. Finally sanity returned and I said to myself, now, Smith, you know you've got to get that top down from there. In the logging woods we used to call such broken tops widow-makers, for valid reason. So I spent considerable time working it free and clearing it off the trail.

I cut a block off the butt of the tree and carried it up to the cabin to see how well it burns. The good news is that it is excellent firewood. But I found that carrying a block a hundred yards up this steep mountainside is more than a chore. It made me appreciate how easy it was at home to get up in the morning and turn up the thermostat.

From this thought I went on to calculate why it takes me longer to do my housework than it does my wife at home. It takes 110 steps round trip to get water from the spring. It's 140 steps to go to the "bathroom," and 150 steps to visit the "refrigerator." The kitchen stove requires attention every fifteen or twenty minutes. The only easy operation is garbage disposal. I simply walk out the front door and heave everything as far as I can down the mountainside. Everything biodegradable, that is. At first this was offensive to my notions of sanitation, but the Clark's nutcrackers, gray jays, and chipmunks do a very efficient job of cleaning up, so I decided this technique integrates naturally into the alpine ecosystem. How's that for a rationale?

When the air is still and the sun is out, it is quite comfortable even at this elevation. I can go without a shirt much of the day. But if there is wind or cloud it immediately cools below the comfort level. It's now a little after 11 a.m. and I have a low fire going in the kitchen stove. I'm sitting here by the stove trying to get my number 12 boots inside the small oven to keep my feet warm. Even though I am wearing very heavy socks, my toes are stiff with cold. Usually I keep warm by alternating between the sedentary and active states. Carrying a pail of water or chopping some wood is usually enough to restore circulation.

Last night when I was walking up to the heliport to scan the countryside for big game, I heard a grinding noise nearby. The first thing I thought of was the pack strings of horses coming down trails back on the Salmon River in Idaho. There was always something loose in their packs that would make a heavy rustling or jingling sound. But as I came out on the bench where the heliport is, I saw the tailend of a porcupine vanish into the brush. It has been making a dinner of the roof of the weather shelter, which is still not installed and is easily accessible to ground creatures. The roof is made of ⅝-inch plywood, and the porcupine had chewed and apparently consumed an area that measured seven by eleven inches. I hope that if the splinters don't get him the lead in the paint will. It's difficult not to think bad thoughts about the porcupine when your weather station is being eaten.

This morning I've been watching two marmots playing on a snowfield a short distance from the cabin, chasing each other and sliding on the snow. They are probably a male and a female. At first it appeared they were males fighting over territorial rights, but I am now convinced that their screaming and squalling are just the domestic strife that seems to occur in the best-regulated households.

The slope above the cabin seems to be sort of a community playground where marmots congregate from all directions, and although it was a cold and dreary afternoon, they were all out there. At one point I heard a sound like two babies crying; it was two small marmots racing around a stump. They would roll and tumble and appear to be biting each other. All of the marmots seem to be getting more accustomed to my presence. At first they would all scatter toward their respective dens whenever I opened the door. Now I'm able to walk around the cabin area and even to approach to within fifty feet before they take off. I can identify several of them, and know that when they split up and flee, a large light-colored one will head toward the rock outcrop area above the cabin, and a smaller dark one will dash back toward the cabin; this apparently is the one that lives under the kitchen floor. A third marmot always runs into the rockslide near the spring.

Another anthropomorphic observation. I'm convinced the gray jays like to have me out and around where they can see me. On two mornings, after an especially long hike the day before, I got up fairly late, about seven-thirty, to find the jays hopping around on the catwalk in front of the cabin, making an unearthly racket. As soon as I got up and came outside they quieted down and resumed more normal activity. They do not make nearly so much noise on the mornings I get up early. Well, I wouldn't stake my professional reputation on this reasoning, but my behavior does seem to affect theirs.

The country is becoming noticeably greener. There is a change every day as new plants emerge from the snow and older plants put on new growth. There must be thirty-five or forty species flowering in the general vicinity. Some of the flowering plants are beginning to develop seeds already. This is a typical alpine adaptation; organisms must complete their life cycle in a very short time. Some plants actually begin to develop seed heads within three weeks of emergence from a snowbank.

July 7

Last night at about six o'clock it finally settled down and began to rain in earnest, a steady drizzle on into the night. One of the nice things about having a roof with no insulation is the gentle sound of the rain. It is soothing and makes for excellent sleeping. I sleep perfectly all night up here, except for those rare occasions when I have to make a wee-hours trip to the bathroom. That is rather traumatic, coming down the stairs and going through the cold cabin and out into the colder alpine night. It does, however, offer the compensation of moon and stars. You've never really seen the Milky Way until you've seen it from here, above all the smog and dust.

This morning I awoke to find that the rain had stopped and fog had arrived. Clouds are floating past the cabin so close I can nearly reach out and touch them. It is wonderful, really; so quiet; and after the rain it smells fresh with everything a bit greener than the day before.

When I was chopping wood outside today I heard a crack like a rifle shot. It came from the hillside directly in front of the cabin, about two hundred yards away. For a second I wasn't sure what was happening. Then I realized that an avalanche of rocks was starting down the face of the mountain. I heard this same sound two or three weeks ago, at midmorning when the temperature was rising. I assume that the surface rocks tend to lose their grip then, as the frozen soil begins to thaw in the sun.

This morning's rock-rolling was doubly eerie because it started up in the cloud where I couldn't see it. Finally a dozen or more boulders came bounding into view, then quickly disappeared into the fog downhill. In the more than three weeks I've been here I've never felt anything but safe. But I must admit that I was unsettled by this rock avalanche.

July 8

Maybe I've been up here too long already; I had to go look at the calendar to find out what day it is. Well, it's the eighth, and it was a routine day. As usual for the past week, I awoke totally convinced that the helicopter would be here, bringing the radio relay station. When it wasn't, I went up and over Brown's Pass, reshooting the stationary photo points I had first photographed about two weeks ago. After finishing those I came back to the cabin, where a good-sized marmot was waiting near the kitchen door. I began filming it beginning from about sixty feet away, and I kept on until I was about thirty feet distant, when it dove under the catwalk. It is encouraging to be able to get closer to these animals.

Later I collected several early-flowering plants, such as snow buttercup and marsh marigold. While I was pressing them I noticed a female robin picking up food particles and flying away with them. I followed her line of flight and located a nest in a spruce tree below the cabin. Robins (*Turdus migratorius*) don't usually nest at this high an elevation, but this one is setting her own rules. Her nest is out at the end of some branches about twenty feet off the ground in an Engelmann spruce. It appears to be made of used toilet paper, old insulating material, and some very large sticks. There is at least one fledgling, which the mother is feeding, so the system must work.

One might wonder how a robin could survive, let alone breed, so far from golf courses, suburban lawns, and juicy earthworms. In fact, robins will go nearly anywhere and eat just about anything; it is the lucky bird that gets a worm. The diet of most robins, for most of the year, is more than half vegetable matter of all types, especially wild fruit when available. Somewhat less than half is animal, although the variety is great, including beetles, grasshoppers, and caterpillars. I can't be sure what this female is eating up here.

This afternoon I thought I would get some movie footage of this hardy bird, but at three-thirty my plans were rudely interrupted when six people on horseback came down the mountain. One of them turned out to be Mark Rodgers, the son of Ken Rodgers, whom I've had some misunderstandings with. He had a party of five people, who were from Kentucky and Texas. At first I thought he might be bringing word or supplies from the Forest Service, so I let him and his guests tie their horses to trees around the cabin. However, I found that he had not been in touch with the Forest Service at all but was simply taking his clients out for a ride with the intention of using Brown's Cabin as his stopping point. They did stop, and he took his guests over to the stamp mill a quarter of a mile from the cabin.

I was disturbed about this because Charlie has told Ken Rodgers that pack trips here would interfere with our program. We have an agreement with Charlie not to have anyone in here, including Charlie himself unless I arrange it with him; and we have a special-use permit from the Forest

Service to ensure this. Of course, we cannot interfere with people passing through on the Forest Service trail, but we certainly can ask them not to make the cabin a stopover. I hastily wrote a letter to Ken Rodgers to this effect and sent it out with Mark.

This may sound like the deed of a mean old man, but there are many undesirable aspects to groups of visitors. By the time all the party had straggled in, there were eight people and ten horses, the latter all tied to trees and depositing manure around the cabin, where it certainly does not belong as part of the local ecology. In the resulting commotion, the wild animals, particularly the marmots, all disappeared. The party had numerous questions about flowers around the place and so forth, so I did not complete the plant pressing and identification while there was still daylight, nor was I able to photograph the robin's nest.

There is some history to this issue. In the group were two young kids who acted as packers for Ken Rodgers. One or both of them, recent high school graduates, I believe, were among the young people who came in with Ken Rodgers last September. At that time they were sporting large revolvers in holsters that they wore low and strapped to the leg in the best western style. They were wearing the weapons again today. When they came in last fall, my wife, Carol, was with me at the cabin and she really put them on the spot. Even though we've been married for nearly twenty-seven years, I'm still unsure sometimes whether my wife is being naïve or just subtle in a devastating sort of way. She began by asking one of these young fellows why he carried a gun up here. He gave some glib response to the effect that you could never tell when you'd need one, but she persisted and asked what specifically you might need one for. He had a story that I'm sure is favored by local guides about the wild animals that might attack him. My wife expressed some skepticism about that, and asked if he knew of any cases of animals attacking anyone up here. About that time I think he realized that he had walked into an ambush, but he said rather lamely, no, well, not specifically, but it could happen. Then he added that you could never tell when you'd run into another person who might give you some trouble, and you'd need a gun.

I think by this time he was ready to change the subject, but my wife kept on. Well, she asked, what might somebody do to you that would make you want to have a gun? It was obvious that he hadn't thought about this very much, and he mumbled that somebody might tell you you couldn't do something you had a right to do, and my wife said, "Do you mean that you'd murder a man because of that?" He answered that he certainly intended to "protect his rights."

This dialogue continued for a little while longer, as I sat there enjoying it hugely. They had been swaggering around with those guns, whose real purpose, I think, was to impress the dudes, and my "dude" wife wasn't impressed at all. I wondered today if they remembered her; I feel sure they did.

Well, that long and windy story doesn't have much to do with high-mountain ecology, but it does give me a transition to the topic of wind. It is howling now about as hard as I've heard since I arrived. It has also been thundering and raining a bit. However, the weather forecast sounds good for tomorrow, so once again I'll be expecting the helicopter.

July 9

I suppose it is not considered ethical to lie to your tape recorder, so I may as well admit that today I have reached despondency. It's the first time I've been depressed since coming to Brown's Cabin. I'm sure that in the past weeks there have been a lot of comments about waiting for the helicopter to arrive. Well, this is related to my need for radio communication. My concern is primarily that Larry Savadove and the Landsburg crew are waiting until there is radio contact with the outside world before they come in. Secondly, and importantly for me, I want to be able to communicate with my family and know that they can contact me if they need to. I'm not greatly troubled about our son Gary—he is the one who graduated from high school and went to Maine—but Carol wrote in her letter of June 24 that he is homesick and upset, so naturally I am concerned.

I suppose that I have strongly expected that the helicopter would be in on at least half of the last eighteen days. This has cramped my work schedule, because I've tried to find chores that would keep me around the cabin in case the electronics technician came in. On all those days I have been able to kid myself out of feeling too disappointed. But today being Friday, with the knowledge that there is no chance for the chopper until Monday, has pushed me into a slough of despond that I can't seem to escape. So I've been feeling a little sorry for myself and have had a severe headache all day. I think it's psychosomatic, but it is nonetheless real. I've taken enough aspirin and Darvon to make me a bit groggy tonight.

That's more than enough on my physical and mental condition. This morning I completed keying out the plants I had collected yesterday and had been unable to take care of because of the unwelcome guests. I also went out to the robin's nest and found that the fledgling has left. I'm sure this is at least partly due to the fact that one of the dudes tied his horse

to that tree yesterday. I had made a ladder and clipped off limbs that were
in the way so I could photograph from a distance of about eight feet. Now
all that has gone down the drain.

I guess the discovery of the vanished robins represented the bottom
of the emotional barrel today—no helicopter, no robins, no friends, no
mail. I really didn't feel like doing a damn thing. I decided the best therapy was some hard work, so I took the saw and ax down to the tree I felled
the other day, sawed several blocks of wood, packed them up to the cabin,
and split them. This way I'll be a little ahead in maintaining my wood
supply, because tomorrow—I'm anticipating again—is the day Stewart
Parks of the Forest Service told me he would be in to help me set up the
weather station and all the instruments. He'll probably stay over tomorrow night and go back Sunday. If he comes.

I have another marmot story to tell. Today I watched the reddish
male marmot and smaller dark female in a dramatic performance. These
are the two who have been having the domestic strife. Today they were
friendly to each other and reminded me for all the world of the story
about Tom Sawyer doing handstands and walking the boards of the fence
to attract the attention of Becky Thatcher. First I noticed the male marmot working his way across the ledge above the cabin toward a spot where
the female was sunning herself on a rock. When he got to within ten or
fifteen feet of her he began rolling over and climbing around the
rocks, much more than marmots do in normal travel. Then he would cork-
screw his tail around. She avoided watching him when he was close, but
once he pulled back five or ten feet she would coolly turn her head
toward him to give audience to his antics. They kept this routine going
for at least ten minutes, he moving about seventy-five feet away from
her, then back and into his Tom Sawyer displays. Showing off, I would
say.

This afternoon I made a reconnaissance trip, circling about a quarter
of a mile from the cabin, looking for blinds from which to photograph big
game. I took two blocks of salt to one site and left them there as entice-
ment. Big-game animals have a marvelous ability to seek out a freshly
placed salt lick. If they find this one, I will have a good chance of getting
pictures from a blind nearby.

I noticed a robin behaving oddly. These birds are normally very
peaceful, coexisting with other species of songbirds without strife. But this
female robin, which probably has young nearby, was chasing the gray jays
and Clark's nutcrackers all over the mountainside. Several times she even

followed them across the draw in front of the cabin all the way into the timber on the far side.

July 10

First thing this morning I hauled a shovel, a bar, a pick, and other tools we might need up to the heliport. I don't want to waste time with hauling once Stewart Parks is here to put up the weather station. I found that the shelter had been attacked again—not by the much-maligned porcupine but by the weather. I had placed it on a large, round rock, and last night the wind blew it over and smashed it to pieces. The sides had been completely torn apart, the roof was lying elsewhere on the mountainside, and eight or nine of the louvers were broken out. So I went back down to the cabin and got a saw, hammer, nails, screws, screwdrivers, and wrenches. By the time I had all the tools in place and had carried the pieces of the shelter back to the site, it was nearly nine o'clock. It took two and a half hours to get it back together, but it is now a lot more solid than it was as manufactured. The boards had been merely tacked together with one or two small nails. I was rather disgusted with the way modern carpenters perform.

About eleven-fifteen I went back to the cabin for more tools, had a glass of milk and a sandwich, then returned to the heliport. I was just putting in the last screw when Charlie Combs and Stewart Parks hove into view on the trail leading down from Brown's Pass. Needless to say, I was pleased they had made it. Charlie had brought a small collection of fresh vegetables and a large bundle of mail, including word that my wife is getting along fine and that my youngest son, Mark, has won the fourteen-and-under division of the Fort Collins tennis tournament, made the semifinals in the sixteen-and-under division, and has been invited to the Colorado state-closed tournament. There was a marvelous letter from Gary, in Maine; he has about as many wildlife stories as I do. He is remodeling log cabins on Moosehead Lake, and the raccoons and other wildlife seem to come and go in a ceaseless parade.

Stew Parks and I tackled the weather station immediately, and this, as expected, was quite a job. We had to dig four postholes in very stony soil, one for each corner. It took all afternoon to put up the structure and arrange temporary anchorage. Stewart and I work well together, because he's probably even more particular than I am. When we had finished, the platform was perfectly level and we were both happy with the result. It is now ten-thirty and we have just finished the dishes, looking forward to sleep.

July 11

We started early this morning and spent all day assembling the weather station's instrumentation: a standard thermometer, a maximum-minimum thermometer, a microbarograph to record pressure, a hygrothermograph to record humidity (the last two are clock-driven, have seven-day charts, and will run for eight days without winding). After installing the instruments, I dug a hole and set a seven-foot post, which will support the anemometer, or wind gauge. This one is a totalizing anemometer, which gives cumulative wind motion rather than wind velocity at any given moment. This motion is measured in miles.

Finally we built a platform, buried it partially, and anchored it with rocks to keep it from moving or blowing away. Then we bolted on a recording precipitation gauge. This, too, has a seven-day chart and a clock drive. The advantage of this device over the old rain gauge with the dipstick is that it tells you not only how much precipitation has fallen, but when it fell.

We finished at six o'clock, and I now have quite an array of technological toys to play with. Stewart packed up and headed for the road. He plans to come back on Tuesday to bring a couple of replacement parts and to see that everything is running properly.

I will certainly write a letter of commendation about Stew, with copies to appropriate supervisors, because his cooperation has been simply outstanding. He took the trouble to gather a great deal of literature concerning weather record-keeping and put in a weekend of hard work with no hesitation or complaint. He won't be compensated for this time; he simply donated it to the project.

Stewart was also a joy to have as a guest. He is simply a wonderful young man, a good husband and father, apparently, who loves his family very much and is happy with his life. He has taken a number of college courses, mainly those with direct application to his work, such as electronics, mathematics, and climatology. He knows his profession very well. However, he does have one definite career limitation—the lack of a bachelor's degree. But Stewart, at age thirty-five, has no intention of going back to college. He likes to be out in the open and in the mountains, where he is at least five days a week. He and his wife enjoy living in the colorful town of Leadville. So although he foresees a salary ceiling, at current salary rates, of twelve to fourteen thousand dollars at the time of retirement, he is perfectly happy with his career. Somehow I found myself envying his simple approach to life and I wondered whether the pain of going through the bachelor's, master's, and Ph.D. programs has been worth it for myself and my family. I suppose if I were to do it again I would fumble through the same routines, but sometimes I rue the cost in lost vacations and weekends with my family during the long time it took. Long time, good God! That's an understatement. It took thirty-three years to get from high school diploma to Ph.D.

July 12

I decided last night that a crisis was in the making. I had not done any laundry for sixteen days, and bed sheets, pillowcase, and Levi's have not known soap and water during the twenty-eight days I have been here. So I put all of these things to soak overnight, and this morning after breakfast I began the long process of doing a complete laundry. As I've said before, I don't like the drudgery of this job, and it certainly has nothing to do with filming the documentary or studying the alpine ecosystem. But it's the only way I can come up with to stay reasonably clean. I won't attempt to relate how many trips I made to the spring, how many armloads of wood it took to heat the water, how many feet of rope to hang everything. I shall just say that I used three big tubs and five small ones, and by the time I had finished I had used most of the trees around the cabin to string clothesline.

July 13

Another disappointing day. I went up this morning to check the weather instruments and see how they were doing. Some of the clocks are running a bit slow and will have to be adjusted. Stewart Parks was to be in early this morning, and I waited for him until afternoon. When I finally decided he wasn't coming, I took a short hike to the little valley below the cabin where I had placed the salt licks. I was pleased to find that some animal had found the salt and licked it.

I also swung around through the timber and through some of the bogs and windblown trees, looking over the prospects for filming the effects of stress in this environment. I still feel hung up on the filming. I have it in my head, but I'm not getting it on film. And I'm getting damned tired of waiting and waiting. I realize that there are other things I could have been doing—studying the literature of alpine biology, for example; or collecting plants and insects. I especially want to learn something of the behavior of the alpine flies in this area. Flies are extremely important as pollinators here. At lower altitudes, bees fill this role, but they are immobilized in temperatures below 50 degrees and need bright light to work in. Flies have lower energy requirements and need less light.

But I didn't get any of these things done. The point of realization that the visit I'm expecting is not going to happen on a particular day does not come suddenly or early in the day. It kind of creeps up on me around noon or early afternoon, when it's too late to start any substantial project. There have been too many days like that.

July 14

The helicopter didn't come in today and neither did Stew Parks. But I did accomplish a fair number of things. First, while still halfheartedly waiting for the helicopter, I collected some new plant species, brought them to the cabin, and got them into the plant press. Then I took temperature measurements of water in ponds and streams to see what kinds of aquatic creatures might be expected. I also began collecting aquatic insects. Later I put together several live animal traps and set them out in an area in the willows where some kind of rodent is feeding. It clips twigs into two- and three-inch lengths, leaving them, completely peeled, on the ground. This feeding pattern indicates some species of mouse.

I then took a hike around the basin to find sites that will illustrate some of the micro-environments in this area. Vegetation is developing rapidly now. Areas that emerged from snowbanks no more than two or three weeks ago are covered with beautiful alpine flowers. The grasses are maturing and a number of sedges and grasses have already headed out in their amazingly short span between emergence and maturity. There is great variety in the soil conditions. One minute you can be walking through a bog where your feet get wet and in the next be on higher ground that is totally dry. The dryness of the soils is undoubtedly responsible for the early maturation of the species growing in it. Midafternoon brought some violent thunder to the area but only a small amount of rain.

July 15

After taking the weather data I made a square rodent pen out of wire mesh. It is about four feet on each side and a foot and a half high. I drove steel stakes in each corner and sank the wire in the ground about an inch so rodents can't dig out. I want to catch some of them, whatever they are, release them in this pen to identify and photograph them, then set them free.

In the afternoon I walked through a saddle that Charlie Combs says serves as a funnel where deer come into the basin. There were indeed many deer tracks, though not as many as I expected. Just as I popped out into the saddle I saw a beautiful red-colored doe. I saw her only for a few seconds and had no chance to film her, but it was good to see big game up close.

I curved downward out of the saddle and moved along the east side of South Texas Creek. There was a fair abundance of both elk and deer tracks and droppings along the route I followed through typical alpine tundra with its expanses of grasses and showy displays of flowers. Among the flowers were various plants, including such colorful species as moss campion and alpine forget-me-nots. Cushion plants have adapted themselves extraordinarily well to this windy environment. They grow low to the ground, the flowers are nearly stemless, and the leaves are very small, offering little wind resistance. They are what ecologists call a pioneer species, leading the way for others. Stubby branches catch blown-in soil which, with old leaves and other plant matter, absorbs moisture and contributes to soil building and stabilization.

Ruth Ashton Nelson, in her *Handbook of Rocky Mountain Plants*, offers such a good description of moss campion as a pioneer species that I'd like to quote it: "It is one of the first colonizers of barren gravel areas in the alpine zone. Each mat of stems and leaves accumulating over many, many years eventually becomes a nursery for other alpine plants." She goes on to say that in the slow progress of this vegetation toward a climax community, the vegetation which had helped make the beginning possible is in turn eliminated and no longer found.

The notion of a climax, or mature, community is a common one in plant ecology, and perhaps I ought to explain it here. It refers to a community of species that is perfectly suited to a certain set of environmental conditions. A climax community will not change unless altered by some environmental agent, such as fire or climate.

A climax community is the final product of "plant succession"—the gradual development that begins with pioneer species in an uninhabited environment, such as solid rock or barren soil. These pioneers—lichens, mosses, cushion plants, others—help break down rock and build up soil, making it possible for larger, more complex plants to succeed them, until finally there is enough soil to support a forest, grassland prairie, alpine tundra, or other climax community.

In the montane zone below here, the typical climax community is the ponderosa pine–Douglas fir forest. If fire destroys such a forest, it may be replaced by a fast-growing and dense stand of lodgepole pine. The lodgepole may then yield, over a period of many years, to the original climax situation. In the subalpine region, which reaches up to Brown's Cabin, the climax community is the beautiful Engelmann spruce–alpine fir forest. A fire in this kind of forest often burns with such heat that the soil's humus is destroyed. The area may return to pioneer conditions, followed by lodgepole pine, and finally by the climax forest itself. All such plant succession takes place very slowly and depends upon the weather, orientation of the site with respect to the sun, and other factors.

At about two o'clock I came to a point on the ridge where I could see the cabin and was surprised to see it surrounded by horses. I watched for some time through the binoculars and finally saw two men. They did not seem to be molesting anything. I thought it was Ken Rodgers, who was supposed to have come in earlier to remove some equipment.

I continued along the Divide for another three quarters of an hour, searching for a suitable route toward Cottonwood Pass, where there may be bighorn sheep. Then I turned and started back, coming in view of Brown's Pass at about two-thirty. There I saw two riders with four horses headed up the Divide toward Kroenke Lake. I could see one of the animals was a mule, loaded with long aluminum pipes and antenna-shaped things, so I knew that the Forest Service, without the helicopter, had finally come to my rescue with the radio equipment.

I didn't get a chance to talk to the two men with the pack string, but as I came down toward the cabin I met Stew Parks working on the weather station. I helped him until about five-thirty, when the other two men, Bob Graves, a packer, and Duane McCrary returned from where they had set up the repeater station. We all went back to the cabin and began working on the balky generator. There were considerable difficulties. Finally, after removing the regulators from the generator and using only the regulator attached to the propane bottle, we were able to get the motor started. During this time we also managed to radio Charlie at Buena Vista, although we were having some trouble, probably because he was unfamiliar with the controls.

I whipped together a crude supper for the fellows so they could eat before they left at eight-thirty. It must have been a long day for them, because they started early and had experienced a good deal of trouble with the pack string. They had tried to come up through the meadow on Denny Creek, but one of the horses had sunk in up to its belly and then fallen over on its pack. So the whole awkward load had to be rearranged, and apparently fell off several times again on the trip up. Fortunately no damage was done to the camera case that had been sent in.

After the fellows left I made my nine o'clock call to Charlie; this is the time we have established for a daily safety check. I was able to talk with him fairly well. Then I turned to what seemed like a huge stack of dirty dishes; I'm not used to so much company.

We had agreed that when McCrary got to Buena Vista he would call me to see if he could straighten out some of the problems Charlie was having with the set. At eleven-thirty the call came through and it was a good clear transmission both ways. So I breathe easier. It appears that we have this communication problem solved at last—after thirty days without verbal contact with the outside world.

July 16

I spent most of the day in the shed working on the generator. When it was set there a month ago the shed was full of ice and snow. When the ice melted the generator had become unstable; it had a definite tilt, and the vibration of the motor would have caused it to slide off the blocks in a matter of days. It's difficult to handle a 300-pound generator alone, but fortunately there is a block and tackle here, so I was able to lift it up and build a stable base. Now it is perfectly level. I use the generator mainly to charge the camera batteries, but as a pleasant bonus, when it is working it powers four electric lights in the cabin.

July 17

I made my circuit of photo points today, which brought me back to the cabin around noon. I was eating lunch when an interesting visitor came into view. He is the first person who has been by the cabin since July 5, except for those who came in specifically to see me. It turned out that he was fifty-five years old and that he had hiked many parts of this continent, including Canada and Alaska. He was dressed in only a pair of shorts and hiking shoes, without socks, but he seemed to know what hiking is all about. He carried a little bag which he said contained all he needed. It was smaller than a ladies' handbag.

He came down the mountain in a strange fashion, moving from one old hollow stump to another, peering inside each one. When we were talking he finally asked me if I had found an ore grinder. He described this as looking like an old-fashioned coffee grinder, and said that people in museums had told him it was used for analyzing small ore samples. He had come across one of these grinders when he was hiking through here in 1965 and had hidden it in a stump. Apparently someone has made off with it during the intervening years.

I talked with him for nearly an hour, and my impatience began to grow toward the end. I've made it a policy to talk very little with the few people who have wandered by, partly because it takes up valuable time, and partly to avoid the inevitable questions about what I'm doing here. I find it interesting that the half dozen people I've talked with have been bursting with curiosity, and yet not a one has come out and asked me. So I haven't told them.

This morning as I was heading up to Brown's Pass I heard shooting. I looked up on the Divide and saw a fellow walking back down toward the pass. When I reached it there were two motorcycles parked there and two men with them. One said he had been shooting at rocks; I suspect at marmots. They said they were trying to decide in what direction they ought to go, so I suggested they should go down Denny Creek. They said that's where they had just come from. I said I knew that, and I still thought it was the best thing for them to do. I'm not winning any popularity contests up here; but they followed my advice and I consider that a small victory for the alpine environment.

July 18

This morning I woke at four-thirty, had breakfast, packed a light lunch, and took off for the Continental Divide. I had promised to take a government sign to post at the radio repeater station, which the packer and Duane McCrary told me was four miles from here. But the hike, going from 11,700 to over 13,000 feet elevation, took me only an hour and seventeen minutes, so I am sure it is much less than four miles.

In the mornings I have been seeing the tracks of a deer, coming down the trail and turning off about a hundred feet above the cabin. This morning, after I had climbed about five hundred feet straight up, I stopped to put on mosquito repellent and I looked back down the basin with the binoculars. I saw a beautiful mule deer doe walk gracefully down from above the weather station, moving at an easy pace, stopping to nibble at grass or weeds, listening attentively but not frightened. As she came to a point about seventy-five feet from the cabin, she stopped, looked it over carefully, then trotted slowly across the draw above my spring into the timber. A little later I saw her come out in the small glade directly below me, where she grazed in some willows for a few minutes.

Aside from the elk, the mule deer (*Odocoileus hemionus*) is the only species of deer living in the Brown's Cabin area. Its close cousin, the white-tailed deer, is primarily an eastern species, though it does occur in Colorado at lower altitudes. Where their habitats overlap, a close look may be necessary to tell the two species apart. The tail is the tip-off: the mule deer's is narrow and black-tipped, quite unlike the startling white banner raised by the whitetail when alarmed.

The antlers offer a more subtle distinction. Those of the mule deer branch into two simple Y-shaped parts; those of the whitetail produce several tines from a single main stem. The mule deer also has much larger ears—and moves with a bouncing gait, quite different from the stealthy movement of a white-tail.

There is little chance of confusing a mule deer with an elk. Even a large deer seldom approaches half the weight of an elk. Nor do the two species compete directly for food. For most of the year, the elk feeds on grasses and forbs, while the deer browses more on shrubs. During severe food shortages, however, either will eat what is available, with the elk taking the lion's share.

From what I have seen so far, the population of mule deer here is modest. Before the Civil War, the species was described by one naturalist as "everywhere" throughout the mountains. But heavy hunting for meat and trophies accompanied settlement of the region, and in 1911 Merritt Cary wrote in the *Biological Survey of Colorado:* "A few mule deer [were reported] in the Estes Park region in 1895, but I heard of none in the foothills of Boulder and Larimer Counties in 1906."

Deer are important to the ecosystem as converters of leaves and other plant matter to protein. Historically, they have supported many predators, especially mountain lions and wolves. They were more important as food to these predators than marmots, rabbits, and other small animals, who do not provide enough of a meal to warrant the effort of chasing them. Coyotes and bobcats also prey on young, weak, and snowbound deer, and scavengers devour the carcasses of the many deer that die each year from other causes. Nowadays hunters and automobiles probably kill more deer than traditional predators, which themselves have become scarce. Consequently, the energy flow through this ecosystem is much different from what it was before human settlement.

A short time after I arrived at the repeater station I heard a muffled roar below me. I looked through the binoculars toward Kroenke Lake and saw the first motorcycle of the day. This cast a pall over the hike. I looked some more around the lake and saw five people fishing, at least one tent camp, and two horses grazing. This is a remote lake and a small one, so it probably receives little fishing pressure during most of the summer. As I continued to look around I saw a mule deer doe with two fawns on a little bench quite far down. They were easy to spot with the glasses. I scanned elsewhere for a while, and when I looked back at the doe she was standing at full alert, staring down the slope. The two fawns had disappeared. Finally, after ten or fifteen minutes, she began grazing again, and within two or three minutes the two fawns had reappeared beside her. Apparently she had given them several signals: first, that there was danger nearby, and second, that the danger had passed.

I learned later the cause of the doe's anxiety. When I got back to the cabin Charlie Combs and his companion, Chuck Comer, were there, and they told me they had been camped in the mouth of the draw below this mule deer and her fawns. They had slept until about eight o'clock and then had gotten up, built a campfire, and eaten breakfast. I had been watching her at around eight-thirty, when, undoubtedly, she had been alerted by Charlie and Chuck.

After posting my sign I started back for the cabin. As I was coming across a flat grassy area, a small songbird flew literally from beneath my feet. I searched the tundra and found her nest. It was a rather deep cup, perhaps four inches, overhung with dry grass, containing four shiny, light brown eggs, which I identified as those of the water pipit (*Anthus spinoletta*). This sparrow-sized bird with long, bobbing, white-edged tail is one of the less than half a dozen species that nest regularly in the rigorous alpine region of the Colorado Rockies. Others that I would expect to find nesting near and above my cabin are rosy finches, white-crowned sparrows, horned larks, and white-tailed ptarmigan.

This nesting pipit probably arrived only a couple of weeks ago from some southern wintering ground, perhaps as far away as South America. Pipits nest almost immediately after arriving on the tundra and incubate their eggs for only two weeks. As with plants, alpine birds nest, incubate, and raise their young quickly in order to complete their necessary life processes during the brief alpine summer.

As I neared the cabin I heard a call from below and then saw Charlie reaching the cabin just ahead of me. We had been talking only a few minutes when two motorcyclists came down the trail and stopped. I gave them the usual cold shoulder, and Charlie went further and told them that they had no business being on that trail, that this area was closed, and that we could get a $100 reward for turning them in. I was a little skeptical about Charlie's hard-line approach, but decided this was not the time to contradict him. The motorcyclists seemed to be nice fellows, and although they were obviously embarrassed by the treatment they were getting, they tried to be friendly and make conversation for a few minutes. Both were carrying rifles slung around their shoulders—which explained the shots I had heard coming off the Divide—and they said they had been shooting marmots. Hearing that made me glad that Charlie had chosen the hard line. The fellows finally got back on their cycles and left. Instead of going down in the soft ground around Texas Creek, as they had intended, our attitude seemed to change their minds. They roared back up the mountain, leaving a shower of gravel and dust.

July 19

After we had eaten lunch, I decided to go with Charlie and Chuck into town. For three weeks I have been bothered by a constant and increasing pain under my shoulder blades. I have no idea what it is and have been trying without success to ignore it.

The next morning I got an appointment with a physician in Salida. As usual in my experience with physicians, I didn't believe what he told me, but maybe there was some therapeutic value in being able to tell him my troubles. He examined me and said that he thought I had a deteriorating disc in my spine. This I doubt because I had a disc operation several years ago, and what I am experiencing now feels different. Also, the diagnosis required much more sophisticated testing than I had today. In any event, he gave me a shot, some pills which I'm supposed to take for the next few days, and the assurance that this will make everything better. I hope so. I have been very reluctant to go to town, but this thing is crippling my efficiency.

I did attend to a number of chores while in town. I called Ross Moser, the district ranger, and asked if he had heard anything about my request for some protection against four-wheel-drive vehicles and motorcycles. He assured me that he had. Bill Lucas, the regional forester, had Xeroxed my handwritten letter and distributed copies to supervisors of the Gunnison and San Isabel forests. They in turn had gotten in touch with their rangers. So Ross was having a sign made; it was just taking a few slow, bureaucratic days because it had to have a special design for this unusual and temporary situation. When I told him about the motorcycles coming in by way of Kroenke Lake, he said he would get another sign and bring both of them out in the next day or two. He also called Bill Conklin, the ranger on Gunnison, and found that Bill had already gotten his sign made and set up on Texas Creek. So something is indeed being done to protect me from this motorized invasion force.

After buying a few things I was ready to get back "home"; I hadn't been away overnight for more than a month. I had a bowl of soup in the café, returned to Charlie's house, and he brought me to the mouth of Denny Creek. At two o'clock I left for the cabin, and had only been hiking about fifteen minutes when a drenching rain began. It continued the rest of the way in. I was feeling some concern about leaving all the expensive equipment inside the cabin while I was away, even though two of the doors are barred and the third has a lock on it. So it was with a feeling of relief that I found everything in order when I got back. It was extremely damp and cold in the cabin, however, and there were puddles where the heavy rain had leaked in. I got the fire going in a hurry and began making supper.

Just then the fog began drifting in. I always enjoy watching it creep up the basin and begin to surround the cabin. There are times when the fog is so dense that it obscures trees that are only thirty or forty feet away, and I become enclosed in a world of my own.

Before leaving home in Fort Collins, I had bought some tape cassettes to use for corresponding with my department head at Colorado State, Dr. Gustav Swanson. I just got a response to my first tape to him, and it was fun to listen to it while I made supper. I had asked him to look up some references on things I did not completely understand and—this is a real great guy—he had gone to considerable lengths to find them and report the results to me. I also picked up some mail at Salida, which I read after supper. It was good to learn that the family is very well and that my son won the runner-up trophy in the statewide closed tennis tournament. Although he was not the winner I am enormously proud of him, considering the fact that some of the Denver and larger tennis clubs have higher-level coaching and competition than our little club in Fort Collins. I think if Mark could get that kind of training he would be a champion-level player.

This may be my anthropomorphism again, but I'm convinced that the animals were glad to have me back at the cabin. As I was coming in over the Divide, a pair of marmots, a male and a female, came quite close, lay on top of a rock in the rain, and began calling toward me. I tried talking back to them and there is no question in my mind but that we were communicating in some way. I wonder what they thought I was saying. Farther along the trail a pika, which is normally a shy little creature, came running down the slope and stopped about thirty feet away from me. It hopped onto a rock and squeaked away as I walked past. Finally, when I reached the cabin, the large marmot which occupies the cellar apartment was sitting on top of the shed. I'd been able to get no closer than thirty or forty feet before, but this time he watched me, writhing around making play movements, until I reached the eaves of the shed only a few feet from him. Then he scampered off. So, whatever the scientific facts may be, I was made to feel welcome, and indeed I felt much happier to be here among these wordless friends than I had felt down in Salida.

July 20

Today was cold, dark, dreary, and dismal all the way through. The temperature ranged from 38 to 49 degrees, and the sun never showed. It didn't rain very hard, but it rained almost all day.

It was one of those days when I barely got out. I spent more time than I liked just keeping the cabin warm. Both stoves had to be kept going, and even wearing two pairs of socks, I had cold feet all day. It was much more pleasant to be outside hiking around, which I did a little. I also read up on some of the relevant literature on alpine ecology. Reading is one of the aspects of this study that I am sure is being slighted. It seems that there are always enough things to be doing outside or around the cabin so that I seldom get time to sit down with books and papers. A bona fide ecological study involves much time reviewing scientific writings. So far I have not found this time.

July 21

Today was another cold day, barely making it into the lower fifties, and it rained intermittently all day. Fog and high clouds drifted through the valley every fifteen to thirty minutes, obliterating all my mountain landmarks, so I stayed close to home most of the time.

I did take a hike to the salt stations I set up earlier to see how much they are being used. Not much, it appears. On the way down an animal leaped into a tree. At first I thought it was a large red squirrel, but when I got closer I saw that it was a pine marten. This is the first one I've seen since the glimpse of my house marten scurrying across the floor of the cabin after trying to steal the Canadian bacon. This one behaved not at all like a squirrel would have in the same situation. Instead of scampering into the upper branches of the tree, it merely circled warily around the trunk, keeping to the side opposite from me. As I got closer it began weaving downward and jumped into an adjacent tree, still coming down. It stopped finally, about four feet off the ground and stared at me, eyeball to eyeball, from ten or twelve feet away. This marten struck me as a rather aggressive animal for its species, which almost never shows itself in the dense forests where it lives.

This afternoon I spent a couple of hours sweeping floors and setting up beds in the two rooms upstairs so that we won't have to spend time on that when Larry Savadove and the fellows from Landsburg get here. They are due in tomorrow, and who knows? I may be surprised by an on-time arrival.

July 22

It was very humid this morning, and a light wind pushed dense clouds down along Brown's Pass until about nine-fifteen, when they began to thin out.

After breakfast I was looking out the kitchen window when I saw a mule deer doe about fifty feet away, walking toward me. She came on until she was about thirty feet from the window, alert but not frightened. I had some pitch knots burning in the kitchen stove, and each time they crackled she flinched. I tried to slip into the other room for a camera, but apparently she saw the movement and changed her course. She didn't run, but walked rapidly across the slope, below the snowfield, and into the timber to the east. I am glad that these large animals are beginning to come closer to the cabin.

I went up to record the weather data, then decided to look at an area where mud is sliding over the snow at the head of Denny Creek. I had just gotten there when a pack string came into view, led by Don Little, who is doing the packing for me. He had brought in Larry, Glen Winters, Vilis Lapenieks, and Paul Desatoff, along with their gear. Right on schedule. So I hustled on back to the cabin to get acquainted.

Larry got right to work, setting up to take a number of shots around the cabin—shots of sawing and chopping wood, walking in and out of the cabin, housekeeping. The weather is terrible for photography, but at least I'll be able to get answers to the questions that have been troubling me.

July 23

This morning when I arose and came outside a mule deer was feeding about a hundred feet below the cabin. When it saw me it trotted off through the timber. The crew is eager to film some big game, but the animals have been elusive.

Again we have a very overcast day, with clouds just at mountaintop level and fog drifting through the valley. The relative humidity yesterday was 94 percent, which is the highest it's been since I have been reading the instruments.

Despite cold, windy, gray weather we filmed more of my activities—entering the cabin, leaving the cabin, attending the weather station, investigating a mine above the cabin, walking along the ridge above the snow. We also filmed an Indian paintbrush as a backdrop for the rodent pen.

This plant species—or group of species, really—is well known to laymen for the bright beauty of its reds, oranges, pinks, and whites. But few people realize that the flowers themselves are inconspicuous. The colors are found on the calyxes and leafy bracts that surround the flowers in brushlike patterns.

July 24

This morning early I made the mistake of alerting the fellows to a beautiful sunrise. The rich light was touching the peaks of the Three Apostles while Texas Creek below was filled with a pure white fog. It was a mistake because Larry came out about that time and decided we ought to put a basin of ice-cold water on top of a nearby stump and film me washing my face, with the sunrise and fog in the background. So my day began abruptly.

Last night the temperature dropped to 32 degrees, and the ground was covered with frost this morning. But the day was clear and full of filming. I won't try to detail it all; just assume that everything within telephoto range of Brown's Cabin is now somewhere in the movies.

July 25

Before we went to bed last night we set up a remote-control camera on a stump aimed at the meadow near the cabin where the deer have been seen. This morning Vilis, Glen, and I got up early, ready to operate the remote system, and found the glass housing around it so dew-covered that we couldn't see through it. So Vilis slipped down through the timber and Glen went in another direction with hand cameras. Neither found a deer. They took a few final shots Larry wanted, then the packer came in, loaded up the crew, and I was alone again.

I have a number of reflections about the past four days. One is that I feel less sure of my ability to judge people. I certainly misjudged the crew that Larry brought in. They came up through Denny Creek and when I first saw them they were already fairly close. Vilis and Paul both have long hair and beards, and I formed the impression of an unprofessional-looking group who would probably waste their time and mine. I even wondered if Larry had picked people off the sidewalks of Los Angeles who just wanted a trip to the mountains.

But after having worked with these fellows for a few days, I am eager to correct my mistake. I now know that they are outstanding at what they do. They worked with great energy, and not only at their own jobs. They also pitched in and helped with the routine housekeeping chores in a totally unforeseen way. I felt extremely grateful.

I have met Larry Savadove before, but again I was impressed with the dedication he brings to these assignments. I must say that I didn't agree with the way he did everything, but I really admired his determination to get the filming completed. Glen was quick and efficient, and Paul was just darned helpful in everything he did. Vilis is quite a character, and even though he is older than the others and admittedly in poor physical condition, he was always right on the job. I was amazed at how well the crew operated, knowing how difficult it is, physically, to adjust from conditions at sea level to the thin air at 12,000 feet. They stayed outside even in the worst weather, trying to wring every bit of value from every minute they were here.

Although it's nice to be alone again, this experience certainly was a good one. I had the chance to ask any number of questions about filming. Of course, I thought of more questions after they left, which always seems to happen. But I certainly feel much happier about my cinematographic situation than I did a week or two ago. I'm still a long way from getting a job at Warner Brothers, but I think I can now do what is expected around Brown's Cabin.

As the pack string was leaving I felt fired up about getting out and exposing reel after reel of film, and it was a letdown to realize that I had to get the cabin and myself cleaned up first. Primarily through the efforts of Paul, though all the crew helped, the cabin was in surprisingly good shape for having held this number of people for four days. Mostly it was a matter of rearrangement; I suppose I spent an hour getting things back where I am accustomed to finding them. Then came a big wash that has been postponed too long, which pretty well took care of the rest of the afternoon.

The day ended with two unpleasant episodes. At about three-thirty there was a brief rainstorm with a little hail, and then four motorcycles came in and parked above the cabin. Six riders got off and walked over west of the cabin, making a lot of racket and as usual totally disgusting me. So I just stayed inside. I suppose that was immature sulking, but I was already scrubbing clothes and didn't want to stop for motorcyclists. I heard them speculating about the purpose of the cabin and whether there was a fireplace inside where they could come in and warm up. I didn't go out to talk with them, just kept on with my business until finally they got on their bikes and roared up Brown's Pass.

They hadn't been gone more than half an hour when Ken Rodgers' son and one of his packers came in with some horses and said that Ken was coming in with guests. I won't go into the details, but I had some pretty short words for Ken and I think he finally got the message not to continue arriving here while I'm filming the documentary. He had brought two guests, two wranglers, six horses. I overheard a guest asking who was this bearded guy and how come he was telling Ken what to do. I didn't hear Ken's response.

Before they left, Ken asked me why Charlie Combs had not hired him to do the packing for me, and I simply told him that it was because I wanted somebody else. I feel that Ken Rodgers is a person you have to be blunt with in order to reach any understanding. I hope we have reached one.

July 26

This has been a good day, for the most part. I got up at five forty-five, got coffee started, and went down to the meadow with my camera at the ready. I saw a mule deer before reaching the meadow and was able to film her until she finally ran; then I saw a second doe higher in the meadow and got some footage of her.

I caught up with some of the weather operations that had been neglected during the time Larry and crew were here, and I cut and split a little supply of wood. We had used all the wood I had stored before they came.

This evening I heard the short, sweet song of the white-crowned sparrow (*Zonotrichia leucophrys*) as I sat in the outhouse above its willow-field domain. This well-camouflaged bird, another of the few hardy nesters in the alpine, is hard to spot. Its speckled wings and streaked head perfectly match the crosshatched pattern of the willow leaves and branches. It constructs its nest in the crotch of the willow branches, protected from below by a leafy canopy. As I listened I gradually became aware of a disharmonious accompaniment, a chattery series of weak notes that signaled the presence of a Wilson's warbler. Although this warbler does not nest here, it shares the alpine willow fields with the white-crowned sparrow during its stay.

While I am on the subject of songbirds, I should mention the red crossbill (*Loxia curvirostra*), whose name implies its salient feature—a long, slender bill with crossed tips, which it uses to extract seeds from cones. I see it often in the spruce stands between here and Texas Creek. The brick-red males with their black-and-white wings are easy to spot, although the crossbill's most attention-getting device is the scratchy, piping sound it makes as it clambers around in the trees like a parrot.

July 27

The weather today has been clear most of the time, with a heavier wind than I have yet experienced.

I took two rolls of film, featuring: a pocket gopher feeding between the cabin and the spring, various species of wildflowers, a marmot in the head of Denny Creek, more shots of marmots in a rock field near Brown's Pass, ravens soaring overhead, two mule deer does just across the draw from the cabin, and some close-ups of a spectacular alpine thistle.

It was a good day of filming, but there was one disappointment. After eating lunch in the vicinity of Brown's Pass, I worked my way up to the Continental Divide, finally arriving in the saddle between my basin and Kroenke Basin just below the radio repeater station. I spent about an hour searching for the water pipit nest I had stumbled upon a week or ten days ago. It had been thoughtless not to mark it, and I muttered this to myself as I tramped back and forth. I know that I was very close because two pipits came aloft to harass me, chirping over my head, probably trying to distract me. But I couldn't find the nest.

After returning to the cabin I went farther down the mountainside and saw a doe bedded near the spring. She remained still as I walked up through the trees to within about fifty yards. I was able to photograph her. Then I saw a second doe nearby and continued on across the marshy area until I was standing at the base of the slope, perhaps forty yards below both deer. They went on feeding but would not let me get any closer. I stopped filming and walked to the cabin, looking back from time to time as the deer still fed around the rocks and among the trees.

These two does have been in the cabin area four or five times now and they show little fear of me. This is the third time I have walked around in plain view of them. They simply watch me carefully, often with their large ears extended, dropping their heads to graze on the grass or stretching to nibble in the willows. If I try to approach closer they drift into the brush or timber, not leaving the area entirely, simply maintaining some unwritten but well-known margin of safety between themselves and me.

When I went up to the ridgetop to radio Charlie, I checked the animal traps and found I had caught a montane vole (*Microtus montanus*). "Vole" comes from the Norwegian word for field, and voles are often referred to as field mice. Actually they are more stumpy-looking than true mice, with shorter tails and legs. Morphologically they are between mice and lemmings. There are several dozen species in North America, and in terms of numbers of individuals the vole genus *Microtus* is probably our commonest mammal, surpassing even the white-footed mouse (*Peromyscus leucopus*).

These voles flourish in moist meadowlands and aspen woodlands. Their most notable characteristic is the construction of networks of runways through the grass, which is their primary food. Within these runways, which are easy to spot, is a well-worn, inch-wide pathway bordered by a supply of neatly clipped pieces of grass. Montane voles do not hibernate, but remain active throughout the winter. Their cheek teeth grow constantly to compensate for the daily grinding against the tough grasses they eat.

Like some other small rodents, voles have a prodigious reproductive rate and may experience lemminglike boom-and-bust population cycles. When the population becomes too large for the food supply, the birth rate drops. When the population drops, the birth rate rises again. Voles breed throughout the warm months. The females bear young in ball-shaped nests of grass along the runways after only three weeks of gestation. Maturation is so fast that females born early in the season may breed that same summer.

I released the vole into my rodent corral, which worked very well. I was able to get good action photos, and now the vole can get back to its food gathering.

Yesterday Bill Nelson, assistant ranger of the Salida district, and another fellow came in by horseback with the posts and signs to close the Denny Creek trail temporarily to motorized vehicles. They were going to place a second sign near Kroenke Lake. Though I have expressed impatience about getting these signs posted, I also feel grateful to these fellows. It's really quite a task to get on a saddle horse and carry a seven-foot post with a heavy wooden sign bolted to it for a distance of several miles.

July 28

Happy birthday to you, happy birthday to you, happy birthday, you grizzled old bastard, happy birthday to you. Well, I'm celebrating July 28, 1971, which marks my first half century on this good earth.

Now back to work. It has been a good day and a busy one, so I'll regretfully begin and conclude the festivities with that song fragment. However, I do want to reflect a bit about what has been accomplished and, perhaps more important, what has not been accomplished in these fifty years, and what brought me to Brown's Cabin in the Rocky Mountains, to prepare a documentary on ecology.

Those years have been bitter and sweet, as I am sure is true for everyone. Without question the best has been my good marriage, which means my wonderful wife and four children, each of whom has been remarkable in his or her own way. In this regard I think of a conversation I had with one of the young fellows in the film crew up here. He made the apparently sincere statement that he felt marriage an unnecessary social institution. He said that a license to have children would be appropriate, but that he saw no good reason for a conventional marriage license, or for any contract between two people to live together until death parts them. Theologically and philosophically I disagree with that position strongly. Were it not for our marriage, in which we shall have persisted for twenty-seven years on the twenty-first of next month, one of the greatest satisfactions of my life would have been denied. This pleasure is only partially sexual;

more important has been the personal bond that has grown between my wife and me through these years.

This is not to say there have never been tough times. There certainly have. During the years immediately following our wedding I spent thirteen months in the Army in Europe. When we moved out to the University of Idaho we lived with a small baby in an eighteen-foot trailer on my stipend of $220 per month, and I worked at odd jobs in order to complete my bachelor's degree. After that we lived in tents and log cabins in remote areas during the two years' research and writing necessary for the master's degree. Things got pretty rough in spots; we were not as mellow and understanding of one another as we are now, and there were times when the marriage seemed to strain at its seams. But always, undoubtedly through my wife's strong religious faith and deeper understanding of human nature, we were able to patch up our differences and continue more strongly than ever. I've heard it said that the first seven years are the hardest, and this proved true for us.

As our children grew up, we shared in their triumphs and their disappointments, and this brought the entire family even closer together. The letter I received a few days ago from Gary coincides with my own feeling about doing this documentary, away from each other. Gary wrote: "Being apart physically will bring our family closer together spiritually." Perhaps this is trite, perhaps it's a cliché; but I think it is an excellent thought and I'm glad that my son is thinking this way.

I've also thought about the disappointment of having not reached anticipated goals by the time I was fifty years old. At twenty-one it seemed that the world was just one big red apple to be relished a bite at a time. Some of these bites I have taken and relished; some have been reluctantly chewed. There certainly have been enjoyable jobs. Perhaps the early years with the Idaho Fish and Game Department as a biologist were the most satisfying, even though they were hard physically. There were many long hikes and horseback rides and outdoor discomforts. I recall around the year 1950 that I had a difficult time requisitioning a sleeping bag that cost a hundred and fourteen dollars. The department was not pleased with such a large expenditure. To prove it was a necessary investment, I kept a record of how many nights I was away from home, sleeping out in the open. During the first twelve months after the purchase of the sleeping bag, I spent 218 nights in it. On our twelfth anniversary my wife and I calculated that I had spent more than half the nights of our marriage away from home. Don't ask me why we calculated it in terms of nights.

At the end of nearly six years with Idaho Fish and Game I was still earning only $400 a month. Because this was the top salary for a Biologist 2, which was the top category there, and because we had three children and a fourth on the way, we moved to Colorado for a better-paying job with the U.S. Forest Service in range and wildlife habitat research. This, too, was a job with many satisfactions. I was able to learn new skills in the fields of botany and range management and to make, I hope, some permanent contributions, including two U.S. Department of Agriculture technical publications, which I hope are proving useful to landowners and natural resources managers. Since I was trained primarily as a wildlife biologist, this Forest Service work with cattlemen and sheepmen in managing grazing land acquainted me with some other views about the use of public land for wildlife, recreation, and aesthetics.

Midway through my nine years with the Forest Service I was shifted to project leader in charge of wildlife habitat research, where I felt at home again. Then in 1965 I joined the faculty at Colorado State—primarily because I had begun to feel that our research results were reaching the resource managers and the public slowly, if at all. I have always had a deep interest in people, so it seemed natural to go into teaching, a job that allowed me to bring information directly to people who could and would use it.

Without doubt the most crucial single event of my life occurred five days after beginning work with the university, on July 5, 1965, when I was in Yellowstone National Park making a first visit to a graduate student whom I would be supervising. That evening I was called to the phone and informed by the Wyoming State Police that my eldest son had been killed in an automobile accident. Alan was only a few weeks short of his nineteenth birthday and had been an outstanding boy in every respect. He was returning from a short climbing trip in the Tetons. He had marvelous physical and mental equipment and probably had a brilliant future. When his life was snuffed out something was snuffed out in me, and in his mother and brothers and sister as well. For a long time I resented teaching other boys of Alan's age. I guess I had the feeling that they were not as worthy, or valuable, as my own son. That was, of course, an unfair and ultimately untenable attitude for a teacher, but that's what happened, and it affected my early university years profoundly.

My academic career has been unusual from at least one standpoint. For a variety of reasons, including seven major surgeries in the last fifteen years, a good deal of procrastination, and other personal limitations, I allowed my Ph.D. program to drag on for an extraordinarily long time. This slowed my pace of promotion at the university, so that I find myself at the end of my first fifty years with an associate professor rank and a brand-new Ph.D. degree. Now that I have it, however, the degree can help me attain a full professorship within a few years, if I stay with the university.

By any yardstick, this has been mighty slow progress. I suppose there is reason for satisfaction in having worked for state and federal agencies in management and research, and in having a reasonable list of publications to my credit. But the general level of accomplishment in these fifty years has been nothing to make headlines.

Now I find myself at Brown's Cabin. In general, I have entered the making of this documentary with great enthusiasm. I have already outlined my frustrations with establishing the radio communications and getting the film crew here to orient me, so I won't mention them again. But I do have a serious concern that has nothing to do with procedures— one that I have been unable to talk about even to my impersonal tape recorder. That is my physical health. This may seem totally unexpected—it seems that way to me. I have been following a rather rigid physical-fitness regime for the past three or four years and have been told by doctors that physiologically I am in better condition than most men ten years my junior. However, about three weeks after arriving, I began to notice a dull pain under my shoulder blades. This continued and increased in intensity until finally I went to the doctor in Salida. I already mentioned his diagnosis of a deteriorating disc, which I doubt simply because he made no detailed examination.

The worrisome thing is that the shot and medicine he gave me to take for a few days have had no effect. The pain seems to have increased in frequency and intensity. There were times when Larry and the fellows were here when I thought I would no longer be able to continue walking and photographing. It isn't the physical exertion that bothers me; I can backpack and do many chores with little pain. But there are certain positions and times during the day when the pain just hums along all by itself. When I'm alone my solution is to live on aspirin and Darvon, and also to stop what I'm doing three or four times a day, lie on the ground for about five minutes, and do some exercises. That helps temporarily.

Well, whatever it is, my attitude now is that I'm deeply into this project and I am going to complete it. I can only hope in the meanwhile that whatever is causing this pain will correct itself.

That was a good deal more reflecting than I meant to tape. But I'll only have one fiftieth birthday and, being without benefit of birthday cake, I had to do something special.

Part III

HIGH SUMMER

July 29

There was a severe hailstorm this morning and fairly high winds throughout the day. Between storms the country looked more beautiful than ever.
Almost all the snow has melted; that which remains is mostly in permanent snowfields that will melt only slowly, to be replenished by the first
autumn snows. The general aspect is now green, and I would judge that in
many areas the peak of flowering is already past, having begun only three
to four weeks ago.

Today was a hard day physically. I hiked out to the Cottonwood
Road this morning and was met by Charlie Combs, who drove me up to
what we both assumed was Osborn Creek. There was no sign, but according to the map it looked right. It was not. I followed the creek for about a
mile before deciding that it was leading me in the wrong direction. It
must have been the north fork of Cottonwood Creek.

The purpose of all that hiking was to investigate reports that bighorn
sheep were roaming this area. I had also been told I might find elk along
the Divide and in the head of South Texas Creek. But they weren't and I
didn't. There were very few tracks or other signs, and I did not actually see
a single big-game animal. Even though I haven't found any sheep yet, it is
exciting to be back in bighorn country. This is the animal I studied for my
master's thesis, and I never tire of watching a herd of them feeding and
playing in their high-country habitats.

The Rocky Mountain bighorn sheep (*Ovis canadensis canadensis*) is
the state mammal of Colorado, and it is an obvious choice. It is the ruler
of remote high places in a state famous for its precipitous mountains. Although some *canadensis* move to lower ranges in winter, others stay near
or above timberline year round. Its sureness afoot is legendary, even along

the scantest of trails and the most treacherous terrain. To us heavy-footed humans, it seems carefree in situations where we can scarcely travel.

The bighorn is a mixture of skittishness and savagery. It is often difficult to approach, particularly during hunting season when it is frequently still in the high country. This challenge has brought out countless hunters who regard a bighorn trophy as the sign of true skill. Bighorn vision is extremely keen, like that of other open-ground mammals. So is their hearing, and a herd may vanish like the dew at the slightest movement. But its behavior is something of an enigma. I have come to within twenty-five feet of ewe-lamb bands in Idaho while studying bighorn in the remote Salmon River mountains, and I have also had a large ram come to within ten feet of me. Later, in the Sun River county of Montana, I walked directly into a herd of fifty bighorn, including sixteen big rams. More recently, in the Pecos Wilderness Area of New Mexico, a bighorn ewe knocked my camera over a cliff while licking the salty sweat off my legs! A lot of romantic nonsense has been written about the wildness of bighorn sheep. Like most behavior in nature, bighorn responses depend on season, circumstance, sex and age of animals—and many unknowns.

When mating season arrives, the rams, in particular, display a nervous energy that often explodes into spectacular fighting. The ewes usually come into estrus one at a time. As soon as one becomes receptive, a male will begin his advances. Typically, the male will approach the female and she will run off a few yards, then stop. He will approach again, she will run off, and so on, until mating occurs.

Often, however, more than one male is interested in a lone female— a conflict usually settled by force. Most of the fighting is done head on in one of the most violent dueling styles in nature. The rams charge toward each other for several feet or yards, finishing the charge with a burst of speed, launching their bodies forward at the last second. Rams may weigh as much as 350 pounds or more, so that the noise of these collisions can be heard across whole valleys. The horns absorb most of the momentum, but there are no rules of chivalry. The rams may kick each other in the flanks, butt against shoulders, and rear to strike with their front hoofs. To the victor goes the privilege of mating—unless a third ram has stepped in to mate with the female while she watched the duel.

Unlike members of the deer family, bighorn rams do not shed their massive horns. They continue to grow each year, accumulating annual rings which indicate the age of the sheep. Ewes have slightly back-curved spike horns, as do yearling rams. The horns of a ram reach farther back and down each year; by the time they reach the bottom of an imaginary circle, the ram is about five years old. After that the growth of the horns slows. In a very old ram, they may actually reach a complete circle, but this is rarely seen in the wild, where the normal life span is eight to ten years.

Outside of mating season, the life of a bighorn is fairly placid. A herd may remain throughout the year within an area no more than a few miles across. Or it may move several miles or across a broad valley to warmer wintering grounds.

The life style of the bighorn is largely defensive: it keeps itself clear of mountain lions and other large predators by escaping into cliffs or rugged, rocky outcrops. Today, however, this species has new enemies that even the mighty rams are helpless to fight. Humans are in several ways a threat—both directly, by occupying or otherwise interfering with their habitat, and indirectly, by allowing stock to overgraze bighorn winter ranges. These stresses—particularly when exacerbated by severe climactic conditions—render the sheep vulnerable to parasites and diseases, especially lungworm and pneumonia. The impact of hunting is a controversial issue. But there is evidence that, unless carefully controlled, hunting may be detrimental to some bighorn populations.

To ease my frustration at not finding any animals, I decided to take the "easier" way back home, down rocky slopes to the willow fields above Hartenstein Lake. These willow fields are common throughout the Rockies, growing densely along stream banks and wherever soil is moist. Learning to distinguish willow species is difficult; there are thirty in the state of Colorado, many of them similar in appearance. But they contribute much beauty to the landscape, and deer, elk, mountain sheep, and livestock browse on their twigs and buds and find shelter in their thickets. I have walked through willows before, but this was the largest and densest willow field I have ever seen. For two or three stretches I walked for a hundred yards or more literally on top of the willows. I doubt that my feet came closer than twelve inches to the ground, and in some places I was probably thirty inches high. The extraordinary experience of living alone and filming an ecological documentary may not have equipped me to walk on water, as I learned crossing Texas Creek, but at least now I can walk on willows!

Earlier in the summer when I crossed the tundra, the attention-getters were the early spring flowers—the alpine forget-me-nots, the snow lily, the mountain bluebells, marsh marigolds, violets, and buttercups. Now that the season is further advanced there is more diversity in the plant communities. I can see the tiny alpine dryad and the bluegrasses;

the sedges and the rushes are beginning to form flower stalks; profuse mats of distinctive alpine avens are in full yellow bloom. Species of *Senecio*, a large genus of yellow-flowering plants, are already past their prime, as are other members of the sunflower family. Indian paintbrush in all its variety is now a dominant feature of the landscape. As I'm sitting here by a stump next to the cabin, I'm looking up toward the Continental Divide above the old mine shafts, and I see that the vegetation on the drier soils has already passed the bright green stage and moved nearer to dull tan or yellow. Summer seems so fleeting here. As soon as I can identify its presence with any confidence, it has begun to move past me.

July 30

The first thing I shall report is the weather, which was generally good today. However, the temperatures have fallen considerably from the highs of late June, when there was still two or three feet of snow on the ground. It was not unusual then to have a peak temperature in the middle or upper sixties; yesterday's high was 56. I don't mind some cold weather but I hope the fair weather has not vanished.

I was able to get some footage of the marmot who lives in the rocks just below my spring. I followed him about for a good while as he was feeding. I also took some photos of brown-capped rosy finches feeding on tiny insects on the snow. These insects are so small that even using the zoom lens I probably don't have what you'd call a close-up. This finch (*Leucosticte australis*) is truly an alpine bird, breeding above timberline in rock crevices or under boulders and feeding on insects and seeds blown to the heights by strong winds. Typically it is found in flocks hunting for seeds and chilled insects along the edges of snowfields, its feathers fluffed against the cold, hopping about and chattering incessantly. The whole flock may swirl restlessly into the air at frequent intervals, as though blown by the wind.

Tomorrow I plan to leave for a short backpacking trip. I want to scout for big game and to toughen myself up a bit for a longer trip. Traveling up here with all my camera gear is no easy thing. All of this country seems to be straight up or straight down, with very little level ground in between.

July 31

I left for Magdalene Basin carrying a pack of about fifty pounds. I had a chance to photograph myself crossing Texas Creek—something I don't get to do every day—because I chanced to meet a hiker at just the right time. I set up the tripod and then returned across the creek to re-enact the scene. When I yelled, the hiker pushed the trigger and I splashed back through the water. This passage was not as exciting as it was on July 4, when I nearly fell in. The water is considerably lower now. Even so, it was deep enough so that I had to put on the waders and watch my step.

I succeeded in finding an ideal location for a tent camp. It was good to get away from the cabin for a while and to find this beautiful spot, sheltered by some Engelmann spruce and the surrounding terrain. A granite boulder about six feet in diameter served as a good back wall for a campfire, and another rock about eight feet away offered a comfortable backrest. It was pleasant in the evening to sit and watch the fire and to feel the heat reflected from the boulder. Of course, campfires demand work in return for pleasure, so there was limb chopping and stump up-rooting to be done.

As much as I enjoy a fire, I wonder sometimes if backcountry areas can continue to supply campers without becoming barren. Perhaps my new mini camp stove is a better solution. It cost $9.95 in Fort Collins, and is small enough to slip into a pocket—five or six inches in diameter and maybe an inch and a half high. I think even the Idaho Fish and Game Department would have approved the purchase. When assembled it stands six or seven inches high, and you plug a tiny propane bottle into it by means of a stem and grommet. It takes about fifteen seconds to assemble and light. The fire is so hot I was able to boil water in three or four minutes. Therefore, thanks to freeze-dried turkey Tetrazzini, my supper was ready in five minutes, presto.

August 1

Another month has passed; I am now reporting on the first day of August. I spent a very comfortable night in the tent, although it must have been cold outside. Even at ten o'clock this morning, after two hours of bright sun in the basin, all of the small water areas were still frozen, and a pane of ice lay on some of the small ponds.

After a quick breakfast, which consisted of instant hot cereal and coffee, I was on my way up into Magdalene Basin a little before eight o'clock. The sun didn't come up in most of the basin until after I'd left, but when it did it was truly a beautiful sight. As I neared the place which ultimately became my next campsite I saw two elk on a slope half a mile away. With the binoculars I was able to count five altogether; and across a small ravine nearby a huge old bull was lying under a tree, apparently staring back at me. Unfortunately I was scouting for a tent site at the time and had left my telephoto lens behind in my pack. When I started back to get it this bull and another one took off.

Elk react differently than deer in this kind of situation. Deer tend to wait until you are quite close before spooking. Then they bound off for a short distance, stop, look back, and may settle down again to resume feeding or whatever they were doing. Elk, on the other hand, may watch your approach for some time without moving. Then, when they're convinced that you're really coming within threatening range, they will literally leave the country. When they take off through a basin it is a spectacular sight—and generally the last sight. So I was disappointed but not surprised that I couldn't get closer to these elk.

I continued on up the mountain toward the Magdalene mine, trying to find ptarmigan. They are reported to live along the ridges near the old mine site. After about an hour of exhausting climbing I reached the mine and a cabin in very poor condition. I don't know much about the history of the mine except that a man named Paul Smith was the principal miner, and he shut down sometime in the 1930s. He must have had a considerable crew up here, to judge by the evidence. They seem to have dug tunnels a great distance back under the Continental Divide; I found a number of ore buckets and hundreds of feet of cable that had been used to winch the buckets in and out of the tunnels. There is a remarkable amount of heavy machinery lying around, including a steam engine, a boiler, a huge winch and track, and all the buckets.

I sat for a while near the mine to take in the view. I was at an elevation of 13,000 feet, just below the jagged peaks of the Divide, and it was breathtaking. I tried to pan across the whole horizon, but I doubt that the camera can bring to a viewer the same feeling of awe I was experiencing by being there. I felt as though I could see the entire country.

I then walked on across the northwest edge of the basin and climbed again to some high benches where there was another cabin, smaller and more run-down than the other. A couple of shafts had been dug and ribbed with heavy poles. I have no idea how deep they were because each hole was filled with water. Here, too, was a beautiful location, with alpine meadows behind the cabin. Obviously the mining activity here was nothing like the operation in the Magdalene mine.

After an hour or more at the mine I went back into the basin, through typically steep Krummholz, expecting a ptarmigan behind every willow. Suddenly out of the matted Engelmann spruce there came a great sound and a burst of movement. It turned out to be a young mule deer buck. He was moving so fast that even if I had practiced the quick draw of the camera recommended by Vilis, I'm afraid I wouldn't have gotten more than a brief glimpse of his rear end.

Very late in the evening I saw the five elk in the meadow again, and I watched them until it was almost too dark to see. Just before night fell, they seemed to be disturbed by something at the lower end of the meadow; one cow and then another looked down, saw something she didn't like, and began her escape behavior. They moved away rapidly through the willows until each was completely hidden within the heavy timber at the edge of the meadow.

August 2

I awakened to hear the rain pattering on the top of the tent; a soothing but unusual sound. After getting up and starting a campfire outside I prepared breakfast inside, on the propane stove. Hot cereal and fried ham. I also fried some freeze-dried beef patties for lunch later in the day.

The rain alternated with clear, sunny weather, and it was not until ten o'clock that I could get everything packed up. I left a clean campsite and walked down through the wet willow meadow and over into the spruce timber. Yesterday I had seen what appeared to be two elk wallows in a meadow about a mile from my camp and I wanted to investigate. Elk are creatures of habit, often using the same routes to and from different feeding grounds, or the same wallows, for many years. It could be that later on the bulls will use this wallow in conjunction with their courtship activities. It would be a fine photo site. Sure enough, shortly after entering the spruce timber I discovered an obvious game trail, which led straight to the wallows. I then spent half an hour in the meadow looking for a campsite in the event I come back later in August.

When I reached Texas Creek the water was so much lower I was able to walk across on dry rock. I stopped to photograph an area roughly six feet by six feet carpeted with Indian paintbrush. There were eight distinct color variations ranging from yellowish white to deep rose. Still later I found and filmed a patch of a tiny cloverlike plant called Sibbaldia. Along with a few buttercups, it was adding its own tiny yellow flowers to the edge of a snowbank melting in the sun. These plants are a sure sign that a snowfield has just melted away. In a few weeks, Sibbaldia will turn crimson and be much easier to see.

It was good to get back to Brown's Cabin, which I did at about four-thirty. However, I was disturbed to notice as I climbed the final fifty yards of trail that the shed door was open. I was certain that I'd had a visitor, because this door is kept closed and fastened from the inside by wire. Upon arriving I was relieved to find Stew Parks, who had come in to work on the weather station. He had been driven back from the weather station by an electrical storm and had taken shelter in the shed. He was in the process of writing me a note explaining this when I arrived.

Much as I like Stew it is a little disturbing to have people coming and going at the cabin. Charlie Combs was in the day before I left for Magdalene Basin to do some necessary work on the roof, to help put up the radio, and to bring me some supplies. Now Stew is here, and his work, too, is necessary. It is disconcerting to be alone, yet not alone.

I spent the rest of the evening getting the cabin warm, unpacking and drying some of the camping equipment. At eight o'clock I made radio contact with Charlie, and we had fairly clear communication although he still has difficulty hearing me at times. I suspect that I have been talking across the mike, as I talk for the tape recorder, rather than directly into it. Tonight, quite by accident, I spoke straight into it and Charlie heard me better. I started the generator to charge the camera batteries; then went to bed a little early and did some much-needed reading by electric light.

August 3

I just made my call to Charlie and he has agreed to meet me at nine o'clock tomorrow morning at the bottom of the Denny Creek trail. I regret leaving the cabin for civilization, but it seems necessary. I need some material to make carrying cases for two of the movie cameras and the tripod—something waterproof—for long backpacking trips. And I need to ask local wildlife biologists for advice on better places to film elk, bighorn sheep, and mountain goats. I have general information from packers and other people, and I know the habits of big-game animals. But before I put in days of hiking I want better odds that I'll find them.

Charlie is still having problems understanding me. I'm becoming more convinced that it is less a mechanical problem than a Charlie problem.

I had a disturbing confrontation with representatives of the outside world today. Two men and six teen-aged Boy Scouts arrived at four-thirty with the intention of spending the night at Brown's Cabin. One of the boys walked right into the cabin and started unpacking. I asked him to wait a minute so we could talk about it. The two adult leaders became rather belligerent and said the boys were completely played out and had to stay here, that it was out of the question for them to return to their cars at the road. I told them what we were doing and they said, yes, a forest ranger (who turned out to be Stew Parks) had told them last night that someone was in here making a movie. As of now I don't exactly know what Stew said, but it did not dissuade eight of them, with packs, from coming here to stay overnight. I told them they could not do this, that we had a special-use permit from the Forest Service for exclusive use of the area and a contract with Charlie Combs. They were disappointed and angry. I didn't help matters when I criticized the way they had planned a trip without knowing whether they could spend the night at their destination. Then the leaders said that two of the Scouts were ill and couldn't make it back, but I was adamant and simply told them they would have to camp on the other side of Brown's Pass.

Well, the way things are going, I hope this project is a winner, because it's leading me to make more enemies in a short time than I have made in the rest of my life. There's no question but that Ken Rodgers and his sons are upset that this operation co-opts their favorite hunting site. Then I had pressured Ross Moser to erect the trail sign at the bottom of the meadow on Denny Creek. Two or three days later one of the Forest Service permittees brought his motorcycle up the trail, right past the sign, to Brown's Pass, where I met him. Later I wrote a short note to Moser telling him that the sign was not effective. I told him what I thought was wrong with the location, the wording, and how it should be changed. Now the Boy Scouts of America and a couple of their leaders are very unhappy about being turned away from a warm cabin. I hope that Landsburg Productions provides a good retirement system for people who have worked six months for them.

Speaking of Landsburg reminds me that several times now I have spotted a weasel that Larry Savadove saw while he was here. One evening it was scurrying across the snowfield above the cabin, and this morning I had a glimpse of it darting under the catwalk and then through the trees. Tonight it was at the dump and running through the woods below the cabin, but it never pauses long enough for me even to think about getting a camera.

These long-tailed weasels (*Mustela frenata*) are probably the most abundant carnivore in this area, especially along stream valleys and around rocky, brushy areas where rodents abound. And it is probably the busiest. Weasels always seem to be hard at work hunting mice, voles, chipmunks, pocket gophers; I have seen one carrying a pika in its mouth. Unlike the marten and some other carnivores, it seems to have no curiosity about humans, preoccupied with its constant travels and search for food.

Weasels have little choice about their near-constant need to eat. The long, thin shape of their bodies retains heat poorly and they burn up a lot of energy staying warm at this altitude. The rate of their metabolism is so high that they must consume up to half or more of their body weight in food daily.

I reported a few weeks ago that two gray jays were chasing a chipmunk, seemingly in some type of play activity. There was more of this today. A small songbird, which has been moving so fast I can't identify it, has been chasing a chipmunk, and again the chipmunk doesn't seem really to make an effort to escape. One result of this tag game was a near collision. I was narrating earlier this afternoon sitting on a stump near the cabin when I looked up to see the chipmunk running full speed toward me. It suddenly saw me when it was about four feet away, hit all four brakes, reversed its field, and ran back into the brush, all in one confused flurry of motion. It wasn't until then that I noticed the small bird in swift pursuit. In the end, however, the chipmunk ran up on top of a stump and sat there for several minutes, unmolested by the songbird. It was as if this were a demilitarized zone, a place where, by mutual understanding, the chipmunk could rest in peace.

August 4

This morning I left the cabin at seven and hiked out to the Cottonwood Road, where I met Charlie. He drove me to Buena Vista and loaned me his pickup to drive to Salida, where I spent the remainder of the day. Mission number one was to get cases for the cameras and tripod. My trip to Magdalene Basin had convinced me that my present backpacking system is inadequate. When I have a full load, including tent, sleeping bag, cooking utensils, enough food, changes of clothing, the two movie cameras, the still camera, and the tripod, I am not only loaded down but also unable to keep the cameras both handy and protected from rainstorms and dirt.

I tried several people, including a shoemaker and two upholstery workers, before finding someone willing to make custom cases: Tom Bainbridge, another upholsterer. He has to get the material from Denver, but he's going there tomorrow and thinks he can have the cases ready by next Monday for about thirty dollars. I think this a real bargain.

In Salida I also found out that there are some herds of bighorn sheep ten or fifteen miles from here. I can hire someone with a saddle and pack-horse and move into bighorn country with enough camping equipment to stay for a week or so, if necessary. There's no substitute for local knowledge about where you can expect to find big-game animals at certain times of year. John Howlett, of the Colorado Division of Wildlife, has assured me that he will send information on where to get some good footage of these animals. He also promised to use some of the division's helicopter time to scout locations for me.

In Salida I had my first encounter with a laundromat. I had accumulated a massive pile of dirty clothing and decided to save myself the half day's effort in chopping wood, heating and carrying water, and scrubbing by hand at the cabin. In the process of my adventure I discovered that little old ladies are attracted to grizzled old men in laundromats. One woman saw immediately that I didn't know what I was doing, so she took me in hand and showed me the ropes: the best kind of detergent to get out of the soap dispenser, tricks in getting the most for your quarter, how to get clothes drier than dry, the whole gamut. She did this with great diplomacy. She gently told me that although the instructions said to put one packet of soap into each tub, it was better to use at least one and a half packets. She refrained from saying that mine was the dirtiest pile of clothes she had ever seen. I shall think of this lady evermore as the Patron Saint of the Salida Laundromat.

August 5

I spent last night in a motel, again wishing I were back in the cabin. Although they are necessary, I feel these trips to town break into the special mood established by living alone in the mountains. I got up at five-thirty and Charlie had me and my supplies up to the mouth of Denny Creek at seven-fifty. I immediately set off on foot for Brown's Cabin. It was a beautiful morning; the mountains stood out sharply against the blue sky; there was very little wind and only a few fleecy clouds. The feeling that I had accomplished something in Salida the previous day must have improved my mental as well as physical condition, because I really felt like striding along. Perhaps part of the incentive was that Stew Parks, a vigorous young man in his mid-thirties, had made the trip in 1 hour and 39 minutes. This considerably eclipsed my times of 2 hours and 22 minutes on June 21 and 2 hours and 8 minutes on June 30. Charlie Combs, at age sixty, recently made it in 2 hours and 10 minutes. Charlie and I were dismayed to learn that Stew had left us so far behind.

For the first two miles up the mountain I felt there was no way I could equal Stew's record even though I was walking quite rapidly. However, about midway in I was feeling good, no physical strain at all, hardly sweating, so two and a half miles from the cabin I began to stretch out and really hike. The punch line of the whole story is that I made it in 1 hour and 34 minutes, five minutes better than Stew Parks!

I expect that to an outsider this business of old men timing themselves walking up a mountain sounds silly, and I guess it is. But when you feel in good physical condition it adds a little zest to the day to meet a challenge of this kind. Now I feel that I was loafing for the first part of the trip—next time I'm going to try for 1 hour and 20 minutes.

Enough on the physical. Soon after I got back to the cabin Billy Carpenter, the packer, came in with the biweekly supplies. He had an enormous pile of boxes on his little mule, and he had handled them all successfully except for the center box, which contained the milk. One of the crosspieces on the pack saddle had poked through a quart container, so the black mule came to the cabin with white milk streaming down its back. Billy stayed for lunch and we talked some about the problem of getting close to big-game animals.

I spent part of the afternoon packing away the new supplies and part putting a screened food cooler under the stairway. There is still an animal problem inside the cabin. I'm not sure what it is—weasel, chipmunk, marmot, marten—but whatever it is it frequently raids my food supplies. This screened-in structure should be not only "critter-proof" but also cooler thanks to Charlie. The stairway is directly over the old cellar, and a cool breeze flows in from between the good-sized cracks Charlie left when he boarded it up. Most of the time the temperature is in the high forties and low fifties, so the food should keep well here.

During the late afternoon and evening I visited nearby meadows to look for deer. I've seen a large buck in the area and would like a close-up view of this beautiful specimen. However, deer do change their grazing places from time to time and I couldn't find him.

I've moved the time for the evening radio check with Charlie from nine o'clock to eight. Charlie apparently wasn't on the radio at eight, but I left my receiver on and he came on at eight-fifteen. After I responded to his call, he said, "I heard you very good," and those were the last words I heard.

August 6

The weather has been good today, except for a brief, severe hailstorm in late afternoon.

Since at noon I had several things on my mind, I decided to sit by my favorite log in the sunshine and do my taping early. Just as I got settled four young men with backpacks appeared, climbing up from Texas Creek. They proved to be a most interesting foursome, and for once I didn't resent the intrusion into my privacy. Two were seniors in high school, one from Michigan and the other from Texas. Another was a freshman from a university in Ohio. The fourth was a sophomore from a college in Corpus Christi, Texas. They were taking part in a training program called the Wilderness Institute, apparently an outgrowth of the Outward Bound program, based in Denver. These fellows were completing their three-day final, which involved hiking from Twin Lakes, about twenty miles from here, over the Continental Divide, down through Magdalene Basin, up along Texas Creek, and past Brown's Cabin down to the road on Cottonwood Creek. They were given a map, minimal food supplies, and their destination. The rest was up to them.

They seem to have survived their three days in the wilderness in good style. They were also the most polite and considerate group that has come through here this summer. I was so impressed with the boys that I invited them inside the cabin for a look around. This is something I have never done before for strangers. They mentioned several of the other mining cabins they had come across, and I knew they were very curious about my mission here. But they were too polite to ask. It was a real pleasure to talk with young men who are interested in their environment and willing to put out considerable effort to see it.

After the boys left I had lunch, then took two cameras and hiked toward the Divide in hopes of photographing pikas and marmots. But today these creatures were not cooperative. The pikas were reluctant to let me any closer than sixty or seventy feet.

After returning I cleaned ashes out of the stove and was beginning to make an early supper when the sky began to darken. In a few seconds I could barely see inside the cabin, and almost immediately a storm began, dropping huge hailstones. The crash of the hail hitting the cabin roof, the catwalk, and occasionally a tin tub in front of the cabin was so dramatic that I recorded it; I also took close-up movies of hailstones hitting the ground. Some bounced as high as two or three feet. By the time I stopped filming there was a pile of hailstones two inches deep inside the open kitchen door.

After the storm subsided I went up to the weather station to see how the instruments had responded. For six hours before the storm, the barometric pressure had been dropping fast. The temperature had plunged just as the storm came through, while the relative humidity and the rain gauge went up equally fast. Nearly a third of an inch of rain fell in ten minutes.

When I returned from the weather station I walked into the kitchen and was startled to find a marten sitting in the middle of the kitchen table. It didn't act afraid, although it did move to the windowsill, where it seemed to be searching for a way out. Failing at that, it slipped to the floor and ran behind a cabinet into a crevice in the logs. There it promptly got stuck behind the chicken wire I had nailed over the hole several weeks ago. I got a flashlight in order to see it better, but it was moving around fast—first out of the crevice, then up the wall until it was looking at me over the top of the cabinet, then down again to the chicken wire. I decided to open the door to let more light in the cabin, but that turned out to be a mistake. It slipped out the door and into the timber below the cabin.

The marten's behavior struck me as unusual in several ways. I had not been gone more than fifteen minutes, yet in that time it had been clever enough to slip into the cabin and make itself at home. The creature was distinctly unafraid of me. Its movements were deliberate, revealing none of the panic I would expect in a wild animal trapped inside a cabin with a human. It even had the presence to look directly at me most of the time.

When I was alone once again I pulled the cabinet away from the wall and nailed another piece of chicken wire securely over the hole. Most of the time I feel I have the edge in this territorial conflict, but every once in a while, like today, that assumption seems ill-founded.

I was confounded again at about one-thirty in the morning when I heard things crashing and thudding in the kitchen. I got my eyes open and, flashlight in hand, ran downstairs to find that some creature had strewn dried soup and toothpicks across the floor, and attempted to haul a package of food behind the cabinet. Then at three-thirty I heard another racket, this time directly in the window under which I sleep. I looked out—or at least I got one eye partially open—and made out some type of animal stretched up against the windowpane, scratching as if trying to get in. By the time I had gotten my glasses and flashlight it had vanished.

Nor was that all. At four-thirty my sleep was broken again, this time by loud thumping on the roof. Something was walking back and forth; I'm certain it was the marten. And yet again, shortly before my alarm went off at six, the terrible screeching of Charlie and Martha, the two marmots that live in the ledge above the cabin, and whom I have taken the liberty to name, woke me. Apparently matters have gone awry in their marital bliss. After the initial quarreling, they seemed to have settled down amicably. I presumed Martha was expecting, although I still haven't seen any young. Maybe the screeching means they can't agree on how to raise the kids, hidden somewhere in the rock pile.

Whoever perpetrated the myth about the solitude and silence of the wilderness must have lived in a city. Brown's Cabin lately has been as noisy as feeding time at the zoo.

Last night I listened to a tape from my department head, Gus Swanson. On it he describes a real human tragedy, the death of a young man near Grand Lake not far from here. According to news reports, the story went something like this. A young couple, plus some relatives, were camping near the lake, and during the night the young man was attacked and killed by a black bear. This is the first time that such an event has been recorded in the state of Colorado. The reports went on to say that the victim was sleeping alone in one tent, and that during the night the others heard a commotion. His fiancée, who had run over from the other tent, was also attacked by the bear and slightly mauled. Finally a brother-in-law came out with a frying pan and chased the bear away. But by that time the man had been killed.

After word of the attack got back to civilization, members of Colorado Division of Wildlife tracked down the bear, killed it, and brought the carcass to the division's laboratory in Fort Collins. There Dr. Swanson examined it and talked to the biologists who had investigated the case. They found that the real circumstances were quite different from those reported in the news. The young man and his fiancée were not in separate tents but in the same tent. They were, in fact, in the same sleeping bag, where they were, or had just finished, making love. The investigating biologist concluded that the odors associated with sexual intercourse had provoked the bear to attack.

This may seem a farfetched theory, but it is not a new one. In another much-publicized case, when two girls were attacked and killed by grizzlies in Glacier National Park a few years ago, it was found that both were in their menstrual period. Then, too, the only provocation for the attack that biologists could come up with was the odors associated with the biology and physiology of sex. It is not known what mechanisms are involved here, but it seems evident there is a relationship between human odors and bear behavior.

Another pertinent fact related to this tragic event is that it happened on a dude ranch where the operators had been putting out garbage to attract bears so the guests could see and photograph them. The killer bear had been coming to the garbage area for some time.

As I listened to this tape it began to dawn on me that I was getting a personal message from Dr. Swanson. I even began to suspect that he was telling this story to warn me about my own behavior up here. I had the thought that he was either underestimating my morals or overestimating my opportunities, or both, if he was warning me against having sexual intercourse in the presence of a black bear. So it was with a feeling of relief that I heard him come to the punch line of his story—to be careful where I threw my garbage!

Fortunately, there is little cause for concern here. There are very few bears in this area, although black bears can be found throughout forested sections of the Rockies. Last September when I came to the cabin I did see some fresh tracks of a yearling bear at the head of Denny Creek, about a mile from the cabin. But since then I have seen no sign of bears. To the best of everyone's knowledge grizzlies vanished from Colorado early in this century. (AUTHOR'S NOTE: Just last year a bear was positively identified in the Colorado Rockies! I'm glad I didn't know that then.)

August 7

Today I photographed an old burn on the side of Mount Yale in the Delaney Creek drainage. These burns are important to the ecology of subalpine areas. I don't know the history of this particular one, but from superficial appearances I would say the fire occurred forty or fifty years ago. This environment recovers from fire extremely slowly; in fact, the only trees on this burn are seedlings.

It is impossible to tell now whether or not this fire was a "natural" one. Statistics show that in this region more than half the fires are started by lightning, with somewhat under half caused by human error, negligence, and malice. The question of fire control in wilderness areas is a hot one, if you'll excuse the metaphor. Many people would like to have all fires controlled, and indeed this has been the traditional policy of the Forest Service. It is of course true that a large fire can be devastating, not only killing all the local plant life but also accelerating erosion, damaging wildlife habitat, and, in extreme cases, killing the animals themselves.

However, as I said earlier, a fire must be considered part of the natural setting up here. If we are being truly consistent in our desire for complete naturalness, then we must seriously consider the possibility of letting naturally caused forest fires run their course—even though a single fire could blacken an entire mountainside and destroy a lot of vegetation for decades to come. This has been so common throughout past centuries that much of the vegetation we see in the mountains today was "shaped" by fire.

At the present time, the Brown's Cabin area is not a wilderness area by legal classification; it is national forest land. Therefore fires here would be brought under control by all possible means, including the use of bulldozers to cut fire breaks. I think that small fires are not sufficient cause for bringing in bulldozers and other soil-damaging large equipment. However, when we get a real conflagration that threatens to burn thousands of acres of timberland, the question becomes more difficult. Does today's wilderness enthusiast really want to see thousands of acres, entire hillsides, even whole mountains completely devastated in order that his successors a hundred years hence will be able to say, ah, this was a natural event, see this fire scar, see how the land is "recovering"? Maybe. But I think we need to do more research into people's motivations and desires. When we know what the majority of the people really want, and have a better understanding of the ecological impact of a "let burn" policy, then we should instruct our public lands managers accordingly.

There has been another definite dip in the temperature. In the last few days, daytime maximums are between 55 and 63 and at night the minimums range from 30 to 36. So unless this trend reverses soon, it appears that the peak of summer has already passed.

Tomorrow morning I'm going to pack my gear and climb Mount Yale. It is one of Colorado's taller peaks—14,196 feet—and it appears appealingly rugged near the summit. I've decided that tomorrow, which will be Sunday, should be my day off. Also, most of my work this summer has been between 11,500 and 12,500 feet, and I haven't taken a good hard look at the extreme elevations. So I'll take the camera and go climbing.

August 8

This is being narrated for Sunday, August 8, even though it is Monday, because I came in utterly exhausted last night and wasn't up to the job of narrating.

Fortunately yesterday was one of those rare days when the weather was good most of the time. There was a brief afternoon hailstorm and a few bursts of high wind, but the rest of the day was unusually fine for this high elevation.

On my way to Mount Yale, as I was climbing the snowfield, I noticed that a Clark's nutcracker was moving steadily ahead of me up the slope. For perhaps a quarter of a mile this creature managed to stay not less than ten or more than twenty feet uphill of me. It would feed briefly, then hop along on rocks, keeping a constant distance between us. We went along in tandem like this for some time.

I had first seen these noisy nutcrackers as soon as I arrived. The bird is aggressive and nearly omnivorous; some people call it camp robber or robber bird because it is so quick to adapt to people and their food. It will also steal ptarmigan eggs while the female is away from the nest feeding. Its slate-gray body with white wing and tail patches was easily spotted and first named by Captain William Clark, during the Lewis and Clark expedition, near the present site of Salmon, Idaho, in 1805. He chose to call it Clark's crow at the time. By now I have learned to welcome its bold sociability; I assume the explorers did also.

The name nutcracker came along as its habits were better known. The bird loves pine nuts. It gets at them by landing on a branch bearing a load of cones. Just as it hits the branch it takes off again, and this collision tends to knock a cone or two loose. Then it swoops to retrieve the cone, takes it to a safe place, and there knocks off the scales to get at the seeds. In the spring, summer, and fall it relies on a modest diet of lupine seeds, insect larvae, butterflies, black crickets, beetles, and grasshoppers.

When I reached the summit I found, anchored in rock, a plastic canister containing a register for people who climb the mountain, a service provided by the Colorado Mountain Club. I was astounded to find that over four hundred people had reached the summit since April 17, when the first three people of the season made the climb. Only one other person climbed the peak today—a young man from the Air Force Academy at Colorado Springs. I was surprised, because I had had the peak in view since about eleven in the morning and hadn't seen anyone going up ahead of me. I assume he came up the other side of the mountain, from Buena Vista.

It was not a killing climb, though I think many people would have difficulty getting up. My route, from Brown's Cabin up to the Continental Divide, down through Kroenke Basin, up out of the basin to the summit, probably covered close to twelve miles. I was thinking all along that perhaps one or two dozen people had done it. But four hundred! So I massaged my ego with the thought that there were probably few others over the age of fifty in the register until I noticed the signature of a man from the Yale class of '37. I was a junior in high school that year!

As I climbed past about 13,000 feet—the first time this summer I've been that high—I began noticing that many of the plant species are the same as they are around the cabin—notably the common alpine bistort with its two-inch head of fluffy white flowers on a foot-long stem; the Indian paintbrushes; the alpine avens that are so abundant now; and some of the erigerons, or mountain daisies. These erigerons (pronounced eh-RIJ-eh-rahns) are often confused with asters, bearing 30 to 150 petal-like flowers in a wide range of violets, pinks, whites, blues, and purples. In the vicinity of Brown's Cabin these species have flower stalks ranging from about eight to eighteen inches. But on Mount Yale, especially when you get up around 14,000 feet, the stalks are stunted by the harsh climate, reaching only one to three inches. The diameter of the flower itself and the length of the petals seem to be the same; only the height of the stalk is dwarfed.

In the way of animals I have the impression of more marmots and pikas from 13,000 feet upward. The pikas were active, particularly in mid-afternoon; I could hear them calling all around the summit. I finally got a brief glimpse of a ptarmigan. I think it was a female, although I did not see any chicks.

What little evidence I saw of human beings was most gratifying. Although about four hundred people have climbed Mount Yale this season so far, the only evidence of human presence that I could detect on or near the summit was one of these short twist-wire affairs used to close a package of bread. It was down among the rocks. I did not see any beer cans or paper or gum wrappers or even cigarette butts. As for that last, I can't believe that anyone would be interested in smoking after so much exertion in thin air, but I am probably wrong. There were not even any tracks near the summit—because of the rocky terrain. Farther down, in some of the rockslide areas, I saw footprints aplenty in fine gravel.

Perhaps this is a logical point to mention the difference in attitude I have noticed between two groups of people this summer. I certainly make no claim to sociological research, but I think anyone could distinguish between those who come in on foot or on horseback and those who come on motorcycles or trail bikes. There is no question but that backpackers and hikers have an entirely different attitude and set of questions than those who come by more rapid transit. For example, backpackers usually ask about the plants and animals they have seen. There are detailed questions about plants—identification, why they have different colors, whether color differences are genetic or related to soil conditions, and so forth. When they have caught a glimpse of some animal, they want to know what it is or how it can survive in this severe climate. Some have also asked about the history of the area after seeing mine shafts and remnants of wagon roads and such, and about how glaciation and other geological forces shaped this country.

By contrast, those few people I have talked to who came in by motorcycle have not had a single query about wildlife or wild plants. They wanted to know instead about the condition of the trail, whether they could go from point A to point B on a motorcycle. This is understandable. They go too fast to see any detail in the flora, and their noise scares away the fauna. I admit that my sampling is colored by the fact that I have not been very friendly with the motor people, but I have no doubt that their behavior is different.

Another point of difference is littering. Along the trails where bike tracks are prevalent, beer cartons, beer cans, pop cans, and so forth are common. I don't have proof positive that this littering was done by motorcyclists alone, but the evidence is strong. The one time I saw two people on one motorcycle the fellow in the rear was carrying a six-pack of beer; another time, some motorcyclists had parked their bikes and were sitting by them drinking beer. I'm making no brief that motorcyclists are heavier beer drinkers than backpackers, but I do believe that backpackers tend not to carry heavy items like liquids in containers that end up as litter. They more frequently carry freeze-dried products and other items that have little refuse associated with them. In talking with backpackers I have found that they normally carry their refuse out with them or burn it before leaving.

After this digression I'll get back to descending Mount Yale and returning home yesterday evening. It was about five when I left the top, and six when I reached a snowfield that was producing a small, icy stream of water. I took my boots and socks off, relaxed, and ate a little more of my lunch. On a trip like this I always nurse my small lunch along so that it lasts me throughout the day; I may even have some left when I return. I certainly recommend to hikers that they take the time to stop one or two times during the day to relax their feet. Best of all, plunge your feet into an icy stream and hold them there until they feel numb about halfway to the knees, as I did yesterday. By the time I had dried off and gotten back into socks and boots my feet felt much refreshed.

There were so many interesting things to see and photograph that it was getting dark by the time I reached Kroenke Basin. When I got home it was nine-fifty and had been very dark since about eight forty-five. I had been away thirteen and a half hours, and most of this time had been spent hiking or climbing. So although I was pleased with the accomplishments of the day, I sort of dragged through making supper and heating water for a good hot bath.

August 9

This has not been an overly productive day. I slept in until eight-thirty, recovered a bit from yesterday, and then walked around the basin observing the seasonal changes that are occurring steadily in the vegetation. One of the best places to see this progression is in the meadow below the outhouse. Early this spring—that is, late in June—as the snow was melting, the white-blossomed marsh marigolds were predominant and the overall aspect of the meadow was white. As the snow completely melted and the weather warmed, other flowers began to dominate the scene, most of them purple and blue. Some of the principal groups were the mountain daisies, mountain bluebells, violets, and on the higher ridges above the meadows, the alpine forget-me-nots. Then, after a bluish week or two, there began an intrusion of paintbrushes, with their varying shades of pink, red, and orange. At about the same time the alpine bistorts, whose white flowers resemble tiny cotton plants, began to mix in. These tall and spectacular plants lasted perhaps longer than any other species. Now the meadows are turning golden as the Compositae family—the broad group of plants generally known as sunflowers—starts to flower, and soon the mustard family will add more yellow to the meadows. Finally, the grasses and sedges (which resemble grasses) and *Kobresia* (close relatives of the sedges) are forming flower stalks. These give the overall scene a dark aspect when viewed from a distance.

Discussing the vegetation reminds me of the heavy hailstorm we had. I don't believe I mentioned some of the effects on the ground and the plants. First I should say that it was not true hail; rather it was what meteorologists call graupel, a German word meaning snow pellets. True hail is precipitation that falls and bounces aloft in air turbulence several times before reaching earth. As it falls it melts slightly; as it climbs it freezes again, growing steadily larger in the process. It acts as a nucleus for condensation of water vapor, which it gathers from the clouds it moves through. When at last it reaches earth it can be identified by the concentric shells it has formed. These shells can be seen easily with a microscope, and sometimes with the naked eye.

Graupel, on the other hand, is a hail-like substance that does not bounce within the clouds but falls straight through them. Consequently they are solid, shell-less pellets of ice. The graupel that fell on August 5 were very large—the largest I remember seeing. The smallest were at least half an inch in diameter, and I measured some at one and a quarter inches. They fell with great force, which I saw illustrated in a nearly dry pond. This pond had a small amount of water in the center, surrounded by mud. Two or three days after the storm I noticed that there was a band about four feet wide around the perimeter which was riddled with holes up to an inch across. At first I thought the holes must have been made by some kind of burrowing animals, perhaps insects, but as I looked more carefully I could see that the cause was the graupel. It had struck the mud with enough force to leave craters an inch and a half deep.

At home in Fort Collins we frequently have hailstorms which cause spectacular damage to our flowers and shrubbery. I have seen hailstorms, of much less intensity than the one we just had up here, that shredded or broke off many of the leaves of even our privet hedge, which is pretty tough. The same happened to other broad-leaved shrubs, like forsythia, prunus, and rose.

Here, however, I surveyed quite a bit of the alpine and subalpine area after the storm and in no place did I see any battered leaves or damage to the showy flowers. The amazing resilience and toughness of these alpine plants are due primarily to the fact that their leaves are narrower and thicker than those found at lower elevations. Apparently the flower stalks and stems, too, are sturdier.

August 10

I traveled today, in unplanned but very profitable fashion. I was just finishing the breakfast dishes when three men came down the trail. They were Fred Barker and Bill Sharp, both of the U.S. Geological Survey, and Bill's son Otis. After learning their plans I decided to go with them to Rebecca Lake near the head of Texas Creek. Fred Barker had been here in 1963, doing a geological survey, and had returned to collect rock samples for use in dating the age of these mountains.

I didn't want to hold them up, and told them to go on ahead, that I would finish my chores and meet them in the basin. I had no trouble finding Rebecca Lake, which is about five miles from here. They were working hard, gathering a good amount of rock to pack out, so we weren't able to spend much time chatting. But I was able to get some bits of information about local geology. At one point Fred showed me a rock glacier on the east side of the basin. It was formed as the snows melted and froze in the cracks and pores of a large mass of rock. This interstitial ice acted as a lubricant for the rocks, allowing them to flow as a glacier. He said that the moraine—an irregular ridge of boulders, gravel, sand, and clay carried in by a glacier—we walked over dates from the late Wisconsin Era, the last glaciation in North America, ending some 10,000 years ago. Behind the rock glaciers was a sort of dish which Fred thought may have held glacial snow and ice up until only a few thousand years ago. These high, cold regions held their ice long after most of the glaciers had gone.

When Fred and Bill had packed up the rock samples in a variety of small sacks, I made the mistake of offering to help carry them out. Before I could reconsider I found myself with a good-sized bag of rocks and an eight-pound sledge in my pack. But the exchange of hauling service for information was a good trade, I felt.

On the way back the four of us made so much noise and traveled so fast we saw little wildlife, although about a hundred yards below the cabin I did catch sight of a pine grosbeak (*Pinicola enucleator*) for the first time this summer. This is the largest finch in the United States, nearly the size of a robin, and often very tame. Its red plumage was in bright contrast to the dark green spruce where it was perched. I suspect that its mate has already nested, probably among the lower branches of a spruce along one of the narrow meadows between the cabin and Texas Creek. When the snows come, this cheerful bird with its beautiful whistles, warbles, and trills will move to lower elevations, then southward for the winter.

Which reminds me that I saw the second red-shafted flicker (just reclassified with two other flickers as the "common flicker," but local people still call it by this name) of the year over in Magdalene Basin last week. This flicker (*Colaptes auratus*) was named for the shafts of its wing feathers, which flash salmon red as it flies overhead. Unlike other woodpeckers, it is predominantly brownish in color and commonly feeds on the ground—on insects, berries, and other fruits. While frequently seen in the alpine, flickers do not stray far from timber stands in spring and early summer. Here, in cavities excavated in a dead tree, the female will have laid six to eight white eggs. By now the juveniles should be at least a month old, and by September or early October the flickers will have abandoned the Brown's Cabin environs for more hospitable conditions in the valleys and tributaries of the lower Arkansas and Colorado rivers.

Fred and Bill do a large amount of field work in the summers and are good hikers, so it was a pleasure to be out with them. They introduced me to homemade pemmican, which was very tasty; the sixteen-year-old boy, Otis, generously left me a small supply of it, plus the recipe.

I was glad to be able to carry my heavy load about ten miles and still keep up with these somewhat younger men. But I must admit that it took a lot out of me. After I got to the cabin it was all I could do to manage dinner, the dishes, and a hot bath before falling into the sack.

August 11

I spent most of today in or near the cabin. I had a number of things to identify, mostly songbirds and plants, so I keyed out some of those, caught up on taping, and photographed the pocket gopher that lives nearby. A storm rolled in a little before three, and by four it was so dark that I needed a flashlight to see inside the cabin.

When I was first thinking about this summer-long project, I imagined that the stormy days would be miserable. I have found this to be true when I am caught outside in a storm; there's no way to romanticize that experience beyond the first few moments. But when I'm near the cabin and can get inside, these summer tempests are really pleasant. This afternoon I spent a few minutes just standing by the window, watching the hail come down and generally enjoying the fury and beauty of rain, wind, and hail. This reaction to stormy conditions makes me think about coming back in winter. I am going to discuss this with Charlie and see if it wouldn't be possible to snowshoe in with my family during Christmas vacation.

As I think about snow settling in around the cabin the idea of spending a winter alone here grows more attractive. I'm not certain whether I would enjoy more a winter alone or with my wife and son. Well, I'm not very serious about this, but it might be interesting, particularly if one had good reading material and perhaps some writing to do. I could probably get a good deal accomplished during a winter of isolation.

During this afternoon's hailstorm I was again impressed by the toughness of alpine vegetation. I observed closely a mountain bluebell beside a stump just outside the cabin door. This is probably as succulent and broad-leaved a plant as occurs in the area. Yet again I could perceive no damage by the hail, which seemed to have even greater intensity for short bursts than the previous storm.

Oh, I might mention the ever-challenging communication situation. I speak each night, in a way, with Charlie, but he isn't able to understand much of what I'm saying. Charlie also has been transmitting to me recently without getting any sound across. I suspect that he forgets to press the button during transmission. So I should say that we exchange grunts and sound fragments. At least he knows I'm alive and I know he's still out there. I did understand from last night's broadcast that he's going to come in Sunday with a wood cart he's built with lumber and bicycle wheels.

August 12

The hail from yesterday's storm has fused into an icy glaze covering all vegetation. On behalf of all my animal and plant colleagues up here I look forward to its melting.

I filmed some ice scenes, deer tracks, and caddis fly cases (these are the homes of aquatic caddis fly larvae, many of which build protective cases of sand or grass roots). Then, since it was beginning to hail and rain again, I returned to the cabin. Just before I got there I met four young girls, probably fourteen to sixteen years old, who are camping their way through the country. They'll be out alone for thirteen days, and they said this was their seventh day. The girls seemed remarkably self-sufficient. They had good maps and knew how to read them. Even though they are all natives of the Midwest, traveling and living in these high mountains did not seem to trouble them.

At about 8 p.m. I saw another girl with a huge pack on her back coming up the trail from the spring. I thought she would stop by the cabin, but she walked on past. I stepped to the door and said Hi, but she only scurried down the trail at a pretty rapid pace. Apparently she didn't trust a bearded old man. I decided not to stop her, although I was somewhat concerned because she was alone and had a good way to hike before catching the rest of the group where they'd planned to camp, on Texas Creek. I guess she thought there were fates worse than being alone in wilderness.

During the heavy rain and hail this afternoon I noticed again the slow water infiltration rate of this soil. The capacity to absorb water is very small here, so that most of a rain runs off downhill before plants can use it. I assume that the main reason is a lack of surface litter and of organic matter in the upper levels of the soil. A mere tenth of an inch of rain is enough to start water cascading down the trails, or any other small depression. This is a sign of how important it is to protect these trails from overuse not only by motorcycles but also by horses and humans. For it is running water that causes erosion. The situation is very different on slopes that have high humus content. Much of the rain in the mountains where there are cloud forests, for example, is absorbed or trapped before it can run off by the soil, leaf litter, and the plants themselves.

August 13

Today is Friday the thirteenth but it has not been an unlucky day—in fact, it's been a productive one. It was my once-a-week day for changing all the charts on the weather instruments, and I found that several of them are not recording accurately. So I decided to go through the manuals on the hygrothermograph, recording rain gauge, and microbarograph. I was pleased to be able to adjust them, and now I think the weather data are going to be considerably more accurate. This technological victory did involve five separate trips to the station, however.

Early in the afternoon I had a visitor from the Kroenke Lake Basin. I didn't get his name—it sounded foreign—but he was a professor of engineering from the University of Colorado at Boulder. He has been vacationing in this area for several years and was able to tell me a lot about some of the wildlife. I must have been a little lonesome—I'm usually short with people who come through, but we got to visiting and over an hour went by without my realizing it.

He was an interesting person. He is a stockholder in the Arapahoe Ski Basin Corporation and an avid skier. He has also made several movies, which he uses in his lectures at CU. He was astounded that I didn't have protective cases for carrying the cameras in my backpack. He has handled movie cameras in backpacks and feels they need strong protection. I described the cases I'm having made in Salida, but he was not impressed. His technique is to build lightweight but rigid frames padded with Styrofoam to cradle the cameras. He slips this whole case into a backpack. Well, live and learn.

After the professor left I went to work on the generator. It has been running rough, and in checking the operation manual I found that there is extensive maintenance work to do at the end of the first two hundred hours. As near as I can estimate, the generator has run at least two hundred hours, so I got out my tools and set about cleaning and checking spark plugs, changing oil, and so on. I discovered that part of the trouble was the propane fuel supply, which was low. So I changed to a fresh bottle. I have now used three bottles and have eight left. It took over three hours to go through all these steps.

By coincidence I learned from Charlie on the radio tonight that the camera cases are finished, and he has picked them up to bring in Sunday. He also told me that a thirty-eight-pound box—presumably film—has arrived from Landsburg. These past two nights communication with Charlie has been good, so perhaps we've got our problem licked.

While working on the generator this afternoon I saw a movement outside the shed and looked out to see a young snowshoe hare, probably six or seven weeks old. This is the first one I've seen here. These animals (*Lepus americanus*) are slightly larger than the common cottontail rabbit. But their smaller ears and larger feet (for which they are named) are distinctive.

There is a more fundamental distinction between rabbits and hares that is not so easily observed. The young of rabbits are altricial; that is, they are born naked, blind, and highly dependent on the mother. Young hares, on the other hand, are precocial—alert, equipped with a coat of fur, ready to move around.

The snowshoe hare, along with the ptarmigan and the weasel, is one of three animals up here that undergo seasonal molt, changing color from brown in the summer to white in winter. The winter molt will begin about a month from now, toward mid-September, and end two to three months after that. It seems to be triggered at least in part by length of day, and these hares are sometimes tricked when the weather is irregular. There is nothing so visible to a coyote, bobcat, or eagle as a brown hare in an early snowfall.

Snowshoe hares are largely nocturnal, resting during the day in snug hideouts. They are solitary, and often hostile toward others of their species. Though their diet consists principally of grasses and forbs, they are known to eat carrion on occasion. They also, like the pika, re-ingest their own feces and may even eat snow.

August 14

Today I photographed a series of Engelmann spruce trees, "following" them from seedling through maturity to death and decomposition. The series began with a very small tree shorter than my jackknife. I brought the tree in after filming it, polished the stem, examined the growth rings through a magnifying glass, and found that it was seven years old! The second tree in the series was about a foot tall. I aged it at twenty-three years. This gives some idea of how slowly vegetation grows in this environment. The effects of the short, cool growing season, wind, and rather infertile soils cannot be overemphasized.

More people have been traveling through the country lately. I saw two backpackers up on the Continental Divide yesterday, and this morning near Brown's Pass I met two more, a Mr. Atkinson and his son from Buena Vista. The elder Atkinson has emphysema and was having a problem breathing at this altitude. I understood that they were going to spend only a brief time in this area, but I haven't seen them come out.

Then at about eleven-thirty I was setting up for some photos near the weather station when I thought I heard a rifle shot. Moments later I noticed a deer standing at the edge of the timber just east of the cabin. She was looking intently down the slope, in the direction of the shots. Then I heard a second shot and the deer took off running into the timber. I shouted, "Don't shoot," and a few moments later a voice from below the cabin said, "We're below the hill." I shouted back, "You're scaring the hell out of the deer." A minute later there was a third shot, and this time I yelled, "Don't shoot," again, along with some colorful profanity. That was the last shot I heard.

Later I was taking photographs near the cabin when several people came up the trail. I asked if they were the ones shooting, and one young fellow said yes, he was. He said he had not heard me shout, nor had he responded, so I concluded that the two men I had seen earlier must have been the ones who answered from below the hill.

It turned out that the young man doing the shooting was a local fellow whose dad handles the boat concession at the reservoir in Taylor Park. The other people were a family from Long Beach, California—a husband and wife, two teen-aged daughters, and a son three-and-a-half years old. They had been spending their vacations in Colorado for eleven years. This year they planned to stay three weeks and take short backpack trips every day within the Texas Creek drainage. They were getting very well acquainted with the country, hiking perhaps only four or five miles each day. I had a nice talk with them and again was impressed with how much more people get out of this kind of recreational experience than they do from a motorized trip.

Autumn seems to be approaching already. In the last few days I have noticed that several of the flowers that bloomed earlier in the spring—the potentillas (or cinquefoils), some of the daisies, alpine avens—are beginning to mature; dry seed heads are appearing. In order to produce seeds in such a brief period (and seed production is the essential work of every flowering plant), these alpine species have a number of special adaptations. For one thing, they are equipped to get an early start in spring. Flower buds often are begun in the previous year's growing season, or even before that. They are usually well formed by the end of summer and safely protected before cold weather sets in.

One consequence of this need for accelerated life processes is that of all the species around Brown's Cabin there is only one annual plant—a tiny buckwheat called Koenigia. The rest are perennials. An annual is at a disadvantage here because it has to sprout from seed and grow a stem, leaves, and roots before it can even begin to produce a flower. There is little time left for making seed. The perennials have already done most of the work and can therefore produce seed faster.

Another adaptation to the short growing season is the storage of large amounts of carbohydrates, primarily in the roots, which are protected from the winter winds. As temperatures rise in the spring, the carbohydrates are converted to starches and sugars to aid rapid sprouting.

Many alpine plants are able to begin absorbing nutrients and achieving photosynthesis as soon as the temperature rises above 32 degrees. For these same functions, plants in the Fort Collins area (5,000 feet elevation) need temperatures around 45 degrees. Also respiration rates of alpine plants are far higher than those of plants growing in temperate regions.

The pikas, too, seem to be preparing for fall. They are beginning to start their hay piles. I've been watching them closely and yesterday was the first time I have seen any of this activity. One of the pikas was clipping a lot of vegetation, which it will store for winter consumption.

I've decided I would like to see the Forest Service or some university undertake a research program on the impact of different kinds of recreation on wildlife populations. I'm thinking of writing a research proposal for consideration at Colorado State. It would have to be a fairly complex study to be useful. Something like this might work: set up two areas and study them for at least two years. In the first year, area A would be open to all types of motorized vehicles and to the use of firearms. Area B would be open only to hikers and backpackers, and no firearms would be permitted. Then in the second year the uses would be reversed. A student or other researcher would live in each area during the entire period of study. If he could devise accurate ways of observing and counting the wildlife, it would be possible to say that, for example, gunfire affects or does not affect elk populations in certain ways, or that trail bikes disturb or do not disturb nesting birds.

It would also be useful to question the people who use these areas. They might be asked how many deer or sheep they had seen, what they found most interesting about their visit, how they think the area should be used. At present there is interest in the Forest Service and other agencies regarding the impact of various users on the environment. But most of the interest centers on physical effects—erosion, damage to the plants, and so on. I think it is equally important to know something about the impact of travel on the wildlife species and the subjective reactions of the users themselves.

The days become noticeably shorter. On June 22 the sun first hit the cabin at seven-ten in the morning. Today I first saw it at eight. On June 22 I could see to hike around outside until about nine-fifteen at night. Now it is dark by eight-thirty.

August 15

It's also getting chilly. The minimum reading this morning was 34.5 degrees. Yesterday's high was 59.5. But it was a pretty day. As the temperature drops I am keeping the stoves burning longer and using more wood. Even though I still have the fires going for only an hour or so in the morning and five or six hours in the evening, I seem to spend an hour a day now sawing, hauling, and splitting wood, so I have asked Charlie to come in with another man to cut enough to last me through the end of this photographing period.

I was to meet Charlie at the Hartenstein Road at ten this morning. He wasn't there, so I went down another half mile. When I still didn't find him, I began filming some sequences of an old forest fire there. Finally about eleven I heard a faint call of "Dwight," and I hightailed it down the mountain to see what was going on. There was Charlie with his two-wheeled cart, piled high with the thirty-eight-pound box of film, some mail and supplies, a huge sleeping bag, some plastic tarp, and several other items that must have weighed over a hundred pounds, which he was trying to wheel up the steep trail. It had taken him two and a half hours to get about a mile and a half. I felt sorry for the old fella and helped him haul the cart up to the old fire scars, where I finished the shots of the burn, then put my pack on and got into the pulling harness he's built onto the front of the cart. He got in behind to push and balance, and we started up the mountain. We must have made quite a sight.

It took about four hours to reach the cabin, a distance of three miles.

I admired Charlie for his ability to handle that load at all, and at the same time was a little annoyed. The packers are coming in with the horses in a few days, and I had suggested that he send the stuff, including the cart, in with them. Instead he spent almost an entire day, and I wasted four hours, fighting that damned cart. We were both exhausted when we got to the cabin. But there was one positive result. Charlie ended up with a feeling of great accomplishment. He was proud of the fact that we could get a load like that in to the cabin, and said he bet there were not many men who could do it. So for him it was a victory, and victories don't come often in life.

August 16

It is about ten in the morning. Charlie is putting insulation in the cracks in the cabin and repairing the door, so I can't do any work or narrating inside. I hiked up close to Brown's Pass, where the pikas are really active. They started sounding off yesterday with great energy, little pikas squeaking in almost every substantial rockslide on the mountain. I've been sitting here for an hour and a quarter. They are harvesting hay and carrying it back into the rocks. The harvest site is a grassy area thirty to fifty feet from me—mostly grasses and sedges, but also some forbs. They feed there vigorously for fifteen or twenty seconds, then, with full mouths, head back into the rocks and disappear. I haven't wanted to disturb them, so I haven't gone up close to see what they finally do with their cargo, but their habit is to lay the plants out on rocks someplace to dry. Then they take them underground or into crevices, where they are stored for winter in what are commonly called hay piles. There are naturalists who dispute the "lay out to dry" theory. But I have seen it done.

The flowering period for most of the forb species has definitely passed its peak. Most of the flowers look old and wilted. I haven't seen any new species come into flower for the last week. I imagine this is due both to the shorter days and to the colder weather, which now features frost.

As Charlie and I were chugging in with the cart we saw the two Atkinsons (the man with emphysema and his son), whom I had seen at Brown's Pass on Saturday morning. They had not gone very far; in fact, they had camped right by the mill, only a ten-minute walk from the cabin, and stayed there the rest of the day and night. They told me that they had just left a note on a block of wood beside my door: "We weren't the ones who were doing the shooting, it was somebody down below us." So I guess they heard the anger in my voice when I was yelling.

Of course I have neglected to say that shooting is technically legal in Colorado under "varmint" regulations, so long as the shooter has a small-game license which legalizes carrying a gun. There is no other law to prevent anyone from shooting marmots, pocket gophers, and the various squirrels and chipmunks any time they want. Most "game" and a few specific species are protected by restrictive hunting seasons and bag limits, or else they have total protection. I think this situation could use some amendment. I feel that in areas where most people are hoping to enjoy backpacking, photography, and the feeling of wilderness, year-round varmint shooting is an undesirable disruption of the peace.

As I have been sitting here the pika have been scampering within fifteen feet of me, giving loud calls every few seconds or minutes. I think the tape must be picking up these whistles and squeaks. This is a pleasant situation for narrating. I must try to use it more often. The camera is set up with the telephoto lens and every time there's an opportunity for a shot I just stop talking and run off a few feet of film. The only disadvantage is the mosquitoes. I thought they would fade with the warm, dry weather, but this morning I've had to rub on repellent as fast as they find fresh spots to attack.

August 17

Yesterday three very welcome guests arrived from Fort Collins—Father Leonard Urban and Tony and Tom Canzona. Father Urban and Tom went immediately to Texas Creek to fish; and in less than two hours returned with twenty trout. Tony stayed here with me. We cut some wood for tonight, then went down to the meadows below the mill to look for elk. Earlier there had been five on the ridge southwest of the cabin—two spiked bulls, two cows, and one calf. They seemed unaware of or unconcerned about my distant presence, and fed and played in full view for ten or fifteen minutes before disappearing into South Texas Creek drainage.

Today Father Urban, Tom, Tony, and I hiked up there, and while Father and Tom did some more fishing, Tony and I scouted the basin for elk tracks. They were abundant all the way down through the timber from the ridge to the meadows, along with fresh droppings. I also came across several active beaver ponds along Texas Creek and some huge beaver houses. These houses, or lodges, may be six feet or more in height, and more than fifteen feet in diameter. They are built in six to eight feet of water, and the entire structure is basically hollow. The walls are built of logs, limbs, and sod, narrowing toward the top.

The beaver (*Castor canadensis*) is the largest rodent here, and indeed the largest rodent in North America. Appropriately, it also has a more extensive and conspicuous effect on its environment than any other mammal. The effects of its huge dams, which may be six feet high and several hundred feet long, are far-reaching and long-lasting. The dam creates a habitat where new species can live—muskrats, mink, waterfowl, fishes. A broken dam can flood large areas.

Most important, however, is the dam's effect on the area immediately behind it. The backed-up water saturates the soil beneath it, drowning the firs, spruces, and other species that cannot tolerate much moisture. Water-loving plants move in, especially willows, alders, cottonwoods, and aspens—the same species whose bark provides the beaver's favorite food.

Eventually, however, even the grandest of beaver dams succumb to a natural process that the most hard-working beaver can do nothing to prevent: siltation. Any dam, as human engineers well know, slows the flow of water so that suspended sediment settles to the bottom. The bottom rises, the water becomes shallower, and the beaver finally moves out to build elsewhere. Gradually the dammed area becomes a meadow, and perhaps even forest again as the trees close in from the sides.

These beaver have apparently had no effect on the fishing in Texas Creek, and for the second consecutive evening we had a big trout feed. It certainly was a welcome change from my diet. Father Urban and Tom and Tony are excellent guests. Well, I can hardly call them guests. They have pitched in and done most of the work while they have been here—cooking, washing dishes, cleaning, cutting wood. Tom, who has taken industrial arts at the university, sharpened my knife, the ax, and the saws, and made other tool repairs around the cabin.

This evening at seven-thirty Father Urban, using a few drops of wine salvaged from an old bottle and a slice of my regular bread, said mass and performed communion. I have never considered myself particularly devout, but I have been surprised to find myself missing being able to go to mass and especially communion. It was truly a beautiful mass, although slightly unorthodox, since we had had to rummage through the dump to find a wine bottle with anything in it. The experience was exceptional for all of us.

As part of the mass, Father asked me to read Psalm 104, which is described as "a hymn in praise of creation." I want to repeat a few verses here, because they seem so close to my own experience this summer in the high country:

> Bless the Lord, O my soul!
> O Lord my God, thou art exceedingly great!
> Thou hast stretched out the heavens like a canopy,
> Thou hast built thy upper rooms above the water,
> Thou makest the clouds thy chariot,
> Thou walkest upon the wings of the wind,
> Thou makest the wind thy messenger,
> and the blazing fire thy ministers.
>
> Thou didst found the earth upon its bases,
> It shall be steadfast forever and ever.
> Thou didst cover it with the ocean as with a garment;
> the waters stood above the mountains. . . .
> The mountains arose, the valleys sank down
> to the place which thou didst prepare for them.
> Thou hast set a bound which they may not cross,
> lest they cover the earth again.
>
> Thou commandest springs to flow down into brooks
> that run between the mountains.
> They give drink to every beast of the field; . . .
> the birds of the air lodge nearby;
> they pour forth their song amid the branches.
> Thou waterest the hills from thy upper rooms;
> the earth is sated with the fruit of thy works.
>
> Thou makest grass grow for cattle,
> and herbage for the service of man . . .
> The trees of the Lord have their fill, . . .
> There the birds build their nests. . . .
> The high mountains give refuge to wild goats,
> the rocks to conies.
> Thou hast made the moon to mark the seasons;
> the sun hast known its going down.
>
> How many are thy works, O Lord!
> Thou hast made all things with wisdom;
> the earth is full of thy creatures . . .

May the glory of the Lord be forever,
may the Lord rejoice in his works,
who looks upon the earth and it trembles,
who touches the mountains and they smoke!
I will sing to the Lord as long as I live;
I will sing praise to my God while I have my being.
May my speech be acceptable to him;
I will be glad in the Lord.

As the four of us sat around the kitchen table I strongly felt that we were sharing not only the mass, the communion, the sign of peace, but also the fuller recognition of our closeness to God and His Creation. I doubt whether any of us here believes that God has personally supervised the creation of every tree and rock, or of each event that has shaped our environment, but I think we might all agree there is a grand design for the universe. The alpine, like every other environment, is part of that design. I think this viewpoint adds important perspective to what we are trying to do as ecologists, and in what I specifically am trying to do in order to bring this story to the public.

The overall forces of nature—formation of rock, development of soil, evolution of plant and animal life—are still, at their fundamental level, largely incomprehensible to even the best scientists. I think all scientific studies are really struggles to understand the grand design within which all these processes are ordered. Certainly we understand fragments of the design. We wrestle with them under various labels: physical geology, speciation, cell biology, ornithology. But here, in the midst of this vast scenery and these physical wonders, I cannot help but be filled with awe and reverence for the magnificence of nature. I witness a constant panorama of life and death. I witness the interrelatedness of all things—insects, songbirds, marmots and pikas, deer and elk, climate, plants, and the land itself. I cannot imagine any of them existing separate from the others, and I am made acutely aware of how damage to any one of them threatens the fabric of the whole.

Now to more mundane things. Yesterday evening I had put my dirty laundry to soak, so this morning, while Father Urban and the two boys hiked around the basin, I did the wash. After that we hiked to Texas Creek. The weather was good until early afternoon, when we had light rainstorms until evening. It was enough to soak the willows and therefore us.

On the way up Texas Creek we met three motorcyclists. They

stopped as usual to ask directions and trail conditions. I took the opportunity to give them my unsolicited views on the use of motorcycles on forest trails. In such encounters I try a soft-sell approach so as not to alienate the recipients to the point where communication breaks down. Two of the men received my message reasonably well, the third seemed more hostile.

Farther up the trail we met two young fishermen who asked where we were going. When I said to Brown's Pass, they said, well, there's a guy up there making a movie, so you probably can't stay at the cabin. Apparently the word is getting around even though I try to keep my mission as quiet as possible. To the fishermen I simply said, yes, I heard that someone was staying at Brown's Cabin this summer.

August 18

This morning we got up early, and Father Urban, Tom, and Tony left at about eight. It was a beautiful day until about twelve-thirty, when it began to storm. Before that I made a tour of the three salt licks I've set up and was pleased to find that all are now being used by big game.

There is more evidence that we are moving rapidly into fall. Only three weeks ago I mentioned that the entire countryside was turning deep green. Now it is moving to yellows and tans. When I look carefully I find that this is caused primarily by the leaves of only a few species. The alpine avens are beginning to turn a dull red. The leaves of the dwarf huckleberries are becoming mottled with yellow. The same applies to the mountain dryad (a white-flowering plant that is important to the diet of ptarmigan) and Sibbaldia, a dwarf cushion plant that will soon be crimson. This change from summer to fall shades is so fast as to be almost shocking, like the aging of Dorian Gray. I assume it is caused by the heavy frosts we are having almost nightly.

Part IV

VISITORS

August 19

Charlie Combs is bringing in his son and his son's family to stay at the cabin from August 20 to 23. I had agreed to move out during this period, and I've decided to go down to Texas Creek where I saw the beaver ponds and houses. I spent most of this drizzly day writing letters and getting ready to leave.

August 20

The action began early this morning. I had finished breakfast and almost the dishes when I looked out the kitchen door and saw a young mule deer buck. This is the first time I've had a buck so close, so I abandoned the dishes and got both cameras set up. I managed about 250 feet of the buck feeding in the willows and grass. His antlers are still covered with velvet; he appears to have two points on one side and three on the other. I would judge that he is a long yearling (about fifteen months).

I took all this footage with a camera on a tripod set inside the kitchen. Again it was apparent that I need more than this one tripod. To switch from one camera to the other I have to remove one camera from the tripod and mount the other. This is a project in itself—and very inconvenient when dealing with fidgety animals.

I was ready to go when Charlie and his family arrived with Billy Carpenter, the packer. They brought some grocery supplies and mail for me. After lunch with them, I shouldered my pack and took off toward Texas Creek in a persistent drizzle. It continued to rain all afternoon and when I found a suitable camping site near the beaver dam at about four o'clock I was pretty well soaked. I got the mountain tent set up, stowed my wet pack and equipment inside, then began the task of starting a fire in the rain. It wasn't too hard to do, and within a few minutes I had a warming blaze.

From six to about seven the rain paused, and I got out my trusty propane stove and cooked supper. Then I went down to some of the nearby ponds to see if any beaver were active. It began raining again, and no beaver were visible, so I went back to the campfire and stood by it for a few minutes. Since I was getting wetter from the rain above than dry from the campfire below, I gave up and crawled into the tent and into the sleeping bag, wet clothes and all. I must say that I have been more comfortable in my life, but I suppose I'll be dry by morning.

So here I am narrating. The sleeping bag is a down one of my own, and the mountain tent is a really fine piece of equipment. It has a fly suspended above it so that the rain doesn't hit the tent itself, although I can certainly hear it coming down.

There have been few times since I have been at Brown's Cabin that I have felt any loneliness, or a strong wish for some companion, but this evening is one of those times. I suppose the reason is that I was forced inside the tent at twenty minutes after seven and I am just lying here, not yet sleepy. I generally don't go to bed until eleven or later at the cabin.

My tent is pitched under a stand of large spruce trees, and the fog has been drifting up through them all evening. I can almost imagine I am in a rain forest, as the water drips continuously from the high limbs of the spruce and all the dim wetness reduces visibility to just a few hundred yards.

Well, it continues to rain. I hope it clears by morning or I won't be able to do much filming. The willow meadows around the beaver ponds are extremely wet and it is hard to walk through them in a rain like this.

August 21

This morning it was not raining, although the sky was overcast until ten. The sun broke through intermittently until early afternoon; then the sky closed over again for good.

The air inside the tent was damp, so I opened it wide and draped the wet things over tree limbs to dry. One nice thing about this camp, compared with the one I had in Magdalene Basin, is that there is little wind and better firewood. Up there I remember having smoke in my eyes most of the time and insufficient heat. Here it is warm and comfortable by the fire, and not smoky. The fire lasted through the night, even in the rain; when I put on some dry limbs I simply had to blow on the ashes a while to bring it to life. The mini stove with the 95-cent propane bottle continues to win my heart. This morning it produced freeze-dried buttered eggs and hot coffee in only five minutes.

After breakfast I went out to look over the three beaver houses near my campsite. There are perhaps a dozen small ponds near the houses, but I saw no activity in any of them. I got into my waders and made a closer inspection. It is rather a strange situation. There is some evidence of fresh beaver work; in one of the ponds, for example, quite a few willows had been freshly cut. They still had their leaves and were buried on the bottom of the pond, perhaps as future food or patching material for the dam. But the houses don't have any new work on them and the face of the dam shows only a small amount. I'm not sure what's going on. It may be that only one or two pairs of transient beavers work this part of the valley. Tomorrow I'll get up shortly after daybreak to see if there is any activity; if not, I'll probably go up Texas Creek and look at some other ponds, or perhaps back to Magdalene Basin, where I found two elk wallows.

I met two young couples backpacking today. They had stopped at Brown's Cabin on the way up, looked in the window, and seen some mail on the table. They were wondering who Dwight Smith was. Again I didn't let on. Then just beyond the beaver ponds I saw a fisherman coming down Texas Creek, fly-fishing as he came. So today has been a people day for me, somewhat welcome after last night's loneliness.

I want to tell a little about the spruce grove I am camped in. These are large trees for this high altitude, averaging seventy or eighty feet in height. I would say that one out of every ten trees is a dead snag, and lots of them have fallen, so you can't walk directly through the area without clambering over tangled windfalls. Many of the younger trees, perhaps twenty-five feet tall, have been bent over by heavy snows. One of these is right beside my tent. The top is stuck in the ground like the head of an ostrich, and I took advantage of this by leaning five or six small logs against it to make a campfire reflector. As I lie here on the ground narrating, the heat is reflected against my back and I am comfortable. This helps that mean pain in my back, which, incidentally, my doctor diagnosed by mail as bursitis. Heat is the recommended treatment.

At the moment I feel perfectly content. In fact, I seem to enjoy camping out with the tent even more than I like living at the cabin. Maybe this is because I am free of the disruptions caused by visitors, and the many housekeeping chores.

As I lie here tonight and look through the stand of tall spruce, the sunset is still bright in the west and the sky is almost completely free of clouds. I suppose a poetic way of saying it is that the trees have tall, slender spires, some of them with grotesque limbs reaching out to the clear sky, totally black in silhouette. As I turn over now and face the fire, ooo-eee, some of these dead trees and spires are really spectacular. I'm looking at three of them straight above my head and I can just imagine that my wife, who has been taking painting lessons, would really get excited about some of these forms.

There's the first interruption of the evening, a damn jet is going overhead. There are a lot of planes passing over this area—I suppose twenty or more a day. But I've gotten so accustomed to them I barely notice. I'm convinced that taking the tape recorder on these trips and narrating on the spot is the ideal way to do it. If I wait until I get back to the cabin I have forgotten half of what I might have said. It does occur to me that I'm only fifty yards off the trail, and that a fisherman or backpacker could easily hear me talking to myself. I wonder what he would think.

Today while I was looking at the beaver pond my thoughts went back about forty years to when I was a ten-year-old boy and used to visit my uncle and aunt in Idaho. Their house was next to a large pond filled with frogs. I could hear them croaking all through the night. This reminded me that I haven't heard or seen a frog since I've been in here. I'm sure there must be some; at least one species lives in these high basins, the only cold-blooded animal that does. I did, however, see a boreal toad, at the edge of the first creek downstream from Magdalene Basin.

There was a strange event while I was eating dinner tonight. I had a pan of water beside me and an open dish. One moment the water was clear and the dish empty; and the next moment both were covered with tiny black insects. They were smaller than the lead in a pencil and too numerous to count. I threw out the water and cleaned the dish, and in the following minutes only a few more insects appeared. So the fall occurred during a one- or two-minute period. My conclusion is that the rising heat from the fire reached into the lower branches, where these little creatures must live, and caused them to drop in a cloud. I could feel them crawling around in my hair. I've never witnessed anything like this, and I don't know what they are.

I think I'm just in a visiting mood tonight. It's getting so dark I can hardly see. The smoke from the campfire is filtering up through the branches above me, and it looks soft and appealing. Even the sound of Texas Creek is soft, halfway between a murmur and a roar. Between me and the sunset the black dead trees and snags are standing out more and more sharply in black relief. Speaking of relief, that's just what I've got to do, relieve myself, and then I'd better hit the sack.

Well, I'm still up! I just went for a cold drink from a spring 150 yards above the camp and, as my teen-aged sons would say, it's really neat sitting here in complete darkness. There is no moon, only the campfire flickering in the trees. It's still warm a foot and a half from the fire. Although I'm not very good at describing this sort of thing, I know this is the most pleasant, relaxing, and wholly satisfying evening I've spent in a good many weeks. It's nine-fifteen now, and I can hear coyotes howling close by.

August 22

It surprises me that I thought of yesterday's date, August 21, several times last night, yet its significance escaped me utterly until this morning. August 21 was our twenty-seventh wedding anniversary!

August 22, too, has been a good day from the standpoint of weather and productivity. I completed more than four rolls of film, including scenes of the scales of lodgepole cones being harvested and dropped by squirrels, of me making breakfast near the tent, of a weasel in a tree, and of two weasels playing on a rock. Later I got some shots of ants on a trail carrying eggs, a butterfly feeding on an aster, a black caterpillar with a row of red dots, glacial boulders strewn across the Texas Creek valley bottom, a chipmunk, another rock glacier, and the toe of a small moraine.

I just listened back to see if the tape recorder is working and the sound of my voice startled me. It sounded so high and squeaky that I think the recorder batteries must be getting low—or maybe mine are. So unlike last night, I'll make this rather short.

I went out to the beaver ponds shortly after daylight, as planned, and saw nothing, as expected. It was, however, a beautiful sight just before the sun came up. Each beaver pond has its own plume of fog rising from the surface. It was cold and the meadow grass was covered with frost. After breakfast I climbed to the head of Texas Creek and on into some high country, where I did that smorgasbord of photography I just mentioned. I didn't get back to camp until six-thirty, exhausted. I had to sit and eat a candy bar before I could summon the energy to wash up and fix supper. Night falls so early now I could no longer see to write by eight-fifteen, so I pulled the sleeping bag up around my shoulders and went to sleep.

August 23

I got back to the cabin a little past noon, weighed down by my heavy load. Charlie and his family were still here. Charlie helped me off with my pack and thought it was so heavy we ought to weigh it. We had to unpack it and put one piece at a time on the spring scale I have for weighing water in the rain gauge. If anyone's interested, the pack contained two movie cameras and one still camera; several extra lenses; a tripod; ten rolls of film; binoculars; extra clothing including two jackets, poncho, waders, and extra shoes; a tent; sleeping bag and foam pad; hatchet; cook kit; a stove with a propane bottle; first-aid equipment; a tape recorder; and toilet articles, including a roll of toilet paper. It came to 65 pounds, 11 ounces, so I feel proud of making it the four miles uphill from my Texas Creek camp without once taking it off. I must say that I needed about twenty minutes on a chair, three glasses of Tang, one glass of milk, and two cups of tea before I felt ready to move again.

Everything at the cabin was in good order. Charlie and his son had seen quite a bit of wildlife. The smaller animals have been preparing for winter and the large animals moving to new, more sheltered areas. I saw that several elk had crossed the trail below the cabin and I continue to see deer tracks. Charlie said the marten had gotten into the cabin twice while I was gone, and that two days ago they had cornered it on a rafter in the upstairs bedroom. Apparently they were poking at it with a shovel handle to get it out, and it bit the handle and showed its teeth in hostility. I'm sorry this happened because the marten had been appearing more and more in daylight and I had hoped to get some film of it without having to trap the animal.

Billy Carpenter came in at three to pick up Charlie and his family. Bill said that he had had a real problem with the two empty propane bottles on his last trip. When he reached the timber on the other side of Brown's Pass the valve jiggled loose on one of the bottles. It seems that even when a bottle is too "empty" to operate the generator, it still holds enough propane to make a loud hissing noise when released. The mule began bucking when it heard this hissing, and of course the more he bucked, the more it hissed. This cycle continued until the mule had completely torn up the pack saddle, part of the countryside, and thrown both bottles clear. Bill says he doesn't want to pack any more propane bottles out, and I can understand why.

As I was coming up the Texas Creek trail I felt a little despondent about returning to the cabin. It seems that I accomplish more when I'm out in my tent. I suppose that's because the regular chores don't have to be done. What I found myself dreading most today was washing clothes. Even though I washed eight days ago, I didn't wash everything and I've gotten tremendously dirty on this pack trip. I knew I was in for the whole routine: pack water, heat water, wash hair, take a bath, put the clothes to soak overnight; then scrub the clothes tomorrow.

The urgent item of real importance is big game. I want to get over to the Mount Yale area as quickly as possible to find the elk and bighorn herds. It will not be long before these large herds will be breaking up. The bull elk, in particular, go into their courtship and mating phase soon, ending the amicable association of males. I sent a note to Ross Moser telling him that I simply had to get over there and asking for somebody in the Salida or Buena Vista area who knows the country to take me in by horse.

One aspect of my camp at Texas Creek that I did not mention was the rabbits. I've seldom seen as high a concentration of snowshoe hare droppings. There were areas close to my tent literally carpeted with rabbit pellets. I saw no fresh sign, and I saw no rabbits, so there must be a large winter population there.

The vegetation has changed rapidly in the three days I have been gone. Much more yellow and gold are showing around the cabin, and even more at higher elevations.

Another sign of approaching autumn is that for the first time the horseflies are congregating in the cabin. This behavior is an indication that the cold is bothering them outside. I shall not be surprised to wake up one of these mornings to find a blanket of snow.

August 24

Today was the much-dreaded wash day, and it took about four hours. But it is caught up now and I don't anticipate doing any more for at least three weeks.

Right now I'm near Brown's Pass sitting among the rocks of a boulder field, filming pikas. Last night Charlie told me that Ross Moser, the district ranger, and Bob Cermak, supervisor of the San Isabel National Forest, would be in to see me this morning at ten. It's ten-thirty now, so I expect them soon. I'm at a good vantage point to watch for them while doing a little photography and catching up on my narration. It is a good morning, clear, cool, no wind, just a few light clouds coming in rather low on the mountaintops and shrouding the peaks around the basin. I just saw the first hawk that has soared close enough to identify. It's a red-tail, and it seems to be hunting. The preferred foods of this omnipresent bird are mice, voles, gophers, and squirrels of all kinds, though in hard times it will eat anything it can find. There is a pika about ten feet from me, and a chipmunk feeding nearby, both fair game for a red-tail.

Well, here they are, arrived as scheduled. After my firsthand experiences with some of the users of federal forest land here, I am eager to talk about official policy. We went to the cabin where I made coffee, and we ate lunch and visited for several hours. I recorded what Bob Cermak said, and think that his ideas are important enough to summarize.

When Cermak came to the San Isabel a couple of years ago, the public was just getting interested in the environment. Over the years the Forest Service had *wanted* people to be interested, but for some reason they weren't, or the Service failed to get the message across.

He said that land use first became an issue in the West. World War II made some major population changes, bringing a lot of people out here and a great demand for timber to supply the tremendous boom in housing. This boom created new roads, dams, and reservoirs, and more water recreation areas. There didn't seem to be much doubt that the National Forests would be asked to meet a different set of demands, but when the Forest Service people looked at their multiple-use plans, they could see that the plans were inadequate. First, they began to look at Forest Service lands as a whole, and then at Colorado in particular. What kinds of uses were these areas suitable for. Answers had a lot to do with the local soils, water, and geology.

They looked especially hard at the mountains, and saw that there are over a million acres within the San Isabel Forest. Of this, more than 350,000 acres are alpine or subalpine, with over twenty peaks higher than 14,000 feet—the highest block of forest land in the country. A little farther west of the San Isabel are other high ranges—the San Juans, the Elks, the West Elks. Since the prevailing winter storms come generally from the west, they have to pass over this high country before they get to the San Isabel. A lot of that country is at 12,000 and 13,000 feet, so the clouds cool and drop precipitation. Once they reach the San Isabel they are pretty well wrung out. Some of these eastern slopes are almost like deserts.

As a result of the dryness, the organisms that form soil—bacteria, lichens, fungi, earthworms, and so on—are not very active. And because of the altitude the warm season is not long enough for the soil-formers to do much. Without good soil, timber growth is poor. The timber is dwarfed, bent, and slow-growing. To complicate the situation, the trees grow on steep slopes, where they are difficult to get at. What timber there was here was cut during mining days for charcoal, mine props, and buildings, and since it grows so slowly it still hasn't come back. There is very little timber anywhere in this forest that has commercial value.

An important use of other federal lands is grazing. But cattle don't do very well in high country where there is not much good forage for them. This area was grazed by large herds in the past, but the practice is just not compatible with the terrain or with the alpine vegetation. In the 1940s and 1950s there were severe struggles between the Forest Service and ranchers in the San Isabel. The Service wound up closing most of the land to livestock to protect the soil and vegetation, and it is still closed. There are only a few bands of sheep left.

So the Forest Service counted the resources of this forest and saw there was little timber to harvest, little commercial forage, and few minerals left after years of mining. The resources that remain included the natural resources of water and wildlife. And some other resources that haven't in the past been included in planning—what Cermak calls social resources. He describes them as resources found in the mind of man. One such resource is scenery. Wildness and open space are lumped together as another. He doesn't call this wilderness; he says that wilderness has become so tied to the Wilderness Act that he thinks of it only with a capital W. He uses the term "wildness" because it indicates a real condition rather than a technical classification. And the open space part of this condition means the absence of limits such as power lines and roads and fences, which tend to spoil the feeling of wildness.

History and archaeology make up the third kind of social resource. Any of these three can be broken down or rearranged where needed. In the Sawatch Range they consider geology a separate "social use," because the geology there is so unusual and dramatic. It's important to recognize that all these social resources have value, just as natural resources have value. And they must also have protection. In some cases they can even be improved; in other cases, they can't.

Around Brown's Cabin, Cermak sees as our primary resources water, wildlife, and the social resources. Of those, the primary use is recreation, such as four-wheel-driving, hiking, mountain climbing, and snowmobiling. They're trying to get a measure of the quality of these experiences and what they mean to the land. Cermak feels that when they can get this done they'll be in a better position to know what kinds of activity can be allowed while still protecting the natural environment.

To reach that point they divided the forest into five planning areas and then subdivided the planning areas. The Sawatch Range, for example, is one area, but because it is so big—over half a million acres—it is broken up further. Within each unit they would sample the natural and social resources and the major recreation uses.

There is strong feeling among Forest Service people that the standard type of multiple-use plan must be improved if they're going to succeed. So they have come up with a new procedure. It involves numerical rating forms, brief descriptions of each planning area, assumptions about what might happen in the next ten years, and setting down three or four possible ways to manage that area. For Brown's Cabin one alternative might be: make it all wild. Cut off the Cottonwood Road, seed the old roads, and call it Wilderness. Or at the other extreme, develop campgrounds the length and breadth of every flat spot here. There might be five different possibilities just for this one unit. The next step is to get together with the rangers, look at these various summary sheets, and read them over carefully. Then bring all of the parts of the planning units together to make a "management unit."

Now here's the really crucial part of the process, the one that goes far beyond the old multiple-use plans: communicating directly with the public. In the Sangre de Cristos, for example, Bob Cermak's people have gone all-out to make the public aware that there really are problems, and that everyone has a stake in helping decide what to do with this national forest that belongs to them. They have talked to approximately 8,000 people in two years—to hundreds of groups from college classes to motorcycle clubs—to anyone who would listen. They went talking their way through every county on the forest, through two dozen towns and cities. Then they assembled a group with representatives from every recreation user group—four-wheel-drive clubs, motorcycle clubs, the Colorado Mountain Club, the Sierra Club, the Wilderness Society, the local Audubon club— all the way from Canōn City to Pueblo and even Colorado Springs. They made a point of contacting the urban as well as the rural people, because city-dwellers are major users of these areas now. They asked everyone for written comments, and this next Saturday they're going to take people out in the field and show them what they've been talking about. There were also three or four television programs in the Pueblo area and illustrated articles in seven newspapers that reach a total of several thousand people.

One of the most interesting exercises Bob told me about was actually bringing these users together. It was the first time many of them had communicated at all. They were so far out of touch that Sierra Club people wouldn't talk to a motorcyclist or a four-wheel-driver, and vice versa. But when they all got together and started talking about how their grandchildren might experience the same things *they* thought were valuable, it turned out that they agreed on a good many things. The initial hostility comes down to a few specific sources of irritation on both sides. Even the people who disagreed with the Forest Service approach had some good ideas about what should be done with these lands. Some of the more stringent proposals for the Sangre de Cristos actually came from the motorcycle groups and four-wheel-drive clubs. When Cermak laid out some alternatives of what could happen, he was astonished to find that the Pueblo Four Wheel Drive Club wanted to ban cross-country travel!

When the Forest Service announced about three weeks ago that they were closing the whole Sangre de Cristos range to off-road and off-trail vehicular travel, there was not a single complaint. Cermak said that if they had tried to do that out of the blue two years ago, they would have spent the following year and a half trying to explain it, and nobody would have been happy. Worse than that, everyone would have felt alienated from the decision-making process. It is easy to see why people might be tempted to break rules made unilaterally.

Before Bob Cermak came to the San Isabel he was a deputy supervisor of the Black Hills Forest Service district, where he and Ken Scholz, the supervisor now, worked out another new approach. Every national forest is different, after all. The Black Hills, for example, has to fit timber into any resource plan; in fact, what they do is start with timber, and from that point work to the other resources. They knew, for instance, that there were areas subject to erosion when it rained, so they drew up a whole set of cutting instructions to protect the soil. They made other instructions to favor the growth of browse for deer. They deliberately reduced the potential for timber in some areas in order to enhance the deer population.

This is actually a type of zoning, the kind that might keep vehicles out of some places. Apparently, the Forest Service does have zones in some plans. In the Sangre de Cristos and the two areas they intend to propose for the study of wilderness, they won't allow horses overnight. And they don't want *any* horses on the tundra. There may also be places where horses, vehicles, even people must stay on the trail. As Bob said, we've got to consider what we're going to have fifty and a hundred years from now, not just five years from now. We've seen in just three years a tremendous increase in people using the Sangre de Cristos, and Bob said that in California the traffic is even heavier.

"Hell, I walked into the so-called Minaret Wilderness and in one morning I counted 550 people. Last year 25,000 people walked up the Mount Whitney trail; a mile on either side of the trail there's no wood left and there's a pile of trash behind every boulder. You can't really call that wilderness, with or without a capital W. We're going to have to start setting limits to use, no matter how distasteful that is. Even a motorcyclist doesn't want fifty other bikers parked around a wilderness lake at 12,000 feet."

August 25

I'm still thinking of yesterday's interesting conversation with Bob Cermak. I think that Bob's attitude offers an outstanding example of some of the good, new thinking in the Forest Service today. He is about forty years old, relatively young for a forest supervisor, and obviously dedicated and articulate. It gives me faith in the rejuvenative powers of even a bureaucratic agency.

The point of particular interest to me is the public involvement phase of decision-making. If people don't agree with the way a forest is administered, they should be encouraged to say so, in public. It is the public, after all, that owns the public lands. The Forest Service used to regard its job primarily as protector of natural resources—timber, water, wildlife, forage, soil. I am pleased that what Bob calls "social resources"—that is, what people want—have come in for some attention.

Bob also mentioned the importance of new thinking coming from the ground up. We tend to think that the chief forester in Washington or some regional forester should have the good ideas, and that everyone should recognize how good they are. In my experience the top people can have all the bright ideas in the world, but nothing happens if the rangers don't agree with them. The man in the field wants to be, and should be, an integral part of the decision-making process.

Now, in spite of my enthusiastic endorsement of the Forest Service's new concepts as described by Cermak, I feel compelled to state my doubts that very much will change. First, I suspect that Bob is more forward-looking than most Forest Service administrators. Second, plans are useless unless they are implemented. And, before any of this "new thinking" in the Forest Service can be transformed into effective management practices, an enormous bureaucratic inertia will have to be overcome all along the line.

I do have hopes that recently passed legislation, such as the National Environmental Protection Act of 1969, will improve the quality of natural resources decisions and subsequent Forest Service actions. This act requires planning, proposals of alternative courses of action, and public response before final decisions are made—much the same procedures Cermak mentioned during our discussion yesterday.

A key ingredient to future success will also be the alertness of the public and their willingness to participate actively by expressing their concerns during the decision-making process. A concomitant responsibility of the Forest Service will be truly to seek public input and honestly consider it in final decisions. The next decade or two ought to be exciting as we confront the challenges described by Cermak. If only I could turn the calendar back a quarter century and again be an eager young biologist with a fresh diploma in hand and utopian dreams in my head. But the future belongs to the young—although I believe that the young-at-heart (or of mind) can help nudge it along.

Well, Charlie has told me by radio that a man named Alfred Meyer would be in sometime soon with his family. Mr. Meyer is going to be working on this project for Alan Landsburg, but I haven't heard if he arrives today or tomorrow. Here I have another one of those periods when I can't get too far from the cabin, so I've decided to get a little further along in narrating my "life history." I just checked back on the tape and find that I only got through the eighth grade. I really became involved in the details of my early life; they are much more interesting to me now than they were in real time.

My high school years were rather unhappy ones, so I am going to lump them all together. Also I don't remember many of the details. It seems that one's memory blocks out unhappy experiences. I do remember that we were terribly poor, undoubtedly one of the poorest families in the community. Dad was too ill to work during the first two years I was in high school, and during the last two he was on WPA, which I mentioned before was a source of great embarrassment to him. Looking back, I'm sure that Dad was not only embarrassed by having to be on WPA but also deeply depressed by being unable to take care of his family properly. During my first two years of high school our only income was from the huge garden that Mother and I planted and from two or three hundred chickens we raised. I added to that income by beginning early in the spring to plow gardens for neighbors who didn't have horses. This was done with what was called a walking plow. I suspect that few people today have seen one. It had two handles and was hooked to a team of two horses. You walked behind it, guiding the plow by the handles and the horses by the reins. It was hard work. I first began this sort of farmwork at the age of thirteen and continued for the next five springs.

Following the season of plowing and planting I would begin haying. This was also done with horses. There were jobs like mowing, raking, shocking, hauling, and stacking. In the fall we would begin grain harvest. In northern Idaho we used stationary threshing machines. The grain was cut with a binder, which tied the grain into bundles. These bundles were then shocked, pitched onto wagons, and hauled to the threshing machine. I worked at most all of the jobs involved in this process—pitching the bundles onto the wagon, driving the horses, loading the bundles, sewing the sacks of grain (a "prestige" job that paid $3 a day). In addition, each spring I planted from one to fifteen acres of potatoes; then during spare time in the summer I would hoe and cultivate them. For three to four weeks in the fall after the rest of the kids had begun school I would harvest the potatoes and haul them to nearby mining and logging communities in my 1929 Model A Ford pickup.

I also fed and took care of the horses, cows, and pigs. My mother took care of the chickens, but was afraid of the larger animals. I did all the milking.

Perhaps as a result of these responsibilities, I was a shy and rather insecure youngster during high school years. I didn't participate in any social or athletic events because there was always work to be done at home. I did attempt to play in the band for a time, but after a few weeks of having to walk five miles home at night after band practice, and then do all the chores, I gave it up.

My main outside activity was 4-H work, and this organization was good for me. I was twice chosen the outstanding 4-H boy in Benewah County and received $100 scholarships to take agriculture at the University of Idaho. Also I was selected twice for the livestock judging team that went to the livestock show in Portland, Oregon. And in 1938 I won a trip to the Livestock Show and Exposition in Chicago for leadership activities in 4-H. These were literally the first times I saw the outside world and met different kinds of people. By outside world I mean anything beyond a twenty-mile radius of the town of St. Maries.

Actually, as I think about it, these were not altogether unhappy years. I enjoyed most of the work. I recall particularly the plowing in the spring and the sight and smell of the clean, brown earth as it was turned. I took pride in making the furrows straight and turning all the earth completely. I enjoyed disking and harrowing the plowed soil so that it would be well cultivated and clean for planting. I enjoyed, too, the experiences of working with the older men during haying and grain harvest. They would tell my dad what a good, hard-working kid I was, and this probably made me work even harder. The wages, however, were not good. I recall getting $2.00 or $3.00 a day alone, and up to $5.00 for me, my team, and my wagon. And those were usually ten- to twelve-hour days.

There were some disadvantages in this no-play–all-work regimen. One was that I graduated twenty-seventh in a class of fifty-two. I would accept this at face value except that subsequent university records indicate that my potential was considerably above this. I also never learned to play or relax. In the past twenty years of professional employment, during which I have probably accumulated somewhat over 400 days of annual leave, I have not taken more than 100 days for recreational activity. And some of that was used for writing my dissertation and for other work-related projects. My family could scarcely tell the difference between work and "vacation" time.

Looking back, I wonder why I did work so hard during my early years. Certainly my parents never asked me to. In fact, they tried many times to get me to go fishing or just fool around with the other kids. I was the one to veto the idea. I remember a corner of our small farm that was covered with brush and small trees and stumps. Whenever the chores were done I would hitch up the horses and start pulling stumps in this corner, trying to clear it to plant alfalfa. I never did get the corner entirely cleared and never did plant the alfalfa.

Even in recent years I have had a tendency to plod away at some job that I never get done to my satisfaction. My wife has chided me for being unable to relax and enjoy doing something just for the fun of it. I've thought about this a lot this summer. Many things that other families enjoy seem to be just outside my grasp.

As I think about it, I would say that on three out of four weekends and at least 50 percent of my weekday evenings I go into the office. I do not say this with pride, but in fact with some shame. Certainly what I achieve there at such times is not commensurate with the time and effort put in.

To give a somewhat less bleak picture, I should say that there are occasions for relaxation; several times each summer we have friends for a barbecue dinner on the patio, usually preceded by a couple of drinks and maybe badminton on the back lawn. For a few years I went downhill ski-ing eight to ten times each winter; I still enjoy swimming, and tennis with my youngest son. The problem is that I usually feel guilty about taking time for these pursuits. Likewise I belonged to Toastmasters for several years, then decided it was taking up too much time and quit. The same for square dancing with my wife, and for watching television or going to a movie. I probably do not watch one whole program other than the news during a month of television. Often this is frustrating because I will ac-tually want to watch something. But I have such guilt feelings about just watching a show for entertainment that they spoil the entertainment. During our twenty-seven years of married life I can only recall three or four bona fide vacation trips. These were enjoyable and I wonder now why we have not taken more. Certainly my wife has wanted to. I guess I am deciding out loud that some revision of my living schedule is in order— for the sake of my entire family.

Back to my "life history." I graduated from St. Maries High School in the spring of 1938. I was sixteen. My parents decided, and rightly so, that this was too young to go directly into college. Since I didn't have enough money to start college anyway, I stayed out of school for the next fifteen months. That spring I rented fifteen acres of river bottom land and planted it to potatoes. During the summer I worked for nearby farmers haying and harvesting grain, and in the fall I became a logger. Two men worked together with a crosscut saw, a two-handled affair about six feet long. We would fell the trees, then limb them on three sides and cut them into logs twelve to twenty feet long. Sometimes we worked in two or more feet of snow.

The next summer, 1939, I worked for the Forest Service in a blister rust control program. Our job was to remove currant and gooseberry bushes, which are the secondary host for white pine blister rust. I worked as a crew member, a crew foreman, and a checker at the comparatively high wages of 50 to 60 cents an hour. I recall vividly receiving $114 in the month of August. That was the most money I had ever made in one month in my life.

That fall I entered the University of Idaho, planning to become a county extension agent or an agriculture teacher in high school. Before the beginning of World War II, I had completed two and a half years. Like many other students who had little money, I lived in a cooperative dormitory. We shared in the work and were able to live for $27 per se-mester for room, and about $18 or $20 a month for board. I recall that there were only three cars parked in the small lot back of our 160-man dormitory. One was a 1936 Chevrolet owned by the full-time cook we employed; another was a 1926 Model T Ford owned by a friend of mine; the third was mine, a 1930 Model A Ford. I considered myself one of the luckier students.

I had few nonstudy activities, but I did serve one term as dorm representative on the student council, and president of the university 4-H club. My social life picked up, too, in relative terms—from having no dates in high school to taking fourteen different girls during my sophomore year to the exchange and holiday dances that were so popular then.

I also remember my first drunk. This began at a dance downtown and resulted in, among other things, getting slapped by the girl I was dancing with, turning her over my knee and paddling her behind, and the police coming out on the floor to have a conversation with us. They decided that the spanking was justified, but before the evening was over I had also gotten into a fistfight and driven my Model A all over somebody's lawn. I doubt that the police would have had the same attitude toward those activities. Finally I was unable to climb into the upper bunk of my double-decker. For this my roommate demoted me to the lower bunk, where I slept for the remainder of that school year.

In spite of expenses at college and helping my parents, my finances were in better condition than those of many of my friends. I had the $100 4-H scholarship, $600 profit from my 1939 potato crop, and $550 from a Sears Roebuck sales scheme. During my high school years, Sears would send you order blanks with your name on them. If you persuaded a friend to order through the catalogue on one of your blanks, a tiny percentage of that order would come back to you. Prizes were given—telescopes, roller skates, sleds—and this is what most of the kids worked for. If you didn't want the prizes, you could convert the points earned into cash. Of course, I took the cash, and much to the amazement of Sears and Roebuck, I made this a regular business, going from house to house throughout St. Maries asking people to use my order blanks. By the fall of 1939, even though my cut of each order was only about 1 percent, I had earned over $550. This means that people using my order blanks spent over $55,000 on Sears, Roebuck merchandise. At the prices being charged then, this represents a lot of consumer durables.

I had various jobs during summers and vacations. One was cutting Douglas fir timbers—the kind used to reinforce mine shafts—for my uncle. The trees varied from sixteen to twenty-eight inches in diameter at the stump. I worked alone on this job, felling a tree, limbing it, then peeling the bark from it, another instance where I enjoyed being alone in the mountains. One summer I worked for Weyerhaeuser Logging Company, first as a bulldozer pimp. This inelegant title might be translated as "assistant to the bulldozer driver." We were using a D-8 dozer to make skid roads. I would drive the Caterpillar out in the morning, gas it, oil it, grease it; then stay with the driver all day, using an ax to cut overhanging limbs and windfalls out of his way as he gauged roads down from the steep country. Later I went back to felling trees, which I enjoyed more. To conservationists this makes me suspect, I know, but the clear ringing notes of axes hitting wood and the singing of a sharp crosscut saw are sounds I remember with great pleasure.

However, even at that time I was dismayed by the lack of concern for soil and vegetation displayed by the typical logger. I remember one bulldozer driver who, when he had finished working, would sometimes raise the dozer blade to maximum height, open the throttle, and head straight down the mountain for camp, knocking over everything in his path, including trees twenty to thirty feet tall. It is hard to believe now, but there was no opposition to this kind of behavior then. We were tearing hell out of the countryside with the logging operation anyway, so I guess no one was concerned about a little extra mayhem.

Around the same time I also worked on a log landing—briefly. One day a log was rolling toward me and I caught it, as usual, with my cant hook. But the momentum of the log was greater than I expected. It flipped me in a somersault onto my back and my career on the log landing was over. I was hospitalized for a few days, and I've had all sorts of trouble with my back since then, including a laminectomy operation.

All told I have spent a significant part of my life in various hospitals. Today I jotted down my operations, the ones requiring general anesthesia, and I found there were a total of eleven.

Despite this ragged health history, however, I began a program of exercise about four years ago and have been in excellent shape ever since. I ride my bike to work, to church, and frequently downtown shopping. I also go to the CSU gymnasium four days a week when possible, where I run three miles, lift light weights for fifteen minutes, spend fifteen minutes in the sauna, then shower and back to work. This has done wonders for my general well-being and has reduced my resting heart rate from 75 beats per minute to 58. I'm hoping that once I get back to Fort Collins and into my exercise regimen my back pain will disappear and I'll be able to fend off the infirmities of old age at least for a few more years.

August 26

It seems to be tourist season here at Brown's Cabin. This morning I heard voices and later saw three teen-aged boys coming down from the upper mine. The family of one has a cabin on Little Cottonwood Creek about ten miles from here. They had been traveling a good deal this summer, camping out in the high country, and they were able to give me a good rundown on the mountain goat, bighorn sheep, and elk herds in the general area. They had seen a herd of about forty mountain goats in Mineral Basin, which I have heard is an excellent area for game. They also saw about thirty bighorn on the slopes of Mount Yale, where I plan to go in a few days.

A little before lunchtime Bill Conklin, a district ranger from the Gunnison National Forest, and Dick Stillman, also with the Gunnison, came in to see how the project is going and to bring some information I had requested concerning the grazing, mining, and timbering history of this area.

They were here for three hours, and shortly after they left, Alfred Meyer, his wife Pamela, and their young son Paul arrived with Billy Carpenter. Since it was getting late I did not attempt any further outside activity and we got the Meyers settled in the cabin. After dinner we had a very enjoyable conversation about The New Explorer series and life in general.

August 27

Al Meyer went up to the weather station with me, and I described the instrumentation to him.

What we have is a standard Forest Service weather shelter, four feet off the ground, about the height of a big-game animal. If it were higher or lower, the measurements would be quite different. A man named Geiger has written a book called *Climate Near the Ground*, in which he shows how important a few inches can be. For example, he says that on Pike's Peak one clear summer's day the surface temperature was 140 degrees, while the temperature five feet above the ground was only 70 degrees. At the same time, a few inches beneath the surface it was 55 degrees. And it may have been freezing a few inches deeper. So it matters a great deal how we position this station if we are to describe accurately the environment where elk—and humans—spend most of their time.

The instruments include three thermometers—a standard, a minimum, and a maximum thermometer. The standard is the control that is used to check the accuracy of the others, which measure the lowest and highest temperatures that have occurred since I reset them. The minimum thermometer recorded 37½ degrees last night. But from the control, which has been calibrated in the lab and is more accurate, I know that the minimum thermometer is two degrees off, so the minimum really was 35½. I reset the minimum thermometer by moving the marker up to the current temperature. When the temperature falls again it will take the marker back down and leave it at its lowest reading. To reset the maximum thermometer, which recorded 61½ yesterday, I have to spin it, somewhat like shaking a bedside thermometer, so that centrifugal force will move the mercury to whatever the temperature is now.

The hygrothermograph shows current temperature and relative humidity. Relative humidity is the actual amount of moisture that the air at a certain temperature holds relative to the theoretical maximum it might hold at that temperature. If you hear on the Denver radio station that the humidity is 78 percent, which it was this morning, that means that the air held 78 percent of the theoretical maximum for the current temperature. The higher the temperature, the more water the air can hold. So a relative humidity of 78 percent on a cool day feels a lot more comfortable than 78 percent on a hot day.

The third instrument is the microbarograph, which gives the barometric pressure. This has a seven-day chart, and shows whether the pressure is going up or down. I've noticed that before some of these afternoon rainstorms the pressure started falling sharply six to eight hours before the storm began, then frequently fell again right in the middle of the storm.

Precipitation is measured by a recording rain gauge. Rain falls through an opening eight inches in diameter and is then funneled into a bucket that sits on a balance. As the bucket fills it forces the balance down and an arm upward. A pen on the arm makes a line on a seven-day chart. The chart is wrapped around a drum driven by a manually wound clock drive, as are all of the instruments. So I get continuous records, minute by minute, for a whole week.

Finally there is the totaling anemometer, which I've mentioned before—the machine that gives the peculiar reading of "miles of wind" blown. Today's reading was 852 miles. To make sense out of that, you subtract the previous reading—say, 840 miles—and divide the result by the number of hours that have passed. If the previous reading was made an hour ago, you would have had 12 miles of wind, or an average wind of 12 miles per hour.

After we had finished at the weather station, we walked to the mine shafts nearby, then to the pika area, and eventually back to the cabin, where we spent the rest of the day discussing various aspects of alpine ecology, and introducing Alfred's son Paul to mountain wildlife.

August 28

I didn't get much sleep last night, so I got up at four-thirty to watch the dawning of a new day. Soft white clouds had surrounded the cabin most of the night. At about seven-thirty they began to break up, letting the blue sky and vistas of distant mountain peaks through. There was a gentle rain last night, so the grass was bright and shining when the sun rose. In the early afternoon the rain began again, and around six we had two bursts that were as heavy as any I have seen here. All of the organic debris that had accumulated in the trails and open spaces since the last heavy storm was washed away. Sometimes up here the scenery is so powerful it almost makes you hurt. In the logging camp where I used to work two of my roughneck acquaintances had their own terms for this. One would say, "It's so pretty it makes my gut ache." The other would say, "It's so damn beautiful it makes you want to shit." That's not very elegant, or maybe even appropriate, but the feeling is real.

The Meyers left this morning, and once again I am glad to be alone in my cabin. It was a real pleasure to become acquainted with Pamela Meyer. She has wide experience in photography and anthropology, yet has maintained a simple and straightforward manner. Alfred, too, seems to be a perceptive, sensitive person, aware of the details of his surroundings. I was impressed by his comments about the beauty of the flowers and animals. But I have to admit that a family of three overwhelms my sense of housekeeping, and although Alfred and Pamela tried to minimize the disruption of my schedule, the last two days have been difficult. I'm sure they didn't realize what the simple presence of three extra people means to someone who has been alone for two and a half months. The first night the crying of young Paul—who was much affected by the change of altitude—was not too disturbing, but the second night I slept practically not at all. I was weary and cross in the morning, and so tense when he woke me at four-thirty that I didn't even try to get back to sleep.

Also, I did not feel free to go through the rather noisy procedure of back exercises I do every night before bed, and I have had more back pain

last night and today than I've had for several weeks. My nerves generally
have been on edge since early this morning. I have a splitting headache,
which twelve aspirins haven't dissipated. Well, I won't be petulant and
blame all this on the Meyers; I should say that I am not very good at cop-
ing with company.

I walked to Brown's Pass with Al and Pamela and Paul because it is
my day to repeat the permanent photo points. At about nine we said
goodbye; Al was carrying all their gear and Pamela was carrying Paul in a
special pack for children. After they had gone about two hundred yards I
happened to look down and they had stopped, turned, and were waving
goodbye. I waved back, hoping that in spite of my tenseness I had been a
reasonably good host.

As I took the permanent photo point shots I reflected on the importance of solitude to me this summer. I had not realized before how pre-
cious it has been. Other than the times when I needed help installing the
radio transmitter or with filming this documentary, I don't recall a single
time when I have wanted human visitors. The sight of a distant backpacker who might be headed toward the cabin provokes in me a feeling of
apprehension that my solitude and routine will be interrupted once again.

Though I miss my family deeply, even the prospect of mail from
home has not been exciting. One can easily get used to going without
mail. I recall the winter of 1951, when the whole family spent the winter
in the wilds of Idaho. During the entire stay we got mail only three times,
by a special ski-equipped airplane. Later we realized that we had fretted
less that winter about receiving mail than we do in town, where we get it
every day.

All that being said, what should happen today but that more visitors
should arrive. Two backpackers I had met before on their way down Texas
Creek were coming back up, and they decided to drop in. I thought they
would only stay a moment, but they wanted to talk. I finally had to say,
well, I'm going to go ahead with my chores instead of being a good host.
When I went upstairs and began rolling sleeping bags, the two hikers at
last got their packs assembled and took off up the trail. I don't like to be
that rude, but I wanted desperately to be alone, and I was willing to do
almost anything to bring that about.

My meeting with Alfred Meyer has triggered some thoughts about
the documentary itself, and I might as well get them off my chest. I am
concerned about the scientific value of this film we are making. It seems
to me a very difficult thing for one man to make a unique and original
contribution to science in five months, especially if that one man is

spending a lot of his time taking stills and movies, keeping a dusty cabin clean, and entertaining a near-constant stream of visitors. I wonder if those who conceived the idea understood what was involved when they instructed me to conduct a study as well as portray the ecology of the alpine. I have been associated with studies in which the man-hours put into the planning phase alone exceed what I shall spend on this entire project. In order for studies to have much value they have to be carefully planned, and must usually be set up on some statistical basis. In other words, sampling must be replicated, and statistical analysis is necessary. The observations, whether they are the measurement of plants, recordings of animal behavior, maintenance of rainfall records, or what have you, must be done over and over. An isolated fact or two has little scientific value. What we have here, really, is a rather human story of a scientifically trained man who lives more or less alone in the wilds for a few months, observing and thinking about the environment he is living in. To advertise it as any more than that could be misleading and tremendously embarrassing.

Since this is a night for philosophic rambling, I want to discuss what is apparently another misconception on the part of the planners of this documentary. That is the myth that we are dealing with a "natural" environment, in the sense of primeval. I think it is fair to say that there is no such place in the contiguous forty-eight states. I've traveled extensively through the national forests and wilderness areas of the half dozen Rocky Mountain states and am positive that if you know what to look for you will see signs of past human use on almost every acre. This is certainly true of the Brown's Cabin area and adjacent regions that I am photographing. Yet I still think we made a good decision in choosing this area; it is probably as "natural" as we could find.

The reason I bring this point up is that otherwise we are implying a virginal landscape that simply no longer exists. The stories we like to tell about the Wild West and its great unspoiled spaces are stories of Hollywood, not of the real world. I'm quite concerned about people like one recent visitor who told me of his despair in watching "our great land" go down the drain. Although I think some of this attitude derives from exposure to large cities, where conditions can indeed seem depressing, such negative views do not match the historical evidence in the mountains here.

I do agree that we are losing some of our natural areas in an irreversible process—the continuing expansion of urban areas, which in turn means more highways and parking lots and the sprawl of suburban developments. Heavy industry is always accompanied by pollution of air, water, and quiet. We are fortunate to have groups such as the Sierra Club, Wilderness Society, and Rocky Mountain Center on Environment that are fighting to preserve wild areas.

However, alarmists and fatalists who see only darkness ahead do us a great disservice. One reason they spread such pessimism is that they lack an understanding of history. There is no question that much of our public land has been raped, desecrated, and abused. Some of this abuse was done knowingly, in full awareness of the consequences, through the greed of our ancestors. Some was inherent in the opening of a new land to settlement and through ignorance of ecological processes. But I find it difficult totally to condemn the early sheepman, stockman, miner, logger, or trapper. As a matter of fact, I doubt that we would now be in a position to enjoy this land at all had it not been for these early pioneers. True, they did mistreat the land, each other, and the Indians. But as I reflect on the social and moral standards of those times, I wonder if the West could have been settled much differently. Thank God we are now more aware of and concerned about other people's rights and humanity; perhaps this awareness is an outgrowth of the sins of the past.

The central Rocky Mountain area first began to attract the white man in large numbers toward the late 1850s, when gold was discovered. The historic mining towns—Cripple Creek, Central City, Leadville, and many others—started to grow, to attract fortune-hunters, and to spread in unruly exuberance over the landscape. Miners built wagon roads to bring heavy equipment into the mountains. Loggers cut vast amounts of timber for building houses, mine and mill structures, mine shaft supports, and for fueling steam engines, like those still found near Brown's Cabin. More timber was cut to make charcoal for processing ore. Horses, mules, and burros were brought in, and their grazing stripped many high mountain meadows and fragile hillsides. Other mountain meadows (at lower elevations than Brown's Cabin) were plowed and planted to oat, hay, and other crops for both animal and human consumption. These immigrant farmers were unfamiliar with the harsh environment of the Rockies, and unaware that most agricultural enterprises had no chance of success. Even today the trained eye can see the scars left by their misguided efforts. So common are these vestiges of failure that scientists use "abandoned field" as the formal term for one of the commoner ecotypes here.

Following the miners came the sheepmen and cattlemen. Again there was great misunderstanding about the capacity of the environment, again the lands were drastically overgrazed, particularly in the ponderosa pine zone and up into the Engelmann spruce and high mountain meadows. Heavy grazing began in the 1880s and continued with great intensity until the early 1900s.

Then came the establishment of the U.S. Forest Service. If my memory is correct, the first national forest was established in Colorado, in 1907. In those early years the restrictions on grazing and other uses were minimal, enforcement nearly nonexistent. But the very presence of a forest ranger here and there did provide some restraint on the headlong exploitation of resources.

Slight progress was being made in reducing destructive practices in the remote areas of our public lands when the Great Depression hit. The Forest Service was forced to back off. Logging restrictions were liberalized, especially for operations thought to be vital to small, impoverished communities. Likewise, grazing rights on public lands were made available at low cost for livestock men who were facing bankruptcy. Mining picked up again in the backcountry, as it did here with Charlie Combs and Homer Brown. Many people left the towns to eke out an existence in the mountains. Many mining claims were filed and stripped of timber between the years 1929 and 1941.

Not until after World War II did we have the leisure to sit back and see what we were doing to our public lands. We saw that it was destructive, and regulations began to be enforced again. The late 1940s and early 1950s brought tremendous conflict between users and regulators, which included the Forest Service, Bureau of Land Management, and Soil Conservation Service. Congress held public hearings at which emotions ran high.

During this period of turmoil many important things happened. Range and wildlife scientists discerned that the environment could not long support our bad habits, and grazing was sharply reduced in the early 1950s; by now I would judge that sheep grazing on public lands has been cut 75 percent from peak times. Cattle grazing on public lands also decreased, although in recent years it has been on the rise because better range management and reduced competition from sheep have improved grazing conditions. There is more surveillance of mining, as well as amendments to the original mining law, which was passed in 1872.

The areas around Brown's Cabin are good examples of what was really happening during the "good old days of unspoiled wilderness." Let me paint a picture of this basin as I think it might have looked fifty to eighty-five years ago. First, there was a lot of tree-cutting. The miners were toppling one Engelmann spruce after another. They used them to heat this cabin plus another cabin on the far side of the basin, and to fire the blacksmith's forge. They also used them to reinforce mine shafts dug back into the mountainsides, and to fuel the steam engine in the mill. They probably cut every mature Engelmann spruce within skidding distance.

Then there were the trails and roads. A major wagon road ran from the mouth of Denny Creek over Brown's Pass, down to the cabin, over to the other cabins, and behind the mill. This road was undoubtedly raw and rutted. Because it traversed steep inclines and fragile soils, there must have been severe erosion problems, and we can assume that deep gullies developed. The road probably had to be moved frequently as gullying made it impassable. Tracks still etched in the landscape indicate this was so.

And there was grazing. The miners kept livestock, primarily mules and burros, for use in transporting ore and supplies. Most of the upper basin was fenced as pasture. Then came the cattle and sheep. I have records from the Forest Service that show heavy grazing of this whole area.

We also know there were numerous forest fires in the early years. People were careless about burning slash—the woody by-products of logging operations. They were equally careless in tending campfires and fireplaces. Many log cabins burned down, often taking acres of forest with them. There was a fairly large fire less than half a mile below Brown's Cabin, covering several hundred acres. The results are still easily visible. Another large area just below the Hartenstein Lake turnoff burned around 1920. The signs of these forest fires are muted today, but obvious to the trained eye.

The astonishing fact is that the land is now recovering from these abuses. Already there are beautiful stands of aspen in the burn areas. Young Engelmann spruce trees left standing have now matured and are curing the scars made by the logging that went on around them. The overgrazed areas, too, have largely healed. On some former ranges it is undoubtedly true that close study would reveal plant communities different from those in ungrazed areas. But to the casual observer it is not readily apparent that the land was once eroded and the vegetation largely destroyed. Even in the harsh climate of this environment with its slow recovery time, we already have a landscape that is pleasing to the eye and which many people would accept as pristine wilderness.

My message is that conditions are not as gloomy as many environmentalists think. I would guess that half of our public lands today are in better, more "natural" condition than they were fifty to a hundred years ago. It is important to recognize that most abuses now occurring on these

"I am about 12,000 feet above sea level, near the Continental Divide, at Brown's Cabin, which was named after Homer Brown, who prospected here for gold."

"In these distinctive Krummholz zones, the spruce, fir, pine, and other trees all have a 'flagged' or 'sheared' shape." (*Above*) "A lot of romantic nonsense has been written about the wildness of bighorn sheep.... I have had large rams come to within ten feet of me." (*Below*)

"The elk is one of nature's noblest creations; there are few animals anywhere that can rival the grandeur of an elk against the backdrop of the Rocky Mountains." (*Above*: Bull Elk. *Below*: Spring Creek Meadow, Mt. Yale in the background.)

"I saw an animal leap into a tree. At first I thought it was a large red squirrel, but when I got closer I saw that it was a marten." (*Above*) "When a pika sits bunched up on a rock top it looks as much like a furry egg as an animal." (*Below*)

"I have been feeding stale or moldy bread to the gray jays, and they have become tame." (*Above*) "Marmots are best described as large, bushy-tailed squirrels that live in holes in the ground. They are stocky and quite bow-legged, so that they waddle more than they run." (*Below*)

Alpine forget-me-not

Sedge

Marsh marigold

Western yellow violet

Indian paintbrush

Globeflower

"The wildflower season here is startling for its beauty."

"Ptarmigan have evolved a seasonal camouflage that makes them nearly invisible year-round. The ground up here is a mottled brown in summer and white in winter, and so are the ptarmigan."

"The forecasters were right; the storm really came.... I didn't get much done except for survival chores. From 6:45 when I got up, until 5:15, I ate only one meal, a good substantial breakfast."

lands are mild indeed compared with those inflicted from 1880 to 1910, the heyday of resource exploitation in the Wild West.

This is not to say there is no reason for current concern; there certainly is. But I do want to leave this subject on an encouraging note, and to deny that this country is going down the drain. I believe that as long as there are concerned managers like Bob Cermak involved in our land agencies, and we the public remain informed and active in expressing opinions, things should get even better.

August 29

Today was Sunday and I didn't get a lot done, partly because I did so much talking and complaining yesterday and partly because I planned it that way. I went to bed last night after midnight, exceedingly tired, my head aching, and slept fairly well until eight-thirty, the latest I've slept since I've been up here.

Believe it or not, I left out one complaint yesterday, and I would like to call this chapter "The Saga of the Chip Bucket." When Charlie Combs and his family were staying at the cabin, a two-gallon galvanized bucket disappeared. I had kept this bucket by the kitchen stove and tossed into it chips of wood, scrap paper, eggshells, used matchsticks, dirty paper toweling—all the burnable items that accumulate in the cabin. Each time I wanted to start the kitchen fire I would dip into the chip bucket for kindling.

Well, I can't find it anywhere. This seems to be symptomatic of all my problems and frustrations. In the overpopulation of Brown's Cabin in recent days, the salt and pepper, the butter, the syrup, and the other little things have been moved from where I expect to find them. I sometimes feel like sitting down and crying like a small boy, "And I can't even find my chip bucket." That is probably the most irritating of all because it seems that every five minutes I get something in my hand and start to toss it in the chip bucket. And of course it's not there.

Back to today. After a late breakfast I spent about two hours on rather piddling chores, like moving all my pitch wood from under the eaves of the cabin, where it was catching water. This brought back my headache and a rather severe pain under my shoulder blades, so I took a hot-water bottle upstairs and lay down to do some reading—*National Wildlife, American Cinematographer, Natural History.* One article I particularly enjoyed, in *Natural History,* described a tavern excavated by archaeologists in New England. I guess I'm an incurable romantic. As the author discussed how people lived in the late 1600s and early 1700s, it reminded me of the way I daydream about the mining days at Brown's Cabin. As I walk along the paths that are still cut into the mountainside, I like to think about how the miners were dressed, how they would swing along to the blacksmith shop, the mine, the mill, and back to the cabin. In my mind's ear, I even hear the mule skinners shouting as they wheeled their six-mule teams down the mountain, bringing in supplies on high-wheeled wagons.

My wife says that I should have been born at least a hundred years ago, and my mother, before her, used to say the same thing. I always felt cheated in not having been born when everyone lived in log cabins, traveled on foot or horseback, and had no electricity. Perhaps that is why I'm completely content living at Brown's Cabin. I feel the lack of absolutely nothing. The only things I can think of to complain about have been the weather station, the radio communications, and the fact that I don't have all the right photo equipment for the job. In fact, I would say there is no better place to live if it weren't for the documentary. Of course, I don't mean that completely—some aspects of the filming have been downright enjoyable. But I could putter around up here happily without it.

Well, the day is about over. I'm going to get to bed because I still haven't recovered from tense nerves or too much socializing or whatever it is that ails me.

August 30

This has been a good day. I rested up last night and got a good early start this morning. Fall is really on the way; minimum temperature last night was 34 degrees and the maximum 53. The days continue to shorten. On June 22 the sun rose at seven-ten; this morning it rose at eight-thirty. A month ago it was perfectly light at nine in the evening; now it is dark at eight. I am very much aware of this from the standpoint of how much filming remains to be done. Also, I realize that any time now I'll be getting a snowstorm. The small wild creatures of the basin seem to work with more urgency. The pikas work hard on their hay piles; the pocket gopher pulls food down into its burrow; the marmots are fattening themselves in preparation for hibernation. Elk sign is more abundant in the basin as they break free of their summer herding patterns. For the first time I heard a bull elk bugling today, so courtship seems to have begun.

Tonight, I listened to an address on the radio by Stewart Udall, who used to be Secretary of the Interior. Udall is considered a Gloomy Gus by many of my university colleagues because he dwells on the shortcomings of our society at such length. However, I feel that he is essentially an optimist; in fact, he said in his speech that he is optimistic about eventually solving our environmental problems. This is in contrast to the fatalistic predictions of many of our environmental activists. For example, when Alfred Meyer was here, he mentioned several times David Brower, formerly executive director of the Sierra Club, now head of Friends of the Earth. I must say I don't share Alfred's enthusiasm for these organizations. In fact, I couldn't belong to either the Sierra Club or Friends of the Earth. This is not to say that the groups have not made substantial contributions to the welfare of our natural resources. Unquestionably, they have. But I feel that many of their efforts have been misguided, and sometimes based on false assumptions about the basics of land use and ecological balance.

I had an interesting insight into how this might have come about. About a year and a half ago David Brower was invited to Colorado State as the principal speaker for Forestry Day. His speech was good, though impassioned and, I felt, biased in several respects. The morning after the address I invited Brower to our house for breakfast. We had an enjoyable visit during the meal and sat around chatting for about two hours.

Several things surprised and disturbed me. One may seem picky, but David told me that only once in his life had he ever spent a night alone in the wilderness. This seemed incredible for a man who has been one of the nation's most prominent wilderness advocates for the last two decades. He went on to say that it had been the most miserable night he could recall. He was terrified by the night noises and simply felt out of his element.

Of course, Brower has been on many group trips into wilderness areas—more than I have. But these trips are made in the company of other people, frequently large groups on wilderness trail rides where everyone is well equipped with modern camping gear. Elegant foods are brought along, and cooks to prepare them. Packers care for the horses, even helping riders to mount, if necessary. It seems to me that this sort of trip merely transports urban social amenities to a wilderness backdrop, and I am cynical about the "wildness" involved.

Something that disturbed me more deeply about Mr. Brower grew out of our talk about ecological relationships. I came away with two impressions: One was that a deep bias characterized Dave's remarks; the other, that he was startlingly ignorant of ecological relationships. Perhaps this is an arrogant statement on my part, but I'm simply reporting my reaction at the time. I recall his description of an overgrazed range in Wyoming, and I asked him how he measured grazing use. He said, well, on that range there was so little vegetation you could look out a hundred yards and see a cow pie. Knowing the natural vegetation of the plains and desert areas of Wyoming, I'm not at all sure that the visibility of a cow pie at a hundred yards is unusual. I went so far as to chuckle at Dave's statement, but he seemed to be quite serious.

Following other statements which did not coincide with my knowledge of ecology, I finally asked him where the Sierra Club got its scientific information. He said it was easy to come by, that any number of engineers, biologists, ecologists, lawyers, and others were interested in the aims of the club and willing to contribute their knowledge. I asked him if he didn't feel that this information might be biased, and he said, why no, these people were specialists in their fields, why should they be biased? Well, it has always seemed obvious to me that there is no such thing as a truly unbiased scientist, any more than any other kind of human—and membership in a strong "advocate" group indicates a strong possibility of bias to me!

This leads me to a related topic. I once talked to an environmentalist who said he was upset about taking some courses at Cornell which, along with other activities of the New York State Department of Conservation, were largely supported by the sportsman's dollar. He seemed to feel that the money was somehow tainted because hunting is brutal and unnecessary. We should instead introduce predators, he said, and re-establish the original balance of nature.

Well, I won't go into great detail about this, but predator-prey relationships, like other ecological relationships, are not nearly as simple as this man apparently believed. I don't think he understood how drastic would be the effects of a ban on hunting today.

I no longer hunt myself, and I'm not an apologist for the sport hunter; but I think he has played an important role in the management of our wildlife. And in financial terms he has been the primary supporter of wildlife research in this country. I wonder if the new environmentalists understand this. The ranks of sportsmen have included, of course, the bloodthirsty and troublemaking. But they have also included those who hold the natural environment and its creatures in highest esteem. It is too simple to dismiss hunting as bloodlust.

The monies for wildlife research—life histories, population dynamics, plant-animal relationships, alterations of habitat—derive primarily from two federal programs. One is the Pittman-Robertson Act, which provides that an 11 percent excise tax on the sale of ammunition and guns go into the Treasury for wildlife research. The other is the Dingell-Johnson Act, which puts a similar tax on fishing tackle and gear for fisheries research and the maintenance of aquatic habitats. In addition, the money paid for hunting and fishing licenses and park permits helps support our state game and fish departments as well as some federal agencies. I shudder to think how ignorant we would be about wildlife without the research and management efforts supported almost entirely by the sportsman's dollar.

Well, this has been a windy approach to the subject of Stewart Udall's radio address, but I want to mention some of his comments, since they parallel some of my own thinking. He said, first of all, that it is essential to redefine "progress" and to redirect our technology. I agree with that. He also challenged the news stories we read about "natural" disasters. These are not natural disasters, he said, but environmental disasters. He talked about Pakistan, where half a million people recently drowned in floods. He said that because of the tremendous population pressure there, people were living in places they shouldn't live, places that are almost certain to flood periodically. They were, in a sense, violating nature.

At the same time, Udall used several times that important word "optimistic"; he is optimistic that we are beginning to recognize our problems, to see what we are doing wrong. He said that we are finally seeing that in our crusade for ever greater material well-being we are letting other, perhaps more important, values go down the drain. As I sit here in the primitive environment of Brown's Cabin, it is easy to agree that this is so.

August 31

This has been a different kind of morning. Never knowing what to expect is one of the reasons living here is exciting. My alarm went off a little before six-thirty, and minutes later I heard an ungodly racket beside the cabin, and then up on the roof. It sounded like a small-animal race, back and forth and around, paws beating at a furious pace. I ran to the west bedroom just as a marten spread-eagled itself across the window. It stared at me and then fled to the ground. I scrambled downstairs myself and watched as the marten crossed the rockslide near the spring and ran into the willows on the far side. The noise from the willows sounded like a herd of deer, but it was only two more martens, one of which was about half the size of the other. This verified my suspicion that I had become godfather to a litter of martens, and explained several auditory events of the past few weeks. During the last evening the Meyers were here, we heard a loud wailing under the cabin below my food cache beneath the stairway. The wailing and screaming came again several times during the night. Now I can assume I was listening to the birth of a marten family.

The other day I was treated to some really exuberant play behavior. I was taking movies of two martens in a tree. I had one camera mounted on the tripod and the other in my hand. While waiting for a better shot I lay down in a small spot of sunlight and apparently fell asleep for a few minutes. When I awakened there was only one marten in the tree and a loud thrashing noise in the willows. I went down to take a look, and while I was there the marten in the tree came scampering down the trunk, leaped out across the slope, and ran directly under the tripod. A minute later both martens were racing around the rock pile near me. Again I had the anthropocentric feeling that they were including me in their play. I even had the notion that the noise in the willows had been part of a ruse to decoy me away from the tree so the second animal could come down.

It was simply beautiful this morning. In the first light I could see fleecy white clouds down in Texas Creek; they soon began rising ghostlike up the valley, the sun flashing unusual lights off their tops. Wind currents shifted the clouds abruptly in almost any direction—up, sideways, then back down the canyon—and swirled them like cotton candy in the making.

I was watching the clouds from the weather station; then I looked at the thermometer: 31½ degrees. I also saw that the wind was blowing from 5 to 20 miles an hour. By coincidence or not, I realized how cold I was and trotted back down to the cabin, where I made a large breakfast— four slabs of bacon, eggs over easy, three pieces of toast, and three or four cups of coffee. By the time I had finished, the clouds had settled into the basin so densely that I could barely see the spring, fifty feet away.

· At ten-fifteen two young men showed up on saddle horses. They were working for a rancher from Gunnison who has the cattle allotment on Texas Creek. They were checking to see if there were any cattle up here; there weren't. They had been riding for two hours and apparently the brush was wet; their boots were soaking and they were pretty well chilled. I invited them in and made a pot of hot coffee, which they drank sitting by the fire. They didn't stay long because they had a lot of riding still to do.

Part V

IN SEARCH
OF BIG GAME

September 1

It is really September 2 and I am camped far from Brown's Cabin in elk country. The cold rain is pouring down and I am in the mountain tent, a day behind in my narration. It is such a cold rain that if it continues all night I predict there will be a good layer of snow in the morning. It was snowing at 12,000 feet today, where I was looking for elk.

Let me go back to September 1. That was the warmest day we've had in several weeks. I had arranged with Don Little, who brings the supplies, to help me get my gear out to the road, and he arrived at eleven-fifteen leading a pack animal. I needed a packhorse to carry all the equipment—approximately 125 pounds' worth—that I'd amassed for the week's stay I've planned here in the Mount Yale area to photograph elk and bighorn sheep.

When we got to Middle Cottonwood Road, Charlie was there to meet us. Charlie loaned me his pickup and I drove down to Salida to have some adjustments made on the three camera cases. While there I stopped by Ross Moser's office to talk, picked up some more maps, and bought supplies. Then I returned to Buena Vista, where I spent the night. John Burt, the owner of the motel (and also the mayor of Buena Vista), does a lot of packing and camping. He offered to lend me his tent, which is lightweight, with more space than my mountain tent. I really needed another tent because the equipment literally fills mine, leaving no room for me. As I lie here in the rain I'm thankful I accepted. I have most of the camera equipment, food, cooking gear, and a small stack of wood in his tent. I am here in my own tent with the radio, clothing, tape recorder, and sleeping bag. I brought the Forest Service radio because I'm not sure how long I will stay. But I've had a hell of a time getting through to Charlie. Last night I heard him plainly but he was not receiving me. He kept saying,

"Dwight, I can't hear you, I can't hear you," over and over. Now I wish I hadn't brought the radio at all; all I've done is to get Charlie excited and confused.

September 2

Last night after I had borrowed the tent from John Burt, I packed up, but I was too tired to tape since I had slept only two hours the night before. I turned in a little after midnight and had a fairly good sleep. After a huge breakfast this morning, I went up to Charlie's house and we drove to Rainbow Lake, where we were to meet the packer at seven-thirty. Billy Carpenter was late, but we finally got the horses packed and off at eight-fifteen. It was a nice ride, although the trail was so steep that we had to rest the horses frequently.

On the way I had an enlightening discussion with Billy. I was surprised to discover that someone who guides fishing guests in the summertime and hunting guests in the fall could be as poorly informed about natural history as Billy. Of course, he is a young fellow and has not had a great deal of packing experience, but he is a native here, of Hotchkiss, a small community of 600 in western Colorado. One would expect him to know more. For example, he didn't know the difference between the spruce, fir, limber pine, and lodgepole pine we were riding past. He didn't know the common shrub mountain mahogany. He didn't know that browsing deer often feed on young woody stems as well as on leaves. As we went along I pointed out various grasses and flowers, shrubs and trees, and he seemed interested. I can't imagine how he answers all the questions his guests must have.

We crossed Silver Creek Pass, which is at an elevation of 11,900 feet, then followed the trail down to Silver Creek. This area was not good for camping, so we took a game trail up the creek for twenty-five minutes until we reached an open, willow-covered meadow with a high rocky bench above it. It should be an excellent campsite, and if the elk visit the meadow a perfect place for filming.

Billy helped me with the mountain tent, and just as we got it up a storm hit. We dove into the tent and stayed there for about twenty minutes until it lessened. Since it kept on drizzling, I stored all the equipment, then rode back to the pass with Billy. He headed for home and I took off for an area that was reported to have bighorn.

I searched for sheep until four twenty-two, but found signs of only moderate sheep traffic. The reason I recall the exact time is that the next storm was so violent I actually looked at my watch as though to record the event. Lightning was crashing nearby, and I left the exposed rocky slopes in a hurry for the protection of some trees. In a severe electrical storm like that you have to use trees carefully. You should not stand under a single tree because it can function as a lightning attractor. Also, you should not choose the tallest trees in a stand, for the same reason. The best place is among trees of similar height. There, any one tree is no more likely to be hit than any other.

I did this, and stood there for a while, getting some protection from the beating rain. I'm usually uneasy during an electrical storm, but I convinced myself that I had chosen the best possible place in the circumstances. Then I looked over at the tree closest to me and saw a large gash down one side of it recently made by lightning. There went my confidence. I tried out the old saying that lightning doesn't strike twice in the same place, but that wasn't much consolation, so I finally decided to get the heck out of there.

Perhaps one of the reasons I have unpleasant feelings about these storms is that I have been caught in the high country before. When the lightning is hitting close in this rocky country you catch the unmistakable smell of ozone and you can feel the hair, particularly on your arms and the back of your neck, just lift away from your flesh. That's when I'd rather be somewhere else.

Despite the storm, the walk back to Silver Creek turned out to be a pleasant one, and I did a good deal of reflecting. It was raining and the wind was blowing hard. I had a feeling of well-being, of personal satisfaction. I was pleased, among other things, that I had let my hair and beard grow for the last three months—but not because of the way it looks; I don't even have a mirror with me. As I was walking in the tundra earlier, I was thinking that it gave me a really free feeling—the words "born free" went through my mind. I also thought of *On the Loose,* a Sierra Club book that I bought for my son Gary. It's about two boys from California who vagabond around the country, footloose.

I guess it was a ridiculous feeling for a fifty-year-old professor with family and responsibilities to have. I love my family and wouldn't have life any other way. Yet I feel that because of the wonderful wife I have, and the strong bond of love we share, I'm able to do something like this, enjoy it, and know that she wants me to enjoy it.

How do I go about describing why I felt so satisfied? I guess part of it was being able to follow game trails back through the timber in the storm. Many times in my role as college professor, and before that when I was a researcher, I felt doubt about my ability to handle certain situations. But here, now, I feel confident that I can live in the mountains alone as well as anyone I know. I guess I feel that I'm a mountain man. I feel that I'm at home in these mountains.

One way I feel at home is a matter of geography, of knowing where I am. I was able to walk back to Silver Creek Pass through a fairly dense stand of limber pine, where I could see only a few hundred feet ahead, at most. In the strict sense of the phrase, I didn't know where I was. But I knew how to get out. I remembered that I had to continue walking to the northwest, because I had looked at my map and saw how the range of mountains lay. I also knew my direction by the trees; the species change with elevation and respond to the prevailing wind. So even in dense timber during a hard storm, I felt no concern about getting back to the pass, although I had walked away from it for two hours and now was going back by a different route.

I felt at home, too, for other reasons related to my training as a biologist. I don't lay claim to being a great naturalist, but I believe that my knowledge of the geology, the plants, the tracks and signs of wild animals allow me to enjoy more fully than most people the experience of being alone in wild country. This is not to say that one must be a scientist to enjoy this situation. The aboriginal Indians knew these things better than I do, without benefit of college degrees. They're simple facts of nature, but satisfying to know. For example, I gained some clues to my whereabouts from the trees, by knowing that limber pine grows at very high elevations; I knew if I left them behind, I was losing altitude. And to tell the limber pine from the lodgepole pine, which they somewhat resemble in a stressed environment like this one, I had only to know that there are five needles per bundle and that the cones are quite large (four to ten inches long). The lodgepole has only two needles per fascicle and lopsided cones that lie tight against the stem. And of course both are easily separated from spruce and fir. Fir trees have whorled, horizontal branches, soft, flat needles, and cones that stand upright on the topmost branches. Spruce trees have four-angled, sharp-pointed needles and cones that hang down.

I saw many other plants—Kobresia, fescues, Indian rice grass, penstemons (the name means "five stamens"), gentians, the various Crucifera (mustards, larkspurs, daisies, fleabanes, reputed to drive away fleas)—that helped me find my way about, ecologically speaking. There are reasons why each occurs where it is; its presence indicates a certain condition of the environment. Certain plants are pioneers, arriving early in areas that have been cleared, bulldozed, eroded. Others are climax species, meaning that they are in a "mature," balanced state. Still others are fire succession plants, which indicate that a forest fire has passed over the area. These plants, the droppings of large animals, their tracks all greeted me like old friends. My knowing about them gave me a sense of belonging among them.

Well, it's five minutes after nine. It is still raining or whatever it's doing outside, hitting hard on the tent. The wind is blowing, and it's really nice to be in my sleeping bag, dry and protected. I'm sure not going to sleep much on a wild night like this, so I might as well go on talking.

This is certainly the heaviest windstorm that I've ever experienced from the inside of a tent. And I've spent a good deal of time in tents. My wife, two children (at that time), and I lived in a tent for six months in Idaho once. Another year I spent a summer in a tent next to a lake, and on still another summer I lived in one for over two months in subalpine country in Idaho. But I've never been in anything like this storm tonight. The wind seems to be gusting over 60 miles an hour, and this little tent shakes violently every time one of those blasts hits it. I'm expecting every moment to hear the fly come ripping off the top and feel the rest of the tent either fly after it or wrap suddenly around my ears. The tent is nylon, with a total weight of five and a half pounds, including the stakes and poles. And the ground here is so soft I was able to push the wire stakes into the ground by hand. I'm amazed that it hasn't been torn away yet. It shakes so hard it rolls me in the sleeping bag; the wind is really screaming through the trees.

Another thing I try unsuccessfully to keep my mind off is the tall dead trees around me. Windstorms in the high country are notorious for upending big, dead trees, and one of them could come crashing down across the tent at any moment. But I just have faith that this won't happen.

The wind seems to be easing somewhat, so I'm going to try for some shut-eye now.

September 3

Good morning, good morning! I'm just faking it to build my spirits up. At five after three this morning I had to get up to pee and my worst fears were realized. As I tried to open the zipper on my tent I found it coated with ice. When I finally got it open I saw that the outside world was com-

pletely white. Three or four inches of snow had fallen and the wind was
still blowing, so by the time I made it back to my sleeping bag I felt nearly
frozen.

Now it's seven o'clock and I'm still in the bag debating, as I have
been for the last twenty minutes, how I am going to get up, what I am
going to eat, what I am going to wear—all those mental exercises to put
off unpleasant reality. I thought I came well prepared, but I didn't think
of this. The wind is again gusting to nearly 60 miles an hour, I would
guess, with a base velocity of 20 to 30. I suspect the actual temperature is
25 to 30 degrees, so the wind-chill factor must be below zero.

I've moved all my clothing for today inside the sleeping bag to begin
the slow process of warming it up. One uncertainty is whether the sky is
clear or not. That seems like it should be easy to solve, but the way these
mountain tents are built makes it a job. The zipper extends so far out
front that I have to climb almost completely out of the sleeping bag to
unzip, and I haven't built up the courage to do that yet.

I *can* tell what awaits me on the ground, just by looking at the sides
of the tent. I can see daylight through it clearly—except on the top and
sides where snow is piled. A little while ago I thumped against the top to
dislodge the snow; instead of being soft, it came off in hard chunks, so I
know it's mean out there.

Last night I recall talking about walking through the country, how I
have grown accustomed to feeling at ease in the mountains. It's a good
thing I got that wind out of my chest last night, because this morning I
feel a little different. I think this weather is really revolting. In fact, I could
best express the way I feel by saying, "I want my mama"—and my cen-
trally heated house in Fort Collins. I did put a small supply of firewood in
the other tent, which I last saw about fifty feet up the slope. But I doubt
whether I could get a fire started in this wind, and if I did, whether I
would feel much heat. My main source of heat this morning is going to be
my own body warmth. And right now I'm going to maintain that by staying inside this down sleeping bag.

As long as I'm lying here, I'll go back to some of my thoughts yesterday about a person's enjoyment of the countryside. I have decided that it
does not depend on being able to identify every organism by name. An
addiction to scientific nomenclature may even be destructive to enjoyment. I know a very fine man in the Forest Service who is admired for
being one of the best plant taxonomists in the country. He knows almost
every plant you can find in the wild down to species, subspecies, and even

variety. But as I've observed him and his exacting nature, I've often had the feeling he wasn't enjoying the plants or seeing their beauty. He might know how many stamens a plant had, or if it had a funnel-form corolla, or if the pistil was extruded—all its mechanistic features rather than its grace or form or how it blends with the greater beauty of the environment.

Still there is a feeling of satisfaction in knowing what family a plant is in, as long as you don't get too obsessed by it, and I was pleased yesterday to use my knowledge of plants to get myself out of the woods and back to the trail. I reached the path less than 150 feet from the pass, so I underwent a short period of self-congratulation and said, well, you old dog, you really knew where you were all the time and you sure do know your mountains. If I'd missed the pass by half a mile, of course, I would have had a different story to tell.

Knowledge of animal signs also helps you keep track of where you are and, perhaps more important, makes you feel that you have company even without seeing the animals. Yesterday, aside from elk and bighorn sign, I noticed some places where a porcupine had been stripping the bark from the upper branches of limber pine. I was surprised because I didn't realize that porcupines worked on trees this high. Over at the border of the timber and the tundra I saw several piles of grouse droppings, which indicated the place where the birds roosted beneath the snow last winter. I also saw a sign of red squirrel activity: pine cone scales they had dropped while feeding and assembling their supplies for winter. These supplies are called middens. They may be a foot deep and twenty to thirty feet across. The largest of them represent the work of successive generations of squirrels working over a score or more years. I have heard that local people raid these middens for the seeds of Douglas fir or Engelmann spruce, which they sell to nurseries. This seems to be a dirty trick on the squirrels, which have labored for months in anticipation of cold weather.

I haven't gotten up yet. I must admit I still feel quite tired. I didn't sleep very well. It may be that my age is catching up with me. This small foam-rubber pad just doesn't seem thick enough to keep my bones off the ground. From three o'clock until seven I was awake more than asleep. Yesterday . . . I guess I'd better identify yesterday. When I first started narrating, yesterday was September 1, but here it is . . . what is today? Saturday, I guess. That's September 3, so now when I say yesterday I mean September 2. I'd better get this straightened out. I'm keeping track of the days of the month by the dates I'm putting on film, but I'm fairly fouled up on days of the week. I told the packer to come in on a Thursday. I'd better figure this out or I'm not going to be ready. Let's see, he came to the cabin on his usual day, which is Wednesday . . .

September 4

It is now the evening of September 4. At least that's what I have decided. Yesterday morning it was rough getting out of bed. But after I had gotten my circulation going, gotten dressed inside this small tent, and stepped out into the snow, it wasn't all that bad. I did have to walk around every once in a while to keep my feet warm, and the wind was blowing so hard I never tried to start a fire. I lit my mini stove in the other tent and cooked a breakfast of freeze-dried hash. I think my taste buds are finally getting jaded by these freeze-dried foods. The hash was most uninspiring. The two cups of hot coffee were very good, however.

Today I have been out all day and am very disappointed that I did not see any sign of bighorn sheep or elk. It has been bitterly cold, not thawing at all in the shade. But I am happy to report that the tent has held perfectly and none of the stakes pulled out.

Well, it's 7:30 a.m., and the darn wind has come up again. Today I was wearing my summer underwear, fishnet underwear, an all-wool shirt, a suede shirt, a blanket-lined Levi's jacket, and finally an all-weather parka, and even so, any time I stopped for five minutes I began to chill. Yet one thing that impresses me about this summer is that although I seem to have been cold more than half the time, I have not had a single sniffle or head cold.

Excuse me, I'm yawning again. I have been thinking back to September 2, when I had a tenuous contact with other humans. About half a mile above my tent camp I saw the imprint of a fairly large log. My first thought was that a bear had moved it, but I couldn't see the log anyplace nearby. Finally I started up into the basin and after about a hundred feet there was the log, set beside a campsite. I was pleased to note that the people involved were high-quality campers. It gave me a warm feeling to think I had shared the basin with good woodsmen. I drifted into fantasy, imagining myself an Indian scout, re-creating the details of the camping scene from clues around the campsite. I decided there were two campers. The log was too big for one man to have moved without dragging it, and there was no sign of dragging. Also the grass and vegetation had been matted down over an area the size of my two-man mountain tent. One sign that they were good campers was that they had brought in a larger supply of wood than they had used, and the remainder was neatly stacked in a dry place under some trees.

The fire site had been prepared with special care. The top layer of soil had been removed with a shovel before the fire was lit. And I could tell that when they left they doused the coals with water. When a fire has been put out this way there are large particles of wood left unburned; when it is allowed to burn itself out, only fine ash remains. Nor were any large chunks of wood left lying together; again they had done the proper thing by stirring them about. When they left, they had carefully replaced the original sod over the ashes. Needless to say, they left no garbage.

Whew, just as I was finishing that tale the wind nearly took my tent away. Tonight I must admit I am really bushed. I'll discuss just one more thing and then try for a good night's sleep. This is something I don't know how to say very well. I guess the first statement would be that, even though it took twenty-five years after marrying a Catholic girl to decide to be baptized a Catholic myself, I'm glad I did. It has given me a great deal of satisfaction and peace of mind. It sounds corny to say that accepting Catholicism has given me an inner source of strength that I never had before, but it has. It certainly has been an important source during my time up here. Perhaps this is illustrated by a recent letter from my wife, in which she quoted Father Urban. He said that I spoke in such a gentle manner when he was up here; that I seemed to be at peace with the world.

I doubt that this is always the case. I don't always speak in a gentle manner and have not been at peace with the world during all of my time here. But perhaps this is essentially true most of the time.

Although my relationship with God has been rather casual, in many ways it is very satisfying, and it has now strengthened a good deal. For many years I have felt the need for prayer, for a relationship with a Supreme Being I always believed exists. But I have been awkward in prayer, never feeling sure I was communicating, not knowing what to say or how to say it. This has changed since I have been at Brown's Cabin. This may be because I live here among the creations of nature. I feel that these creations are close to the Creator, and that in this way I am close to Him as well.

September 5

It's now three-thirty in the morning on September 6 and I haven't slept at all, so I might as well talk some more about yesterday.

I left camp at nine-fifteen, headed down Silver Creek and over the Divide and back, through an area where I have been told I might find elk. I wanted to make an all-out effort. By the map I went about nine or ten miles, and at this elevation—I dropped to about 9,200 feet, and the Divide is over 12,000—I really wore myself out. I did locate the most heavily used game trail, primarily elk, that I've seen this summer, but too late in the day to follow it far. Climbing the last three hundred feet back to camp, I found myself more exhausted than at any time all summer. I literally had to talk myself into taking each step, then the next, to keep from just sitting down.

I tottered back at seven, then washed my hands, face, and feet in the icy stream near camp. I was revived enough by this to get a hot supper, which made me feel somewhat better. I made an unsuccessful attempt to contact Charlie by radio and was in bed by twenty minutes to nine. By nine-thirty I had not fallen asleep and my legs were aching so severely that I went to the other tent and got three aspirins. Once back in the warmth of my sleeping bag I thought it would just be a matter of minutes until I was asleep, but I've been tossing and turning ever since. It seems such a shame because I have now spent nearly half a dozen nights with a maximum of three or four hours' sleep. I guess I'm anxious about not getting footage of the big game I want—nothing of bighorn or elk or goats—no matter what I try.

I suppose, too, I have been examining my conscience a bit about the times I have left my family for extended periods to do things personally satisfying to me, yet not in the best interest of the family as a unit. No serious problems involved, but I've been reflecting on some of my limitations as a father and husband.

September 6

The sun is up now, so I'll change the date. About four-thirty I began to catnap, sleeping about ten minutes, then waking up for about ten minutes, and so on until I finally slept from six to eight forty-five. That's as much sleep as I've had for a good many nights.

I forgot to mention that when I was returning to Silver Creek saddle yesterday, I noticed a coyote had been walking in the snow. The coyote track is similar to that of a bobcat, except that any member of the dog family walks with the toenails extended; tracks of the front two toenails especially can be seen clearly in the snow. Two other members of the dog family also live this high in the Rockies—the red fox and occasionally the gray fox—but they are seldom seen or heard. The coyote (*Canis latrans*) is one of the few large predators to have expanded its range since the advent of civilization, now ranging from the North Slope of Alaska to Costa Rica. Up here they prefer open, parklike situations, woodlands, and rough, brush-covered country.

Part of the coyote's success derives from its broad taste in prey. It finds pleasing things to eat almost anywhere. In the mountains, the coyote's first choice is a rodent, any rodent—voles, mice, wood rats, ground squirrels, marmots, pocket gophers, sometimes beavers. It will also eat less tasty game, including birds, weasels, shrews, snakes, skunks, and, especially in winter, carrion.

This unrestrained diet sometimes spills over to include domestic animals, and many stockmen blame coyotes for heavy losses of young sheep. Coyotes frequently hunt in pairs, and the effectiveness of their teamwork is legendary. Even their most bitter enemies concede a grudging admiration for the cleverness, hardiness, and adaptability of this predator.

The new snow also revealed the activities of other animals I had been unaware of, including chipmunks, mice, snowshoe hares, and red squirrels.

The red squirrel (*Tamiasciurus hudsonicus*), sometimes called the chickaree, is not as red here as elsewhere over its broad range. It is dark grayish brown in winter, becoming somewhat reddish only in summer. Nonetheless, it is familiar to anyone who wanders through the denser forests of the Rockies, scolding any intruder and fiercely defending its one- to three-acre territory. It prefers stands of spruce-fir, Douglas fir, and lodgepole pine at middle elevations.

It prefers these trees not only for their cones, which are the staple of its diet, but also because the thick stands keep the ground below damp and cool. It is here, in deep shade, that the red squirrel assembles its middens, where the high humidity or even standing water suppresses germination of the seeds. The cones are stashed in pits up to a foot deep in the midden and dug up for eating during the winter and spring.

The red squirrel must be alert both when digging in the midden and when working aloft; coyotes, weasels, and foxes stalk along the ground, and the pine marten specializes in catching squirrels among the branches. Squirrels have been known to jump more than twenty feet to the ground to escape a marten.

The only other squirrel hereabouts is Abert's squirrel (*Sciurus aberti*), which cannot be confused with the red squirrel. It weighs three to four times as much, rarely announces its presence, and generally lives in the ponderosa pine woodlands below 8,500 feet. Its distribution is uneven and populations fluctuate, so that a mountain visitor is fortunate to see even one.

Now I'm going back to my discussion about a relationship with God. I must say that discussing this on tape is difficult for me. For this reason I've delayed expressing many deep feelings I have had on this subject. But I have decided that perhaps this is an important part of this experience and should be included in what I narrate.

Well, I'm just stalling, so let me get on with it. I was baptized into the Catholic Church a little over two years ago. Until that time I had simply viewed myself as a Christian. How others, and particularly the One on High, viewed the situation might be different. But I found that with baptism came positive changes. For a long time I had felt sad when my family was able to take communion and I could not. This was something I could now partake in, and it has become very meaningful to me. It opened a more direct avenue for prayer. And at mass I found that I could pray comfortably in association with others.

When I'm alone, as I have been for the past five days, the relationship seems to be informal and easy and natural. I do not hold an anthropocentric view of God; I feel that the world has been created, that it has a wonderful design to it, and that somehow we all fit into this design. I also believe that God exists not as a discrete being but through all of us and all of His works. I think that if I do not see God in my wife, in my children, in my associates, then I won't see Him anywhere.

I believe that the admonition to love thy neighbor as thyself is perhaps the most important and overlooked message in the Bible. When I speak of praying to God, I don't mean that there is someone someplace listening to me. Yet I do feel that somehow we are each of us being considered in some way. I frequently do talk with God in a way that would indicate I think someone is listening. And perhaps I do feel that there is a bond of universal listening and understanding; that it is at least therapeutic to feel that I am sharing this experience with a someone or with others. I don't believe my fate is being guided by God but I do feel that my fate is in His hands, so to speak. I feel that my actions and thoughts and being fit into a universal plan He has for all of us, but that my success in each endeavor is my responsibility. It's up to me to use all my knowledge of the mountains and of ecology, for example, to get safely back to camp. But it is through God's grace that I am allowed to do this.

The other day, during the electrical storm, my feelings were much different than they would have been twenty years before, in Idaho. Then I would have reacted largely with profanity. Profanity seems to be something I still revert to, and I regret this. My wife has often chided me for swearing at inanimate objects; I'm afraid I picked up some rough language in many years of nonacademic life—working as a lumberjack in the Northwest, driving trucks, working in heavy construction, being a mule skinner, spending four years in the infantry.

But during the storm a few days ago I did not swear at God, or even at the lightning. Instead I just sort of talked aloud to Him. The casual comment I actually made was: "God, let's get our ass off of this mountain." This was hardly a profound prayer, but it seemed the natural thing to say, and it seemed to do some "good" for me. I guess I felt I was at the same time on my own and in God's hands.

There have been times in the past when, if lightning struck close or disaster seemed imminent, a real, stark fear would strike my heart—if not for minutes, at least for a few fleeting seconds. But the other day, even though it had started to rain and sleet, and I was in rocky, slippery terrain, and my boots were not gripping well on the wet rocks, I felt absolutely calm. By addressing God, my whole mind and being were released from worry about the storm and I found myself feeling exhilarated about what a good mountain man I was. I watched myself moving through the treacherous hillside, sizing up each rock before trusting its foothold, and I remember thinking: Smith, wipe that damn silly grin off your face. If anyone sees you they'll think you're nuts. I was even enjoying the wind blowing through my hair and the rain and sleet striking my face; I felt attuned to the entire situation.

And I feel this way in general. It is as though my thoughts and energy have been released from worry to more useful areas. I can leave my family, in the confidence that things are going to work out as they should without my constant supervision. I could not always say this—especially in the years after the death of our eldest son, Alan. But now I can.

I forgot to mention that I invented a new technique for starting the campfire. It was born out of desperation. I had been unable to start the fire in the driving rain and snow. This limber pine wood doesn't burn well, even when it's dry. The wind was so strong that every attempt I made was snuffed out. Finally I started the fire inside the tent on the shovel and carried it out, burning. It was really touch and go, because I was trying to film the operation at the same time. But I finally got the fire started on the shovel, set the camera, ran inside the tent, picked the shovel up, set it down in the campfire ring, ran back to shut off the camera, and so on. The final scene shows me eating dinner by the fire. There is a lot of realism in this sequence; misery, frustration, etc.

Some bizarre activity: yesterday when I reached the mouth of Silver Creek on the long hike from my remote camp, the first thing I saw was four young men roaring by on, I believe, 360-cc. Honda motorcycles. They scarcely looked at me as they passed, leaving only a strong odor of gasoline fumes and some dust. Later, as I walked up the Cottonwood Road, I passed several other people camped at roadside. All were aware of my presence and glanced at me, but each turned away just as quickly, saying nothing. Could this be big-city reserve so high in the mountains, where people are usually open and friendly?

And again: A young man camped nearby came down to North Cottonwood Creek where I was eating lunch. He squatted to wash his hands and face in the stream not twenty feet away. All the time he studiously avoided looking at me even though I was looking at him, wondering if this would encourage him to speak. He avoided any eye contact and eventually shook the water off his hands and walked back up the bank without saying a word.

Finally, yesterday, as I was struggling and sweating up to the 12,300-foot saddle on the Divide, I heard motorcycles over in Horn Fork Gulch, where there is said to be a Forest Service trail in fair condition. These big cycles gunning up the mountainside destroyed my inner tranquillity and convinced me even more that vehicular use of these backcountry trails should be minimized, if not eliminated. I simply can't believe this is a meaningful experience for motorcycle drivers. They could just as well be charging over any kind of man-made structures near population centers, where their noises and fumes are already part of the local scene. I certainly can't buy the Forest Service line, which seems to put backpackers in the minority. Certainly when you consider that by August 8 over four hundred people had climbed Mount Yale, which is only one of fifty-three peaks higher than 14,000 feet in the state, you can see how many people come out to the mountains for peace and solitude.

This tirade brings to mind again a thought I had the day of the electrical storm. I wondered if there might not be a use for this documentary that I am only beginning to realize. It is clear that if I, a generally ordinary and average fifty-year-old man, am able to come out to a primitive area, enjoy living alone, setting up a camp, and finding my way about, so would many other people. I think there's a moral and spiritual and physical awakening involved here, a re-creation, if you will. I think the wilderness experience should be available to all those who care to seek it out, and I hope this project suggests to people the benefits such an experience can bring.

Of course, I was not so sanguine about all this last night at three-thirty, when I was trying to narrate myself to sleep. But this morning I am reclining against a warm log, with the warm sun shining on my delightfully pain-free back. My legs have ceased to ache and I can hear the rushing of Silver Creek below me. Above I can look through the trees and see, framed against a perfectly blue sky, Mount Yale and its streamers of white snow down the small ravines. Although there persist the concerns that I expressed in the wee hours, and all the jobs undone, I feel perfectly at peace.

September 7

Today was beautiful. The weather changed suddenly and the temperature soared to about 55, so I traveled in my shirt sleeves most of the day.

I went to sleep at nine last night and woke at one. It was a beautiful moonlit night, and the elk were bugling, so I couldn't get back to sleep again. It was amusing to listen to these early-season buglers—they are mostly young bulls, and like boys with immature voices that crack and break unexpectedly, the bulls came out with some hilarious squawks. But I was concerned as well as amused. On moonlit nights elk tend to stay up and feed and move. I was afraid they would be so active they would move right out of the area. The last bugle I heard was at five-thirty. Immediately I got up, had a cup of coffee, and took off for the place I had seen them the night before. I reached it by daylight, and sure enough, the elk were gone. I hiked down into the meadow and saw abundant signs, but as far as I could tell from their tracks, they had moved up through the saddle and down into an area called Avalanche Gulch. The place was too rough and too far for me to follow with the cameras.

There was one small compensation. During my walk I stumbled across an ideal spot to photograph the tent-pitching sequence Larry wants—a rocky pocket in an isolated area. So I returned to camp and packed up the mountain tent and all the food and equipment necessary to spend the night there. It was sort of heartbreaking to take my tent from its original site. It had been an ideal camp. But I did it, and when I got to Rocky Pocket—that's what I decided to christen my new site—the sun was out and I started filming. It went well until it began to cloud up and the winds came sweeping down over Mount Yale with some force. I decided I'd better abandon photography and get the tent up as quickly as possible, but I was a little late. I had only the inner part of the tent set when the hailstorm hit. All I had time to do was grab pack, camera, tripod, and other scattered equipment, throw them inside, and dive in with them. After fifteen or twenty minutes the storm died down, but it continued to hail every few minutes. It seems that the weather in this country changes so rapidly that I can never complete a photographic project. Just before dark it stormed again in earnest, blotting out my campfire for good. So it was one wet, disgruntled, miserable person who finally crawled into the tent and cooked supper over the mini stove while rain alternated with hail pounding the tent.

A dominant characteristic of my week away from the cabin has been meals of freeze-dried food. This may seem trivial in the light of my heavy thinking of recent days, but let me assure you that on a stormy evening in the wild, mealtime is at least as important as biology or philosophy. Although I accept the idea of using these foods for the sake of convenience and light weight, the taste gets old rather quickly. I've been ordering them from Gibson Discount Store in Salida, which carries two brands—Teakettle and Mountain House. Mountain House offers greater variety, but Teakettle is easier to prepare. I've only found four menus under the Teakettle label: beef almondine with vegetables and macaroni, turkey Tetrazzini with asparagus, chunk chicken with rice and carrots, and tuna à la Neptune. I have four boxes of that tuna. I don't know why I bought so much tuna, because it's not one of my favorite foods.

Now, on the Mountain House side here are the delights I have on hand: chicken stew, chicken chop suey, chili with beans, beef hash, and beef patties, which are like hamburgers and are excellent. The patties present a financial problem—it costs $3.52 for four hamburgers. But they are delicious; I eat them for breakfast and carry them as lunch. There is also, from Mountain House, cheese omelette, eggs with butter, a Mexican omelette, which is tasty, some vegetables, and freeze-dried ice cream—strawberry and vanilla. The vanilla comes in chunks and you just chew it dry. That's one of my favorites.

With the main dishes, you can't beat the light weight and ease of preparation. For example, the Teakettle turkey Tetrazzini has a net weight of one ounce, plus the little aluminum tray. The serving instructions are simple. First you add four ounces of boiling water to the serving tray and stir to wet all ingredients. Then you wait five minutes and eat. I found a good trick was to put in a little less than the four ounces of water to stir and add the rest just before eating it. That makes for a hotter meal.

The Mountain House stuff does not come in one-person servings. The chili with beans has a net weight of 5½ ounces, but with the 12 ounces of boiling water, the serving weight is 17½ ounces. I don't know about you, but 17½ ounces of chili with beans is way too much for this one person. It doesn't come in a box but in sort of a foil wrapper not too convenient for carrying. This time you add boiling water to the *inner* package, which is a kind of heavy plastic, and wait *five to ten* minutes before eating. I haven't found the bag too convenient, so I usually put it into a regular pan.

What else did I eat? I brought a mixture of dried milk, Pream, and chocolate in a plastic bag so I could have a cup of hot chocolate each evening. And I have candy bars, a small supply of beef jerky, and some snack packs of puddings. These last are lightweight, nutritious, and delicious. That's about it for my menu—except that I did bring one small can of stew to break the monotony of freeze-dried food.

At about nine-thirty I was still awake, though my eyes were closed, and I noticed an extremely bright light—bright enough to shine through my closed eyelids. My first thought was that someone was beaming a powerful searchlight on the tent. Of course, this was impossible, so I lay there and thought about it as the lights kept flashing around. Lightning was striking and the wind gusting at 50 to 60 miles an hour. The tent would alternately suck in tightly and then boom outward with a thumping sound as I wondered whether it would stay or go. The tent is made of blue nylon and the lights made the inside look like a miniature discotheque.

Finally I noticed that the brightest lights were flashing across the zipper in front of the tent and along the two metal poles that support the front. I ruled out direct lightning; none was hitting close to me. I decided that it was static electricity; I could actually feel a prickling sensation and see the hair on my arms stand out. Later, the operator of the motel in Salida, John Burt, told me that he has had this same experience during an electrical storm, and it is known as St. Elmo's fire. Apparently the metal of my tent was attracting enough electricity to make it appear that a small ball of fire was running across the poles and down the zipper. I had heard people talk about this but it is my only firsthand experience. It was spine-tingling to have this little mountain tent so full of light flashing from one end to the other. The storm lasted until after midnight and I didn't get more than an hour or two of sleep.

September 8

I must say that with all my trouble sleeping and the resulting fatigue, each time I am greeted by one of the amazing sunrises and calm mornings here I forget all about the miserable night that went before. By ten o'clock I had packed all the cameras and left camp to look for bighorn. I had seen some sign east of Silver Creek saddle; I picked them up again and followed them southeastward toward Middle Cottonwood Creek. I got so low in elevation, about 2,500 feet below the saddle, that I decided it was too far and too late to return to camp, so I kept on going down. I came out at a log cottage where an elderly lady was strolling about. She saw me come off the mountain, greeted me in a very friendly manner, and invited me into the house. I was reluctant to do this because seven days' accumulation of sweat and campfire odors had made me a dirty, disreputable-looking character. But she was persistent. Once inside I met her husband, who was just as hospitable, and who diplomatically handed me a fresh towel and washcloth. They invited me for dinner and afterward drove me into Buena Vista to Charlie Combs's trailer. Their names were Al and Esther Eden, a perfectly delightful couple in their early sixties. Al works for an oil distributor in Colorado Springs.

After dinner I went to a motel in Buena Vista, where I got film and correspondence together and, finally, got my first sound sleep in a week. There are advantages to civilization.

September 9

At 8 a.m., just above Rainbow Lake, I joined Billy Carpenter and Scott, the other wrangler, to go in and pick up my tent camp. We first picked up the borrowed tent and the gear at my original campsite, then worked our way through the timber and along the edge of the cliffs to Rocky Pocket. Because of the horses, this turned out to be a challenge. We got tangled in some rockslides and downed timber and finally had to go down a slope so steep that Billy's horse almost fell on him. To avoid the fall he jumped out of his saddle, and for a while I thought he had broken his foot. It turned out to be just a bruise, so he made it all right through the rest of the day.

We got back to the truck on Middle Cottonwood Road at about two-thirty, which was pretty good time. Charlie Combs, who was going to meet me there, had taken his wife to the doctor, so we tied the horses and drove ourselves to Buena Vista. I bought lunch for the two boys and then returned to the motel. I was about to leave when Bill and Scott roared into the parking area shouting that they had just seen some bighorn sheep, so I grabbed my camera and we went up to a place called Jump Steady. There were indeed a number of ewes and lambs moving up into the cliffs, and I managed to take forty or fifty feet of film.

I stayed overnight at the motel. It was nice to eat a meal cooked by someone else and to sleep in a comfortable bed. At the same time, staying at a motel for two nights did not seem right. I ended up wasting a good part of my chance to live in luxury by lying awake, wondering about the filming that still must be done and wishing I were back at Brown's Cabin.

September 10

In the morning I went to Salida, where I talked about getting a helicopter in to Brown's Cabin around October 1. I'm coming to the conclusion that this may be the only way to get good footage of big game. Also I decided to go into Mineral Basin tomorrow, a place said to be promising for elk and mountain goats.

I was interested to find that the editor of the local weekly newspaper in Buena Vista had written an editorial titled "Discrimination," about the restriction of motorcycles from the Brown's Cabin area. His point was that motorcyclists should be permitted to use trails and roads anyplace in the national forest system, and that it is discriminatory for the Forest Service to close a trail to this one use. I disagree with that point of view, but at least the editor is aware that the Brown's Cabin area is off limits.

September 11

A beautiful warm, clear, windless fall day. Charlie Combs picked me up this morning and we drove up Middle Cottonwood Canyon. As we got to Jump Steady we saw several bighorn ewes and lambs and one young ram. They were just off the road, working their way up an embankment. We stopped and I took most of a hundred-foot roll, even though it was not alpine habitat; the vegetation here is mostly mountain shrubs among some ponderosa pine and junipers at an elevation of only 8,500 feet.

A few sheep were nibbling plants; but most of them were eating soil where the bank had been cut by the road. This is not an unusual phenomenon among bighorn or other large ungulates. In Idaho, in 1949, I found bighorn at four "natural licks," chewing soil in which laboratory analysis showed high concentrates of soluble salts. Later, in 1952, in an effort to find out exactly what the bighorn were after in the soil, I established two "mineral cafeterias" and offered the sheep ten different minerals mixed with soil at each one. The sheep consistently consumed only the three samples that contained sodium in some form and one with cobalt. Of the sodium samples the sheep preferred sodium iodide; the second choice was sodium chloride (common table salt). The mechanisms behind this discrimination are not well understood, but we do know that wild animals have the ability, by selective feeding, to meet their physiological needs.

We went on up toward Mineral Basin, but did not get all the way because of the rough roads. We got out and walked but saw only a few elk tracks. On the way back we met John Howlett, the wildlife conservation officer, who had been looking for elk and mountain goats for us. He hadn't seen anything either.

We drove down to Rainbow Lake, stopped at the small store there for a few things to eat; then Charlie left me at the mouth of Denny Creek, where I set out on foot. It was good to be headed back home again. The willows and bog birch were now a golden yellow, as were a number of other plants. The alpine avens and dwarf huckleberry were turning a deep red. The air seemed clearer than it has been since I arrived. The distant mountains stood out so sharply that I felt as if I had never seen them before.

My joy at being back home was rather short-lived, however. I had asked Charlie to have someone cut a supply of wood for me while I was gone, but he hadn't been able to get anyone. So he had come in himself and managed to get only three or four days' worth of wood.

Then there was the generator. Before I even threw the switch I knew there was trouble, because the switch was in the manual start position. I always leave it in the *electric* start position. I don't know who had tinkered with it—the shed is unlocked—but someone had. In any event, the battery is drained, completely dead. I couldn't get it to turn the motor even once. I have some spare batteries, but they have never been used and are too weak to start the motor. That means I'll have to get new ones before I get electricity.

Another change that has taken place while I've been gone is natural, but saddens me. It is now getting dark by seven-thirty at night. This makes me realize how long I've been here, and how little time I have left. It means I have only a limited period to get the footage I still want, and if I think about it for a few minutes, I get quite upset about the whole thing.

September 12

I worked some more on the generator today. I got the manual out, went through all the procedures, took the spark plug out, cleaned it, checked the gap, checked everything else I could think of, and still it didn't operate. This is doubly frustrating now that time is growing short, because I need the generator to charge the camera batteries as well as to light the cabin after early nightfall.

I noticed in the morning that the pocket gophers have increased their activity. This would seem to indicate that winter is not far away. Also the pikas are still busy working on their hay piles. I haven't seen any piles near completion, so I'm hoping, along with the pikas, that bad weather is still several weeks off. They surely need that much time to store their winter's food supply.

Otherwise the animals have been strangely inconspicuous since my return to the cabin. Though they were all active ten days ago, I have seen few marmots, no porcupines, no deer, no marten, heard no elk bugling. This rapid change in animal behavior is an example of the diversity that I see as a focal point for this study. The seasons change rapidly, forcing animals to compress various phases of their life cycle: for a few days there is frenzied activity of one sort, which is then abruptly transformed to another kind of behavior altogether. Another obvious diversity in the alpine takes place in the vegetation. Because of the complexity of soils, topography, and weather conditions, even a small area may contain several different micro-environments supporting several different plant communities.

September 13

This has been a truly beautiful day, one of those days when you'd like to live forever. I spent the entire time in shirt sleeves.

On the way back to the cabin after a morning of filming, I met Don Little, who had come in with a packhorse, bringing fresh batteries. Don has had some experience with generators, so we put in the new batteries and tried to start it. It did start, although not as rapidly as I thought it should. Don went over it quickly and felt it was okay, but I have some misgivings. If it takes this long to start now, I wonder if it will start at all when the cold weather comes.

Don said that on the way up Denny Creek he had overtaken Charlie

Combs and his sister Pearl. Shortly after we got the generator started they arrived. It was quite a thrilling homecoming for Pearl. She is now sixty-three years old and has lived in Denver for the past thirty-five years. During the winter of 1934 she and her husband spent the entire winter here in the cabin with Homer Brown, and this was the first time she has been back since. With Charlie living in Buena Vista and making frequent trips up here, it seemed an ideal time to come. She was totally delighted with her two or three hours here. She remembered the cabin very well, as well as the details of her winter here thirty-seven years ago. Apparently she had been raised in the city with electricity and running water; she said the most difficult aspect of the winter was trying to keep clean. I guess not much has changed at Brown's Cabin in all those years.

I have said how impressed I am with Charlie Combs's physical condition, but I was even more impressed with that of his sister. Here is a sixty-three-year-old woman who lives in the city but who is still able to walk into Brown's Cabin without seeming particularly tired. She even went down to visit the mill, and the last I saw of her she was enthusiastically striding up toward Brown's Pass. During this one day she will walk more than nine miles at high elevations and it doesn't seem to bother her in the least.

This evening I noticed there were no longer any robins around the cabin. I remember that they were still here when I left on September 1. I suspect they have left for the South.

September 14

Today was possibly more beautiful than yesterday. It reached 60 degrees, after an overnight low of 36½, which is the warmest it's been for several weeks. However, the weather report this morning made me uneasy. Cold air is moving in from the northwest and a storm is forecast in a couple of days. I hope this prediction is inaccurate; there are so many things I still want to film.

One of my chores today was to photograph the heterodyne vegetation meter, which is used to estimate the amount of vegetation covering the ground. Measuring vegetation is an important task for ecologists, who often want to quantify the growth rate or the total production of plants. They might want to measure, for example, how plant production is affected by changes in climate, by seed-eating rodents, by foraging elk, by heavy motorcycle traffic.

To take quantitative measurements is a slow, often inaccurate process, and ecologists had been looking for years for a better way. So when this tool came out, we all rejoiced. The most valuable item of information it gives is an estimate of the total weight of plant matter. It does this by means of a sensing head, which holds an array of fifteen probes eighteen inches long. These probes are arranged on a one-by-two-foot grid. Attached to the sensing head is a transmitter-oscillator, which sets up a radio field within the fifteen probes. Within this field the instrument can measure electrical capacitance, which gives an index to moisture content. So the instrument doesn't really measure plants—it measures moisture.

In order to use this measurement, you have to establish a relationship between moisture readings and plant weight. This is done by a rather complicated process. First, you clip all the vegetation from the same one-by-two plot for which the meter has measured moisture. Then you put it in a paper sack, dry it, and weigh it. (The weight is calculated in "pounds of air-dried herbage per acre.") By doing this for a dozen or so plots you arrive at a reliable moisture/plant ratio, and can then rely on the meter readings alone.

Now let me explain how this information can be used. The amount of vegetation that grows in an area every season is important to managers of livestock ranges and wildlife habitat. We know about how much forage each class of animal needs to eat. For example, as I recall, a cow requires about eighteen pounds of air-dried forage per day. A cow elk might need about six pounds, a female deer about three pounds. If we know how much a habitat produces, we have a basis for calculating how many elk or deer the area can support. Of course, it's not quite that simple, because deer and elk eat only certain species of plants, and of those species they eat only the desired plant parts within their reach. Furthermore, they should not eat more than about half of the annual growth of any plant if the habitat is to remain in good condition. Taking all these factors into consideration, we put figures into an equation and come out with a recommended grazing density, or number of animals per acre. I did a little figuring in my head as I clipped and weighed, and my guess is that in this particular area it would take at least ten acres to support one elk throughout the short summer grazing season.

However, even with our meters and the knowledge we have assembled to date, our management techniques are still crude, especially on these high-altitude ranges. It is very difficult to determine how much wildlife could survive here. Part of the problem is that different plant species reach their peak of production at different times and in different micro-habitats. In some of the cushion plant communities, which are found mostly in exposed sites, the amount of production may be less than fifty pounds of air-dried herbage per acre per season. On the other hand, from some of the sedge and hairgrass communities that grow best on moist sites, I would expect an herbage yield of as much as a ton per acre. And a plant community on a south-facing slope will reach its peak long before a community on a north-facing slope. So all these variations must be considered before we can estimate how many elk or deer or sheep an area like this one can support.

Late in the afternoon I had the movie camera on one tripod and my 35-mm. Pentax on another when a peculiar gust of wind—the only violent gust all afternoon—came up and blew both cameras flat. I held my breath as I went to pick them up. Miraculously there was no damage to the Pentax except that the lens shade was a little askew and some dirt got on the camera. But the 16-mm. movie camera was not as lucky, and I have packed it for shipping back to Los Angeles. This is unfortunate because it leaves me with just two cameras, one of which does not seem to be in perfect working order.

September 15

Today was a good day again, although a little cooler.

This morning I took the camera down into the timber below the cabin and filmed: a few feet of a marten playing around the trees, a chipmunk feeding, some lichens and mosses on tree stumps and downed timber, some fresh gopher mounds.

That young marten again seemed curious about my activities. I was only a few yards from the cabin when I saw it playing, or perhaps hunting, under the trees. It was certainly aware of my presence, but did not seem disturbed. Since martens were not high on my list of objectives today, I didn't pay much attention and continued downslope. But every few minutes I would become aware of this marten's presence. Several times I sat on a rock and waited quietly; soon I would see a bit of brush or grass moving in unnatural fashion close by. I would watch this movement carefully, and sure enough, there would appear a large weasel-like head with bright eyes and round ears, peering over a log or around a tree at me. This continued for quite some time, until I had walked a half mile.

I find this behavior not only gratifying—who could help feeling good about a friendly spirit in the forest?—but also unusual. The traditional ecological wisdom is that when one goes into a wilderness area where animals have had little or no contact with humans, the animals are relatively unafraid. They have no experience of firearms or other associations of danger from humans. But this summer my relations with these animals have been more complex. When I travel away from the cabin, to other lake basins or down in Texas Creek, the pikas and marmots and gray jays are wary. Marmots that have never seen me before will start moving away when I'm within a hundred feet. The pikas do not allow me to get close, and the gray jays make no friendly overtures. But around the cabin, where the animals are used to me, I can approach to within just a few yards of these same species before they make any motion to escape. They greet my return to the cabin with exaggerated play behavior and seem to want to come close to me.

One of my main activities today was to make like a pika and start gathering vegetation—in my case, wood. The weather forecast again included predictions of heavy storms headed this way. Southern Wyoming already has snow at elevations over 6,000 feet. So after I had finished with the photography this afternoon, I chopped wood. I decided to try to bring it to the cabin on Charlie's two-bicycle-wheel cart, but I hadn't gone more than fifteen feet when one of the wheels slowly collapsed into an ellipse. I made three trips with the logs; on the fourth I carried the cart up and retired it to the shed. I hope Charlie doesn't spend any more time on it, although I'm sure he'll be disappointed it hasn't been more useful. He had spent a good many days at Buena Vista getting this contraption together. I guess it is typical of both Charlie's sometimes impractical approach and his generous nature to think of building it at all.

I also found an old log and an old stump with some dry wood, which I sawed and split and carried to the cabin. So now I have enough wood on hand for another three days. That's not as much as I'd like.

September 16

A satisfying day. I took a good, long hike, which always makes me feel better. The storm has not arrived yet, although the weather reports are grim and the temperature continues to drop.

I left the cabin early and climbed up to the Divide. The air was so clear it seemed as if I could see forever. New rich fall colors blended with the usual dark greens of the forest. It was so beautiful that I couldn't help photographing the view from a number of angles.

The wind is beginning to build up, and after my sad experience with the 16-mm. camera I am afraid to use the tripod. I tried some pans across the horizon hand-holding the camera, but each time I got set and squeezed the trigger a hard gust of wind would buffet me and shake the camera.

Then I photographed from above several small lakes at the head of Kroenke Basin. These little pothole lakes are so clear that I could see the bottoms all the way from the Divide. I also filmed a mudflow over a snowfield to show that not all erosion and muddy water are caused by man's mismanagement of nature. This was one of the perpetual snowfields common to the Colorado Rockies. Somewhat resembling tiny glaciers, they may contain snow that has not melted for decades. Some combination of conditions caused the soil above the snowfield to start moving, and it has flowed over the surface of the snow, producing intricate and picturesque patterns. Below the snowfield, water was moving downslope. Water that ordinarily is crystal clear is now brown with mud.

On the way to the basin and back I again experienced the pure delight of going hatless and having the wind blow my long hair; the old man was feeling loose and free again. The only troublesome experience, if you could call it that, came in the descent from the alpine into the head of Denny Creek. In traversing a rockslide, I stepped from a large rock to a fairly narrow ledge in what seemed a safe enough maneuver when it began. But in stepping from that ledge to a lower one, my camera tripod, which was sticking about a foot higher out of the pack than I thought, lodged in a crevice on the rock wall and forced me out away from the face. For a moment my heart stopped and I thought I was going to take off into space for thirty or forty feet. I grabbed at a small niche in an adjacent rock and hung on for dear life. I found myself in a squatting position, which I'm sure would have looked pretty funny to someone who didn't realize how darn scared I was. I was so firmly wedged into a cranny in the rock that at first I couldn't even back out. I finally solved that problem by jackknifing myself as sharply as possible, pulling my chest down tight against my knees. The pack came free and I very carefully backed out and slid on my belly down to the next ledge.

Well, it wasn't exactly the Matterhorn, but for this country boy it was enough mountaineering for one afternoon. Then I got down into the timber and windblown trees, where I encountered what seemed to be an impenetrable stand of willows. This I partially skirted and partially cursed my way through, only to find the willows a prelude to a boggy area, which I might have expected. I had to circle the bogs and stumble through some more downed timber and another rockslide. For a half mile or so, even though I was moving downhill, I was really sweating.

Several days ago I was using some rather flowery language to explain that I had arrived at a calm state of mind in which I appreciated the divine design of our Creator. I said that the natural environment is part of that design, and that I felt the stronger for having to cope with it. Well, most of the time this is true, but there are times like this afternoon when I seem to slip back to the old profane Smith.

I finally got through that difficult mess and emerged at a cool, pleasant stream. I found a place in the sunlight to lay my pack and myself. I ate the rest of my lunch, had a good drink of icy cold water, and felt much better. As I was lying there I thought about the way the terrain was arranged and some of the barriers to my easy travel, and I realized that dissatisfaction with our natural environment is really a problem of our society as a whole. We have never been satisfied with our surroundings as God created them. This is evident in the desire of the Bureau of Reclamation and Army Engineers to build dams across literally all flowing waters. It is also evident in the Soil Conservation Service, the Bureau of Land Management, the Bureau of Indian Affairs, and the Forest Service. All these agencies seem compelled to make drastic changes of one sort or another—spraying herbicides to kill sagebrush and rabbit brush, stopping all forest fires, planting exotic forage plants for cattle and sheep, channeling streams. Yet it is only fair to point out that these agencies are often led into this sort of behavior because large numbers of our people demand natural resource products that can be produced only by intensive management of the public lands.

This afternoon I was showing some of the same arrogance toward nature when I cursed the brush, downed timber, steep rockslides, and boggy areas. A solution to my travel difficulties today would be a totally managed timber stand in which humans come in and remove all the dead material, drain the bogs, and clear the forest floor so I could walk freely. Yet if such an unlikely action should occur I'm sure it would be undesirable. You would lose the decaying material which contributes organic matter to the soil. The soil eventually would suffer deterioration, erosion, and loss of fertility.

I think we should be extremely cautious in changing our natural environment even if it bites, stings, poisons, or burns us. I believe it is foolish to treat any living thing as inherently "bad." Yet a look at the history of North America shows that we have made just this kind of value judgment over and over. We have eliminated some species of plants and animals for the apparent short-term benefit of a part of society. One of the darkest episodes in American history was the eradication of the great buf-

falo herds of the western plains—for our supposed benefit and to deprive
the plains Indians of their livelihood. Once we had rid ourselves of both
the Indians and the buffaloes, we brought in vast herds of cattle. And
those cattle overgrazed the plains within a decade or so.

Right up to the present we have pursued policies of great arrogance.
When grizzlies, mountain lions, or bobcats interfere with our agriculture
or livestock operations, we proceed, through our government agencies, to
kill them off. In my work as an extension wildlife biologist I encountered
numerous programs that clearly stemmed from a policy of human pri-
macy: we behave as though many naturally occurring populations have no
place in our environment. There are extension agents whose titles reflect
this philosophy: animal control agents, nuisance control agents, and so
forth. Some of the "nuisance" species pursued are starlings, blackbirds,
pocket gophers, prairie dogs, jackrabbits, coyotes, and even golden eagles.
Wyoming and Colorado ranchers have been hiring helicopter pilots to kill
off these eagles; the ranchers claim eagles are extremely damaging to
sheep—to lambs, in particular. They have been challenged on this issue; a
number of responsible ranchers say that the golden eagle has a very insignificant effect on lamb crops. Nevertheless, it is by now a western tradi-
tion to shoot first and do the studies later.

Of the dozens of examples, I shall cite one that illustrates how willing we are to spend thousands of dollars to control a species which is far
from proven guilty—the pocket gopher. Even though there is at least as
much evidence that it is a highly beneficial species as there is evidence
that it does harm, our government has worked long hours and spent lots
of money to develop what is called a burrow builder—a machine, pulled
behind a tractor, which digs tunnels that simulate the burrow systems of
the pocket gopher. After these burrows are neatly made another machine
inserts poison bait at intervals along the artificial burrows. Yet after many
scientific studies, all written up in scientific reports, there is no conclusive
evidence that these creatures harm our economic interests, let alone the
environment in a more general sense.

In fact, it has been discovered that in places where the pocket gopher
feeds upon so-called weed species, it tends to eliminate these species. As a
consequence, richer, more balanced stands of grasses come in. This is certainly welcomed by livestock managers. At the same time, this change in
vegetation is an effective population control device for the gopher itself.
Once grasses have dominated an area, it becomes less appealing to gophers and their populations tend to drop. Of course, gophers turn and aerate

the soil as well, increasing its fertility and making it more receptive to water throughout its profile.

What I am suggesting is that everything in this universe has its place, and every time we diminish or destroy one species we tamper with a complex and delicate system that we know very little about. When the Rolls-Royce company sells an automobile, it comes with a locked hood so the owner won't fool around with the engine. We humans have been given a Rolls-Royce with an unlocked hood and we are tinkering around with expensive machinery we understand poorly.

We should have learned our lessons many times by now. One example of misguided intentions was the migration of the sodbusters to Oklahoma, western Kansas, Nebraska, and eastern Colorado to put the plow to millions of acres of tall- and short-grass prairies. In that country much of the soil mantle is too fragile and the climate is too arid for dry-land cultivation—a fact not understood by those pioneers. This was dramatically revealed at great cost during the "dirty thirties," the years of the dust bowl. These droughts not only brought economic disaster to the landowners and townsfolk of those areas; they even caused a fairly large number of fatalities. Some of these lands have now been returned to natural prairie grasses, but Nixon's emphasis on increased food production in the plains may repeat the tragedy.

Another misguided human plan is the phreatophyte (Greek roots of this word mean "artificial well" and "plant") program, a campaign to poison, grub out, bulldoze, and otherwise destroy such water-loving trees as the willow, cottonwood, tamarisk, mesquite, and aspen. These trees put down deep roots for water, and, like all trees, they transpire a good deal of it into the atmosphere. The phreatophytes are especially successful in such arid-region river systems as the Arkansas, the Colorado, the Missouri, and the Platte. The people who dammed and channeled those streams, and the farmers who use them for irrigation, act as though phreatophytes were a tool of the devil himself.

Over the years phreatophyte control has become a staple of porkbarrelers and boondogglers, and millions of dollars have been spent fighting trees. But the fact is that we are largely responsible by our own actions for the proliferation of these "pests." The water resource people tell me that these phreatophytes are growing now in places where sand and sediment have built up as a result of dams and flood-control projects. So we cause to proliferate a plant that we then classify as a pest and pay to eradicate.

Today our engineers proudly assert that every major river within the continental United States is under control (except, of course, for the phreatophytes). But even this isn't true. We still have floods every year. Some of the cause and much of the damage are because we are constantly violating nature's plan with regard to the movement of water. Through ignorance and sometimes greed, industry, agriculture, and municipal builders persist in locating their projects in the path of danger. An example here in Colorado is in the city of Boulder, where luxury homes are being built along a major stream bed, below what, as I recall, is the twenty-year flood line. This means that a flood will more than likely bring water rushing up to or beyond that line about every twenty years. Such a flood will, of course, inundate these homes, no matter how luxurious. Hydrologists have told the real estate people, the municipal planners, and the land speculators that these homes should not be built, but built they are.

Well, I am rambling on; what does all this have to do with the alpine and the subalpine I see around me. I think it has a good deal to do with it, because some of the same pressures are being exerted in damaging ways here, and the laws permit astonishing abuses. I heard on the radio just this morning that something like nineteen legislative proposals have been made in Congress to reform the 1872 Mining Act; this is the act responsible for some of the past trouble here in the high country. The most controversial issue now centers on the Breckenridge ski area, above the little village of Montezuma, where a man who controls a fairly large number of mining claims is planning to strip-mine that entire area. The land lies at about the same altitude as Brown's Cabin—a beautiful, spectacular area.

This is not an isolated case, and a solid foundation of legislation will be needed to prevent this sort of thing from happening in other places. When Bill Conklin, the ranger from the Gunnison National Forest, was here a few weeks ago, he surprised me by estimating that within Texas Creek drainage alone there are 500 to 1,000 mining claims. And most of these are held more or less illegally. Each claimant is supposed to do $100 worth of assessment work on each claim each year, but few of them do, and federal budgets do not provide for enforcement of what little law there is.

Perhaps it seems these points are simply legalistic, or perhaps moralistic. But I am talking about real damage to the environment. Many activities on these mining claims are extremely harmful to wildlife habitat, to the aesthetics of the area, and to the soil. As the law stands, mining claim holders are free to cut down the trees, dead or alive, and people have abused this right to log these claims commercially. This is technically illegal, but again enforcement is so lax that it is seldom challenged.

Mining claimants can also dig holes, cut trenches, and move water around. In hydraulic mining operations, they will dig a diversion ditch from a natural stream, bring the water through a series of successively narrower hoses and connections so that it builds up tremendous force at the nozzle end. This powerful stream of water is played across the land, literally washing the topsoil off the bedrock, so that the miner can proceed to blasting and picking out the ore. It's easy to imagine the results of removing as much as six or seven feet of topsoil and subsoil from a mountain slope. It moves as mud downhill and destroys as much of the area below as that actually involved in the hydraulic mining.

The high country of Colorado is threatened as well by summer and vacation home development. Newspaper, television, and radio advertising hammer at the theme that great profits await the alert land speculator who wants to buy up this country and develop it into summer home complexes. This can lead to real natural disasters.

I have seen developments with rough streets going directly up steep slopes where great gullies had already eroded—even before the homes had been built. There were no provisions for sewage disposal. In some places land developers and homeowners alike were cutting down trees and pruning the lower branches off others for the sake of the view, often leaving the brush in unsightly and dangerous piles. The Colorado State Forest Service, which has responsibility for most of these lands, is horror-struck at the potential for the kind of disastrous fires that are common in the chaparral communities of California, and for tree disease epidemics spread by beetles that breed in these piles. It's really disheartening to find that an affluent and supposedly enlightened society is capable of contaminating such beautiful country with this type of damage. Perhaps this project can help point the way to alternatives.

Part VI

SNOWFALL

September 17

The forecasters were right; the storm really came. I knew I was in trouble as early as last night. I've been sleeping with a cotton flannel sheet and three Army blankets, but soon after I went to bed I added a fourth, then got up and found a fifth, then a sixth, then a seventh blanket, and still I woke up cold. To compound the problem, I drank a lot of tea last night as I was narrating, so I had to get up about three times. As I started down the stairs on the second trip, my eye caught a two-pound coffee can on the floor where it has been catching leaks from the roof. This was as good a time as any to revert to my childhood, when every country boy had a chamber pot beneath the bed; I now have mine right by the foot of the bed, so I don't have to go outside.

When the alarm went off at six forty-five I grabbed a coat and staggered down the stairs. By the time the fire was going my teeth were chattering. The thermometer, which is located in one of the warmest spots in the cabin, registered 31 degrees. It was much colder around the perimeter of the cabin, where the water pails had an eighth of an inch of ice in them. The wind was blowing in hard gusts and the snow was coming down, with about five inches already on the ground.

In fact, the wind was blowing through the kitchen door so freely that I could feel it on my ankles clear across the room. As I walked past either door I could feel a shower of snowflakes coming in, and every window had its pile of snow inside. There was even a crack at floor level beside my bed where I found a pile of snow three inches deep. I couldn't see that it was doing any harm, however, so I just left it there.

I could see that the blankets weren't going to do the job on the bed, so I took two of them off and nailed them over the kitchen door to keep the snow out—the same way they used tapestries in the Middle Ages. I'm going to quit using that door. And I nailed another blanket between the kitchen and living room. I'm going to try to survive mostly in the living room; then I'll have only one room to heat. I replaced the two blankets on my bed with two spread-out sleeping bags.

As you can imagine, this has been an entirely different sort of day, and I didn't get much done, aside from survival chores. In addition, Brown's Cabin was in the clouds most of the time, and it was too dark for even the fastest film. From six forty-five, when I got up, until five-fifteen—ten and a half hours—I ate only one meal, a good, substantial breakfast. The rest of the time was spent cutting wood, stoking the stoves, caulking cracks, fighting a tremendous draft coming up from the cellar, laying down newspapers for insulation, filling all available containers with water.

I went back to another childhood experience to initiate one more emergency measure: a slop pail. When we lived on a remote farm, with no running water, no electricity, no central heating, and no sewage disposal, we used to dump all the dish and wash water into a slop bucket. Most of it would end up being fed to the pigs. I was surprised that the idea of having a slop pail in the kitchen repelled me at first, but it has turned out to be useful. My reason for the pail, and for stocking up on water, is so that I won't have to open the doors any more than necessary. I plan to use only the back door, which leads to the shed. So now, with slop pail, water buckets, wood supply, and pee pot, I can survive without going outside for two or three days, if I have to. I hope that's not necessary.

There isn't much to report about the wildlife because the animals have pretty much disappeared. It has snowed all day, easing off in the evening, when I saw a number of gray-headed juncos feeding diligently on the seed heads of some wheatgrasses that were still above the snow (the second commonest name for juncos is snowbirds). There were a few sparrows in the willows, but I did not see the gray jays, my most constant companions this summer, and I'm wondering where they are. I was surprised to find myself watching for the small mammals around the area and worrying about them. I was worried, too, about the juncos; I'm sure that they are used to more severe weather than this, but this early storm may have caught them by surprise. I wonder if the wild animals are at all prepared. The pikas did not have their hay piles completed, and I haven't heard a peep from them or the marmots. As a biologist I know better than to think like this, but one can't help but worry about his friends!

The cabin never did get very warm today. At breakfast time, when I had both stoves going full blast, the thermometer rose to a peak of 57 degrees. Then it dropped to 50, where it stayed all day. The floor was much colder; none of the drifted snow melted, nor did the ice in the water buckets. I punched holes through the ice when I needed some water. This evening I finally swept up the snow from the floors and threw it out the back door. That seems to offer some psychological comfort. I'll just hope it's not as cold tomorrow.

September 18

My hopes were not realized. It was even colder this morning. I forgot to mention yesterday that I did make a trip up to the weather station and found some of the instruments frozen. I was afraid that the recording rain gauge would break, because it was getting low on antifreeze, so I re-charged it with three quarts of the stuff. And here's why: it had reached a low of 6 degrees above zero the night before last, and a maximum yester-day of 9. This morning the minimum was 3 degrees. It's no wonder I've been so darn cold.

It stopped snowing about noon today, and in the afternoon the sun came out briefly, warming up to a high of 13 degrees. Despite the cold it was a truly beautiful day. The trees are completely covered with snow and the mountains are breathtaking. Again I had a lot of survival chores, but I did manage some filming. One of the things I photographed was my beard, which was full of ice. This is an interesting sensation. I recall in 1951, when we spent the winter in the Idaho wilderness, each time I'd lie down to get a drink from a stream ice crystals would form in my beard and sting as they expanded and pulled the hairs. I'd completely forgotten how it felt until today. It was snowing, and apparently the combination of snow, temperature, and humidity was just right for growing ice in beards.

Then I had an amusing project. I still was uneasy about how long the storm was going to last, so I took the saw over to a large tree Charlie had felled and sawed off two big blocks. Then I took the toboggan over and loaded the two blocks, the saw, ax, and splitting wedge, and hauled it back toward the cabin. I thought it would be fun to film this exercise, so I brought the toboggan to within forty-five feet of the shed door and tested it several times to be sure that all it would take to start it down a small hill was a jerk on the rope. I planned to run ahead of it on my snowshoes, which I have been wearing because of the deep drifts that are forming. Then I set up both cameras just inside the shed door, started them, and ran up to the toboggan and grabbed the rope. My first little tug had no effect, so I gave a harder tug. Then I yanked like hell and still nothing.

Well, the cameras were rolling, and the show wasn't going on, so I moved halfway up on the rope and gave a desperate jerk, and it finally broke loose. It had frozen. I came clomping back toward the camera with a silly grin on my face that should look great on film. I now see why it costs so much to make a real movie.

The tug-of-war with the sled was so typical of the day that I decided to carry on with this theme. So I showed myself unloading the saw and ax, and at one point I laid the ax across one of the blocks of wood to give an idea of how large it was. Then I hammed it up, making a silly face at the camera. I believe this kind of behavior is known as "cabin fever." Later I did something of a repeat—this time rolling off a block of wood and splitting it. I felt pretty good about that scene; I had to swing only four or five times and the big block broke apart very neatly. Then I went over and started slabbing the block and this, too, worked beautifully. Every time I hit the block the ax would neatly crack off a long slab of wood. I must admit to some vanity about my ability as an axman, but I wasn't prepared to have it go this well.

I took quite a few feet of a chipmunk that had emerged from a burrow under the snow where it had made an entrance hole. It would come out and feed on some plants nearby, then dash back into the hole. I first started photographing it from about twenty-five feet away, but every time it went back down the hole I'd move in another five feet and be ready when it came up again. I think there was a bit of the ham in this animal, for after I got within fifteen feet it quit feeding and just sat up and preened and flipped its tail or stood there looking at me. I wasn't able to show as much feeding as I wanted, but this was the first time a chipmunk would sit still for me.

Later on, it and the rest of the chipmunks will sleep most of the winter away in a burrow below the snow. The chipmunk does not truly hibernate, waking occasionally for brief periods of feeding during warm spells.

Oh, yes, I couldn't resist the temptation to film myself sitting in the outhouse in the very cold weather. I don't expect this bit of pornography will appeal to anyone, but I decided to exercise my prerogative as chief cameraman, director, prop man, and star.

Since the arrival of the freeze and storm I have done some reflecting on what this experience means to me, so screw down your hat. I frequently quote my wife, and over the years she has issued any number of quotable statements about me as a person with more obsolete skills than anyone she's ever met. She refers to such things as my abilities as a mule skinner, or how well I can plow with a walking plow and a pair of horses or throw a diamond hitch to cinch a load on a packhorse. Then there is my self-proclaimed ability to stack a beautiful load of grain bundles on a hay wagon. I have twice shared winning honors in the crosscut saw contest during Forestry Days at the university, and I've won prizes in the ax-chopping contest and a cup in the chain-saw event. In short, I have these skills that I'm quite proud of, although most people think them pretty darn useless.

Then comes the storm. I must admit that when I woke up yesterday and found such a sudden bad storm, I knew I could really be up against it. By the time the fires were going I was so chilled I began to wonder if my health was in jeopardy. If I were injured it would be pretty tough to get help. The Forest Service would have difficulty coming in by any means. The snow is not right for snowmobiling, and the visibility much of the time is only a hundred feet or less. I have said before that I like the feeling when the clouds close in around me; but I would be loath to put on the snowshoes and head out for Cottonwood Road in them. It would be easy to lose my way in this blowing snow. And of course airplanes are out of the question. Brown's Cabin is now quite isolated. My first thought yesterday was, my God, this could really develop into a pretty cruel experience.

But after I'd gotten up, warmed the room a bit, had that first cup of coffee in me, and remembered some of my obsolete skills and the cups on my mantel, I began to enjoy the primitive struggle of it all. I thought a good deal about my parents and the things we had done together. I'm sure that many of the little challenges of the past two days were not frightening because I'd met them many times before, in my early life.

In fact, I lived for much of my youth in an old house that was not much better insulated than this cabin. The temperature went to 44 degrees below zero one winter and, believe me, we took turns staying up all night to keep the fires going. As these memories came flooding back, I realized that of course survival in winter storms is possible, and I had the notion that this experience was enabling me to sort of re-create Dwight Smith. I thought of things I hadn't remembered in decades. One of my early concerns had always been the danger of fire. I remembered that Dad used to be very careful in the wintertime; it was fairly common for one of the old farmhouses and various shanties and cabins around the mountain country to burn down during the winter.

Now, as a result, when I go out to cut wood a hundred or so yards from the cabin, I find myself glancing over my shoulder every few minutes to see that no smoke is trickling out from under the eaves. I would be in one hell of a fix if the cabin burned down. As a matter of fact, I make it a practice to wear clothing I could survive in for nine miles through the snow—the distance out to the nearest snow-plowing on Cottonwood Road—if such a disaster should come. I remembered safety lessons like never letting the ashes build up in the ash box, because that makes it easier for live sparks falling through the grate to tumble out onto the floor. With these old wood floors in Brown's Cabin, a bit of burning wood or spark could easily start a fire. I also remembered my mother putting blankets over every door and window at night to keep out the cold.

One reaction that surprised me is related to my alleged fastidiousness, for which I take some ribbing. Even when I'm on a backpacking trip I always take my pajamas, wash with soap and water, and clean my teeth twice a day, all of which make me feel comfortable. So when I got into the business of the chamber pot and the slop pail, I was at first appalled by the idea. But then I thought back and realized that this used to be standard operating procedure when I was growing up. I am at the same time very far away from and very close to my rustic boyhood.

One more note about roughing it: I felt a brief flash of annoyance when the sun came out at midday and brought the temperature up a bit. It was fun to be living a rugged life. It appears that part of me longed for the snow to continue to pile up, longed to battle the elements for another few days. Now it seems that my battle with nature is to be a brief one. Of course, I have to hope this is true because there is a lot of filming still to be done. Also, some of the Landsburg fellows are due in at the end of the month; it would be a shame to be cooped up in the cabin all the time they're here.

September 19

It is hard to imagine how beautiful it has been here today. The trees are all covered with snow, and the skies are bright and blue, without a cloud. The sun was shining so brightly that my dark glasses couldn't keep out the glare.

Last night was even colder than the night before—half a degree below zero. But this afternoon it rose to 32, and the snow was melting fast in the sun. Some of the windblown areas, where there was only four or five inches, are beginning to show bare ground and some grass can be seen here and there. This evening I can even see one golden dandelion blooming bravely.

Today is Sunday, and I celebrated the Sabbath by lying in bed until seven-thirty, putting off the moment when I would have to face the cold. Eventually I pried myself out and got the fires going, and after breakfast I spent the rest of the day outside, making the rounds of my photo points. This took a bit longer than normal, since I still have to travel on snowshoes. I had a little thrill as I moved into photo point No. 6, which is on the edge of a bluff overlooking the cabin. As I came around this small cliff, treading very carefully on a ledge I've always used, I stepped on what appeared to be the ledge, but it wasn't, and I went for a short slide. I won't go into the details, but my heart was pounding fast as I realized how much farther I could have gone down the mountainside. I've mentioned three or four of these incidents and maybe it sounds like I'm clumsy or careless, but I don't think this is true. It's just that the alternative would have been to leave out permanent photo point No. 6. But it has a beautiful view, which includes the cabin, and I really wanted to make it.

Well, this tape recorder and I must be completely incompatible. I'm so damn mad at it. I've talked for fifteen minutes off the end of the tape again. I suppose I should have enough intelligence to figure out how to watch this thing, but by damn, it's a real irritation to have to fiddle-fart around trying to watch that cock-eyed thing at night when it's so dark I have to use a flashlight to see it. It should have a warning buzzer.

Now where in the hell was I? I'm just about out of the mood for narrating, that's where. I have asked Charlie to see if Billy Carpenter can come in for a couple of days to cut some wood. It's not going to be an easy trip, and I hope they don't start out too early in the morning. The kind of snow crust we're getting is hard on wildlife and even harder on horses. When they step through this crust it tends to cut them on the fetlocks. The crust is also dangerous for deer, and can cut their Achilles tendon so severely that their hoofs just flop loosely. I've found deer in the Salmon River country in Idaho that were so badly crippled by crusted snow I decided the most merciful thing to do was to shoot them.

Now that I've calmed down a bit I recall an incident that occurred yesterday while I was eating supper. I looked out the window and saw a weasel going across the slope just below the clouds, which were settling in above the cabin. The weasel had to leap to make its way though the snow; the jumps were short, the back arched high; an awkward movement compared with the fluid way weasels cross solid ground. I watched for a while and concluded that it was hunting, searching for a squirrel or chipmunk without success. The thought struck me that the weasel wasn't ready for this weather any more than I was. Nature has provided the weasel, the ptarmigan, and other animals with the marvelous protective adaptation of changing color in the spring to brown or gray, and in the fall to white. But nature doesn't allow for such emergencies as early snowstorms in September. This weasel looked very, very brown against the white snow, clearly visible to predator and prey alike. It could be a long time between meals if the squirrels and chipmunks can see the weasel as easily as I can.

September 20

I feel a little silly at losing my temper at the tape recorder yesterday evening. But I'll probably do it again.

It's five minutes after one and I'm sitting up here in a rockslide doing some pika watching. They have come out at last. During the first two days of snow I didn't hear a squeak out of them and I was growing concerned.

I have been taking stills and movies of animal tracks in the snow today, while the weather is still good. The forecast this morning was for another eight to twelve inches of snow tonight or tomorrow. I've seen tracks of montane vole, chipmunk, weasel, pika, fox, and some I'm not sure about. The fox tracks were an exciting find, because I haven't seen a fox in this basin all summer. From its tracks, it seemed to be hunting chipmunks and pikas. It would be the red fox (*Vulpes vulpes*). The other two foxes in Colorado, the kit and gray foxes, are not generally found this high.

I haven't expected to see many foxes here for several reasons. For one thing, they are primarily nocturnal; for another, they live in the forested areas. Most often they can be seen at dawn or dusk along forest edges and openings caused by fire or logging. These are the zones they find most profitable for hunting, trotting along the same trails night after night. Foxes hunt by literally "following their noses" for a hundred feet or so, then pausing for a look around, often hopping atop a large rock or stump. They rely on surprise rather than great speed to catch their prey, which is usually a rabbit, pika, or rodent. They are opportunistic feeders, however, and will take birds, insects, amphibians, eggs, and even fruits.

Like coyotes, foxes often hunt in pairs, especially during the breeding season, ranging over a territory of several miles. Once a pair bond is formed it is virtually unbreakable; the male and female hunt, play, and rest together. They mate in winter and the pups are born in a den (in a rock crevice or cave or hole in the ground) seven to eight weeks later. By summer the pups have learned to hunt, and in the fall each member of the family goes its own way. The parents may or may not re-form their bond to mate again.

There was an incident yesterday that illustrates the unexpected hazards of life at Brown's Cabin. The gray jays have been absent from the cabin area for two days, and I was beginning to wonder if they had pulled out for the winter. But yesterday afternoon when I was under a tree urinating, the jays suddenly appeared, flying up from the spruce-fir forest below the cabin. They landed on the cabin, on the shed, and in the tree above me. The trick they've pulled before, one culprit in particular, is to fly directly at my face, so close I can feel the rush of wings. It has never struck me, but I haven't yet developed the sang-froid to stand there without flinching. It did this four or five times yesterday, flying very close, with me backing away each time, when all of a sudden it dove at a lower part of my anatomy, catching me completely unaware. I can't remember such a cruel, swift surprise. I felt a rush of wind and a stinging thump. I did such a rapid withdrawal that about three tablespoons of hot urine, which soon turned cold, spilled down the inside of my pants leg. The air was blue for a little while as I told this degenerate little so-and-so what I thought of it.

I suppose I really brought this humiliation on myself. I have been feeding stale or moldy bread to the gray jays, and they have become tame enough to take pieces off my knee or hand or even, one day, off the top of my head. One jay would land in my hair, and I could feel its talons on my scalp. Taming these easy-to-tame birds has provided a bit of entertainment for me but, it now appears, was responsible for my undoing.

September 21

Late yesterday afternoon, just when I was about to give up on them, Charlie and Billy came in with the horses. They began cutting wood and skidding it over with the toboggan and a saddle horse. I will still have to saw and split it, but I'll be way ahead.

Sure enough, just like the forecaster said, it began snowing about midnight last night; and now there are about four inches of new snow. There's no wind—just nice, soft snow.

Ross Moser has sent in word that a helicopter is scheduled to come in sometime during the week of October 4–8 to bring in a big load of supplies and to take out things I no longer need. I worry about the logistics of supply with this weather. The packer is having problems finding horse pasture, and he'd like to pull all his horses out of the Buena Vista area as soon as he can. I'm expecting the Landsburg people again, as well as my wife and family, so I need to stock up.

Charlie and Billy are gone now. Yesterday they managed to get one six-foot section of tree trunk cut and hauled, but it took them over an hour and a half. It made me realize how time-consuming it is to cut wood by hand. Charlie has a chain saw here, but for some reason he has been reluctant to use it. When I saw how little wood they were processing by hand, I made a strong suggestion that they try to use the chain saw. They did manage to get it going, and this morning they cut up the remainder of that tree as well as a smaller one. So now there is a fairly good-sized pile of short logs in one corner of the shed, which should last me three or four weeks in moderate weather. At three-thirty they left and I was alone.

This darn bursitis is acting up again, apparently because of the cold weather. It usually strikes about midmorning and continues for the rest of the day. In the evenings it is simply horrible.

September 22

Yesterday it started snowing about noon and kept up all afternoon and night. After the storm ended I hiked around the basin scouting for new animal tracks. I followed the trail of a bull elk that came up out of Denny Creek, wandered near the weather station, then zigzagged down into the spruce stand, where I abandoned it. I saw a marten about fifteen feet from the outhouse, so at least one of them is still around. The doorless out-house is an extra-primitive facility these days. I have had to brush from one to three inches of snow off the seat before using it. Sitting down is a chilling experience!

It was warmer this afternoon, and the small animals and birds were more active. The mountain chickadees were singing, the chipmunks were engaged in frenzied activity, and the pikas were out. I haven't seen any marmots since September 16, the day before the storm.

September 23

This morning I arose before daylight, made a cup of coffee, and took off for Brown's Pass to set up a blind from which to call predators. None showed up. The only evidence of a predator I have seen in the past week was the track of the red fox, and if it heard me either it wasn't fooled or it wasn't hungry. As for me, I succeeded in getting chilled to the bone. Back at the cabin I built up the fires and devoured a big breakfast of eggs, sausages, and more hot coffee. Afterward I went over the supplies I'm not going to need and got them ready to ship out on the helicopter. Late in the afternoon I made a circuit around part of the basin in search of animal tracks, or better yet, animals. No luck.

While eating supper I listened to a talk show from Denver conducted by Bill Barker. His guests this evening were three young people from Boulder who are publishing a new ecology magazine called *Dear Earth*. It is always interesting to listen to these young people who are involved in environmental issues. There's no question that they are very sincere, but I often find them lacking in facts. They tend to deal in emotion and opinion rather than quantitative information. Often they even seem unaware of data that is easily available.

I am particularly bothered by their belief that they are the first people who ever felt concern for the environment. They seem to lack any awareness of the people and agencies who are working diligently to protect our environment, and have been doing so for decades. Like many of us who launch ourselves into some new type of endeavor, they tend to feel the problems are simple, and therefore that there must be simple solutions. They also seem to have tunnel vision, seeing only the few problems and solutions that have aroused the public.

Let me give a couple of examples of simplistic thinking in Colorado. First, livestock: the new environmentalists view the use of public lands by sheep, cattle, or horses as synonymous with destruction. I have heard these people say they do not oppose grazing on public lands in appropriate places, but I can't recall ever hearing them mention an appropriate place. They describe all grazing in a derogatory manner, and seem totally unaware of improvements in grazing programs that have been made by the Forest Service and other agencies.

Another example is the use of herbicides. I tend to agree with them in most cases on this issue. But one of the hot issues around here is sagebrush control. Time after time I've heard these people say, we don't want the sagebrush sprayed in order to grow more grass, let's leave it in a natural condition. Well, this is one of those cases of wearing historical blinkers. Sagebrush is not always the natural condition; often it is there because of abusive grazing practices in the past. Much of our sagebrush land was natural grassland before the great herds of cattle were brought in. The environmentalist is thus in the logically ridiculous position of fighting to maintain a condition that was created by environmental abuse.

Another environmental hot potato is timber harvesting. Here again I have heard protectionists say that this is all right in appropriate areas, but I have never heard them say where these areas are. To listen to environmental rhetoric, you would think that anyone involved in the logging and milling industries is, if not actually criminal, at least corrupt and amoral. This is an attitude that bewilders me.

What the environmentalists are saying is that timbering brings ruin to the forests, spoils natural beauty, denies the wonder of trees to our offspring. I have already described all the logging activity that went on around Brown's Cabin, largely between 1885 and 1910. As is evident from all the stumps and skid roads, in terms the modern-day environmentalist would apply, these logged areas must have been devastated.

Well, this summer I have walked through this once-forested mountainside a good deal; I've also walked through other, forested, mountainsides near here where there has been no logging at all. To me, virgin spruce-fir forest is indeed attractive—as seen from the air or from across a canyon. But a solid virgin forest has some disadvantages closer up. Usually it is very dense, and in its natural condition it is cluttered by a network of downed logs which can make foot travel almost impossible.

In the Brown's Cabin area, by contrast, these dense stands of spruce and fir are broken up by little openings where walking is a pleasure. These openings are dotted with old tree stumps indicating past logging activity and, because light can get in, they are carpeted with grasses, shrubs, and various flowers. In dense timber stands like the one down at South Texas Creek, only a small number of shade-tolerant plants can survive on the forest floor. There is also a difference in animal life. Under the virgin timber, the only common species is the red squirrel. There are martens, but they are rarely seen. However, in the small openings created by past logging activity, I see chipmunks, pocket gophers, and a much greater variety of bird life.

I am certainly not making a brief for cutting all the spruce-fir forests in the central Rocky Mountains to make them more beautiful and easier to walk in. I just want to stress that timbering is not a synonym for disaster. However, I believe that the best course is to protect many of these high-country forests from timber harvesting. The reasons for this vary. These forests tend to be remote, in places that should be designated wilderness areas. Logging such forests would require building long roads, producing tremendous erosion on steep lands.

On the other hand, when we have legitimate needs for timber products, as we do, and when environmentally acceptable methods of harvesting are available, as they are, we need not assume that timbering must produce a desolate landscape. For example, the aesthetics- and recreation-conscious Swiss have developed a high-line logging system for harvesting their steep mountainsides with a minimum of damage to the soil and to the beauty of the areas. Such a system involves a continuous cable, like a ski lift, to carry logs down a mountain without using trucks and bulldozers. Swiss loggers have demonstrated their technique in Colorado.

To study how to make logging more visually acceptable, there are now about a dozen landscape architects working in Region 2 of the Forest Service, headquartered in Denver. These architects have developed cutting plans that, when followed correctly, can produce a pleasing pattern of varied vegetation. These variations are brought about by cutting different stands at different times, leaving a mixture of age classes in a forest. Also, a variety of species come in during natural plant succession after timbering. This creates a mosaic of species, heights, shapes, and colors that behavioral researchers have found is more pleasing to the human eye than the monotonous single age–single species stands. I think I could demonstrate this point to any doubter by taking him on a walk from the pleasant meadows and open forests around Brown's Cabin down through the dark, nearly impenetrable virgin forest of South Texas Creek drainage.

September 24

This day probably will go down in my memory as the "day of the bad back." This darn bursitis or whatever it is took over. All evening I've been in such agony I hardly know what I'm doing. Almost everything I've tried has gone wrong; I even upset the tea kettle full of boiling water over my foot. Fortunately I was able to pull off my socks fast enough so that I only burned a small area on top of the instep.

I wish I knew what exactly is wrong. Most of the time it's just a constant, fairly high-level pain under my shoulder blades. Sometimes it's difficult to operate the camera, even on a tripod. Little jerks of pain cause little jerks of the camera. It feels as though someone is driving an ice pick in my back.

After my trip to the weather station I hauled some water, warmed it, and started a batch of clothes soaking. It looks as if there's no way to avoid doing a laundry tomorrow. I made a brief circuit of the basin area; I found that another deer has moved through the area, but no elk. After an early lunch I decided to try to start the chain saw. It would be just right for cutting the short lengths Charlie and Bill had stacked in the shed. I left it in the sun a while to warm up, and to my surprise, it started. I spent three hours sawing and splitting and piling. I now estimate that even in colder weather I have enough wood for about three weeks.

Just before I finished cutting, two men, one about forty-five and the other perhaps eighteen, came by wearing backpacks. They had a large red setter with them, and when this huge dog suddenly appeared about twenty-five feet away I really jumped. The men had walked in from Cottonwood Road, apparently just hiking for pleasure. They said something about fresh air and a good place to camp; I encouraged them to find a site down along Texas Creek. The older one seemed to be hinting that they would like to stay here. But I find that after being alone here for a few weeks my tendency is to talk on and on, if I get started, so the best thing is to keep it short and simple. These two men are the first people I've seen here since late August, except for Charlie and Billy.

September 25

Well, I haven't had a good night's rest and I haven't had any relief from this damn back trouble. Today I've been distracted and distraught all day long, and frankly, I haven't done an awful lot.

Notwithstanding, it was a very nice day. It's continuing to warm up. The temperature reached 47, the warmest it's been since the day before the storm.

After going to the weather station I began washing clothes. I suppose that leaning over the washboard hasn't helped the back situation any. I finished at eleven and came in to make a cup of hot tea. I turned on the radio and there was the pre-game show for the Colorado–Ohio State football game. I had forgotten all about it, but I was just miserable enough to use this as an excuse to stay inside. Which I did.

September 26

It's very late Sunday night, really early Monday morning. After all my complaining yesterday I'm happy to report that I feel better. I indulged myself by staying in bed until eight and this paid off. Now I'm making up for the late start by working most of the night.

It was a routine and fairly short day. I came in at a quarter to five and have been writing letters to people at the university, to my family, and elsewhere. It seems that correspondence is something I haven't cared to deal with this summer. I even discouraged a lot of people from writing. Even so, I have quite a stack of university mail that one of my graduate students has been forwarding to me. It seems that I owe everyone a letter.

I also started getting things together for a trip into bighorn country.

Courtship behavior among the rams should start soon, followed by the breeding season—usually from November to January. I remember the night before I went to the elk meadows; I was up until 4:30 a.m., and that didn't leave me in very good shape for the trip.

September 28

Well, I was planning to take the tape recorder with me to the bighorn country around Taylor Park, but I didn't. It is now October 1 and I have to catch up.

I had a good, vigorous walk up to Brown's Pass, where I enjoyed a beautiful sunrise over the Divide. I had to wade through a foot-deep snowdrift for about fifty yards, but there, marking a neatly precise line along the wind-blown Divide, the snow ended.

I carried a heavy load again, about seventy pounds, and when I reached Middle Cottonwood Road, Danny Herman was waiting to pick me up. Danny is the young man who came to the cabin earlier this summer and had some ideas about where bighorn herds are located. He offered to help me search. Charlie also met me, with groceries and a heart-warming batch of mail, the most I've gotten yet.

Danny and I went on over Cottonwood Pass and down to the Forest Service guard station in Taylor Park, where I am planning to stay and near where Danny's father operates the boat dock and store at the reservoir. After lunch we took off in their Jeep for a place in the high country some twenty miles away where bighorn had been spotted almost daily for the past two weeks. Danny's uncle drove the Jeep back while we worked our way down through the cliffy terrain on foot. It was quite a hike. We did see some tracks and droppings, but all the signs seemed to be at least two or three days old and we spotted no sheep.

We reached the banks of Taylor Reservoir well after dark and used flashlights to signal Danny's father, who came for us in his motorboat. We returned to the dock for a good home-cooked supper, and I was back at the guard station at ten-thirty, where I spent two hours listening to tapes and reading letters. It was nice to hear the voices of my family, and to know that everything is going well.

September 29

I got up at six-thirty, had breakfast, and soon after that was picked up by Danny and his uncle in the Jeep. We drove back to the same area we explored yesterday, then Danny and I took off around the heads of some extremely steep canyons. Danny's uncle drove the Jeep back again and we arranged for a pickup that evening.

This was a miserable day throughout for me. At three in the morning I woke up with a severe headache, and I still had it when I got up at six-thirty. I thought that it would go away in the fresh air, but it didn't. I even vomited part of the day. We were again completely unsuccessful in seeing any sheep.

We reached the far end of the reservoir at about six o'clock in a windy rain. I wondered if Danny's father would see us; but he had been watching with binoculars, and we had been at the shore for only ten minutes when we saw the boat start out across the water. This was a welcome sight because we were tired and already chilled by the cold rain.

Again I had supper with the Hermans, who form an interesting household. There is J.D., who goes by his initials; his son Danny, who is twenty-one; Danny's uncle, Burl Herman; and all of them act as parents to a small boy named Michael, age three. The three men treat him just like one of them; he's out in the boats and the Jeep in all kinds of weather, and he seems to thrive on it. J.D.'s wife Rosie was at their winter home in Montrose.

September 30

After a good night's rest I felt much better. Danny and J.D. picked me up and we drove to the top of Cottonwood Pass to look for ptarmigan. I would like to see if they have changed to their winter plumage yet; if not, their brown feathers will show up clearly against the snow. It was a sunny morning but the wind was high. We climbed from the pass to the crest of the Continental Divide and followed it for half a mile, the three of us fanned out along the slope. It certainly seems as if luck is against me on this trip. I'm convinced that the Hermans know this country and its wildlife extremely well. But the weather was poor and the birds just did not show.

We gave up on the ptarmigan at one-thirty, and after lunch Danny and I took the Jeep into Illinois Gulch. He had seen elk there at this time of year and was confident we could call up a bull elk. Again our best efforts were unsuccessful.

We returned after dark, and it began to rain hard at seven-thirty, so I'm not sure what the weather will be like in the morning. I want to try to call up some coyotes.

October 1

The alarm went off at five-thirty but it was still pouring rain. At about six twenty-five a coyote began howling not far from the cabin. I went to the window and saw that it was now snowing lightly, so I dressed, had a cup of coffee, and got into the Jeep that the Hermans had kindly loaned me. I got within half a mile of the boat docks, where I was to meet Danny, and the Jeep quit running, so I had to walk the rest of the way. It was now snowing quite heavily. Danny got the Jeep down to the dock; then we tried to figure what to do next. We couldn't get up into the high country because of the fresh snow, and even if we could have, it wasn't clear enough to see coyotes, or any other wildlife. I decided at midmorning to return to Brown's Cabin. Danny and I went back to the guard station and packed. He is going with me, since he would like to see the cabin and I have more things than I can carry alone.

October 2

This entry has more to do with human ecology than animal ecology—the human ecology of Taylor Park, you might say. This human community lives in a large park area with a man-made reservoir at 9,500 feet. The park is 30 by 15 miles, the reservoir 2½ by 3½ miles, fed by about 400 miles of streams. Ten to fifteen people make their living there by running various tourist businesses during the summer season. Most of them have been going there for ten to thirty years and are known locally as the "park people." Then there are about twenty-five families who have houses there, where they spend occasional summer weekends and perhaps a two- or three-week summer vacation. The businesses in the park consist of the boat docks owned and managed by the Hermans; a Trading Post with store, café, gas pump, and about twenty-five rental cabins; Cheatham's Cottages, which are also rented; and the Holtz Guest Ranch, with about fifteen cottages. Then there is Tincup, Colorado, which is included in the park population. Tincup has a number of summer homes and a small general store with a gas pump. The postal address for all this is Almont, twenty-six miles down the Taylor River. Tincup has been featured in a number of novels and radio programs; it used to be a mining boom town with a reputation for short-lived sheriffs. It once had a population of several thousand people who, for reasons still obscure, all vanished within a few days.

The point of all this background is that I found—or imagined—what seems to be a frontier spirit still strong in Taylor Park. This was extremely refreshing to behold in our time of stress and impersonality.

This frontier spirit emerged during a series of events that began at seven-thirty last night. J.D. and Danny were making supper when a man came in and announced that one of the summer residents was stalled in a snowdrift atop Cottonwood Pass. This pass, which crosses the Continental Divide, is about eighteen miles from the boat dock, and by then it was snowing hard. Nonetheless, everyone immediately dropped what he was doing, supper forgotten, and we piled into two Jeeps. I went with J.D. while Danny took three-year-old Michael and we headed for the pass. Sherman Cranor, who operates the Trading Post, and his son Roy joined us in a third Jeep. The reason for three vehicles soon became obvious. A weekend was upon us and a number of weekend people were expected. It seemed certain that more people would get stalled on the pass, which is notorious for severe storms. It took about an hour to get there; we could travel only 15 or 20 miles an hour in the blowing snow. Actually the Jeeps were stopped a few times by drifts, which by then were up to three feet deep. We had to back up and blast our way through.

Within perhaps a mile of the pass we came to the stalled car and helped it out. Then we found another and helped it out. It's much easier to say this than it was to do. Each stuck car was a unique challenge that required some strenuous work and maneuvering. I believe that ultimately a total of eleven cars tried to get over the pass, eight of which had trouble. It was quite cold, and a high wind was blowing the gravelly snow across the terrain. At times I couldn't see more than twenty feet.

It was interesting to see how the men worked with one another. J.D. was the one they trusted for guidance in operating the vehicles. Most of the time he stayed in his Jeep and hooked on to one vehicle after another. There were a lot of problems and a lot of shoveling. And that's where Sherm Cranor came in—the other chief. He is a different kind of man, a large and powerful individual who seems to relish physical exercise. He had a large scoop shovel and he moved the snow like John Henry, a human snow machine. His sons are cast in the same mold, vigorous young men who know a good deal about working under these conditions. Two or three times it was necessary to hook both Danny's Jeep and J.D.'s Jeep in tandem to pull a car out—even with the powerful shoveling, pushing, and lifting by the other men. Nor was it simply a matter of getting them out of a single drift. Each car had to be pulled on down the mountain for a mile or two, to where the driving was safer. By and large everyone stayed together to make certain they all got safely off the mountain.

It was two-thirty in the morning by the time we got all the cars and people down into Taylor Park. We were thoroughly chilled, and took great pleasure in the hot coffee and good meal that Uncle Burl had waiting for us. We didn't get to bed until after three.

At nine this morning Danny and I piled into the Jeep and came back over Cottonwood Pass so I could get to Brown's Cabin. On the way we saw another vehicle stuck in the snow, but by the time we got there another Jeep had come in behind it and the driver was using his winch to get the fellow out. We stopped and helped with our scoop shovels. While we were there we mentioned the eight stalled motorists of the previous night, and the young man with the Jeep commented that he bet Danny made a lot of money off those people. Such an idea was so foreign to Danny that he simply didn't have a word to say. Later, as we were driving over the pass, Danny said he couldn't understand how a person could feel that way about simply doing what any neighbor would do. A true western neighborliness still exists in Taylor Park, and I was pleased to have been a witness to it.

At the Hartenstein turnoff Danny and I left the Jeep, divided our loads about equally, and packed into Brown's Cabin. I imagine each pack weighed about fifty-five pounds. I was quite proud of the fact that although Danny is twenty-one years old and considerably more muscular than I am, he still seemed to have more trouble with his load. I suspect the main difference is that I've been carrying a pack most of the time this summer. The fresh snow gave us a good opportunity to see what wildlife had used the area, and again it was apparent there are few large animals around. We saw one set of bull elk tracks, two sets of deer tracks, one set of coyote tracks, and numerous prints of squirrels, chipmunks, and pikas.

It was 30 degrees inside the cabin when we arrived, but we built fires in both stoves and soon it was cheerful and warm. The unpredictable generator was cooperative, so we had electric lights as well. It was truly a beautiful night. I don't think I've enjoyed an evening more or seen more beautiful moonlight since I've been here. The snow was fresh and clean and sparkled as though covered with millions of diamonds.

October 3

The temperature last night dropped to 4 degrees; today it rose to 46. Danny and I worked on the chain saw this morning. He has used chain saws since he was a tyke and he got it working better than it had been. He also detected a dangerous situation I had not been aware of. A considerable amount of gas was coming out through the exhaust system, and he felt there was a real danger the darn thing might blow up. We continued tuning it until finally there was indeed an explosion; I guess we blew out the piston. So that was the end of repairing the chain saw.

Then we got down to business with the good old arm-powered crosscut. We cut down a tree, sawed it into lengths, and hauled some of it in on the toboggan. We also went over the generator, but decided it was running well enough and didn't tinker with it. That was maybe the best thing we didn't do all day.

Danny left the cabin at about three, and I walked with him to the top of the pass. The pikas are still calling; I could hear them as soon as we came outside. I see one of them now, scurrying back and forth in the rock pile by the cabin; apparently they are still getting their food supply built up for winter. It's been over two weeks since I've seen any marmots, so they may have gone into complete hibernation. Most of the birds also seem to have vanished. The only species I see are some gray-headed juncos, the mountain chickadees, and of course the ubiquitous gray jays. The chipmunks are very active, and I have seen weasel and marten tracks. The martens seem to enjoy going into the outhouse, probably for different purposes than mine.

October 4

Another nice day, but crisp. I went up to film the pikas among the snow-covered boulders, but they were so sluggish that I filmed nothing.

The helicopter is scheduled to come in tomorrow morning and I have all the items ready by the door. I took one of the empty propane bottles to a spot seventy-five yards above the cabin and marked off a square with orange tape. I'm hoping the Army pilot can be enticed to set the helicopter down there, closer to the cabin. If they use the same spot they did last spring, it's going to be a long, hard haul to get all the equipment aboard.

October 5

Things began to happen so rapidly so early today I never even got to the weather station. The helicopter arrived at eight-thirty, which is about forty minutes before sunrise now. It circled several times over the area I had marked with tape. I thought I detected some reluctance to land there, and sure enough, they finally settled on the high bench above the cabin. They had some wood Charlie had sent in and also food and mail, which they offloaded on the bench. I started charging up through the snow to where the helicopter sat, and was within about fifty feet of it when suddenly, to my dismay, it rose and moved back toward the spot I had marked. The camera was sitting a few dozen yards from there, and since I'd already had one Beaulieu blown over in a windstorm and couldn't imagine explaining the loss of another, I did a wind sprint down the mountain to get to the camera ahead of the downblast from the chopper. I made it just in time.

After they landed they decided they liked my heliport; subsequently they made two more landings there during the day. I hope we can arrange to use this same helicopter at the termination of the project and that they'll land here again; it's very convenient.

I was amused at the way the Army operates. Apparently this crew is mostly interested in getting what they call high-altitude cargo maneuver training, so they have a very large crew—five men—to take very light loads of cargo. I had no more than a thousand pounds and they made three trips to take it out. But they seemed quite happy doing it that way.

On the second trip they brought me some mail, including a letter from Danny Herman saying the bighorn sheep were back along the reservoir and I ought to come back. This was a pretty hard decision. I had already invested good time in Taylor Park, with no positive results other than meeting the Hermans and getting people off Cottonwood Pass during the blizzard. But I finally decided that the availability of the helicopter was too good an opportunity to pass up. I had about twenty minutes to make the decision, pack my gear, and get aboard, and I did it.

The chopper landed me a short distance from the boat dock, and the Hermans ran out to help with my gear. After lunch we went down to the reservoir, glassed all of that country, and of course, the bighorn were nowhere in sight. This was frustrating. Apparently just two days ago about twenty-five bighorn were up against the cliffs here, where they would have been beautiful photo subjects. We tried a nearby area for elk, with the same result. We bugled for over an hour without a single response. I decided I'm not going to spend any more time bugling and chasing around in the Park. I made some phone calls and arranged to go to Gunnison and then to Lake City, near La Gorita Wilderness Area, where there seem to be bighorn within photographing distance.

October 6

I am now in Lake City, about fifty-eight miles southwest of Gunnison. It has been a long day and I'm pretty tired, having driven a good many miles in the balky, temperamental Jeep I borrowed from Danny.

Lake City is an interesting place. It is the county seat of Hinsdale County, a sparsely populated area. The 1970 census lists a population of 202 people, half of whom are in Lake City. Almost all the businesses are already closed for the winter. The restaurants and gas stations are open only during certain hours, which seem to change daily as the managers go fishing or hunting or somewhere else. I was fortunate to find a cabin with cooking facilities for only four dollars a night. This is a bargain, except that I am quite a distance from the wildlife country.

I arrived about three-thirty this afternoon, then drove to a place nearby where local people said there might be elk. I passed a ranch on the way and stopped to find out if I was getting close. The ranch turned out to be a working headquarters for the Outward Bound program. All the adult leaders were away, but a number of young people were there. The one temporarily in charge held a lottery to see which one might accompany me, and a young man just out of high school in West Virginia won (or lost?). He came with me, and we spent an hour trying to bugle elk. No response, and very few fresh tracks, so we went back to the ranch, where I shared some bread and wine with the young people.

I learned that all but two were vegetarians, which provoked a rather interesting discussion. I made the point that man has long been a meat-eating predator, initially a very primitive one. Through evolution he has become a more sophisticated predator, but still basically a carnivore. One of the fellows said he'd never thought about this before. Only a bit earlier he had been saying that he considered a person who would kill an animal no better than any other murderer!

Then I talked with a young man who said he intended to go on to college and take animal husbandry. He said he wanted to help sick and wounded animals. When I explained that animal husbandry is a branch of agricultural science aimed at the production of beef, mutton, wool, and so on, he was dismayed. *I* was also dismayed. Here was an intelligent young man who had chosen a career he knew almost nothing about. We agreed that what he really wanted to be was a veterinarian.

I returned to Lake City just before ten o'clock to visit briefly with Ron Blumberg, a 1968 graduate of Colorado State who is now wildlife conservation officer in Lake City. He had been out with the civil law enforcement authorities on, of all things, a drug roundup. Thirteen communities were hit simultaneously and forty-five or fifty people arrested. Most of the communities were small mountain towns, and most of the people arrested were those the local folk would call "hippies," who have moved in in considerable numbers lately. There's no question that the sale of marijuana and hard drugs has become a social problem in many areas in Colorado.

October 7

I arose early this morning, cooked a large breakfast, and was on the road by seven twenty-five. Ron Blumberg caught up with me about six miles from where I would have to leave the Jeep, and pointed out the trail and some of the physical features of the land. I set out on foot about ten and arrived a little before noon at what was described as bighorn habitat. It is quite different from the area around Brown's Cabin—broad open benches, ridgetops, and saddles, with very little vegetation. In the snow I crossed a set of adult black bear tracks.

The terrain was gentle and open, which made it difficult to get close to animals. I came to the top of a saddle in open grass and saw a big herd of bighorn sheep, but there was nowhere to hide. I spent about ten minutes getting the cameras ready, and just then three sheep—two ewes and a lamb—appeared in the saddle. They saw me instantly, spooked, and went tearing down the mountainside, as did the rest of the herd. I did get a few feet of this exodus, but not the close-ups I wanted.

I explored two other saddles Ron had described, and got some fair footage of three sheep lying down, but that's about all. As I was working around the contour of the mountain through the snow, I saw tracks indicating that a coyote had stalked and captured a ptarmigan, apparently in its snow roost. It was exactly seven o'clock when I returned to the Jeep, and beginning to get dark. I didn't reach Lake City until ten, when Ron Blumberg poured me a couple of drinks, which I much appreciated.

October 8

When I'd gone to bed at twelve-fifteen I was so tired I didn't think I was going to be able to change film, clean the cameras, and pack again for an early start. So I set the alarm for three, did those chores between three and four, then went back to bed and slept until five-thirty.

Today I was lucky. I came across five ptarmigan and was able to film them extensively. At first they were uncooperative, sitting motionless in the rocks or on the snow, watching me. Eventually I was able to show a ptarmigan starting toward me, a common trick, which sometimes makes the bird look as if it is going to attack. They were feeding on grasses and mountain dryad, a favorite food, and all five were in different stages of transitional plumage. One had turned almost solid white. I tried to show the orange spot over the eye and the numerous feathers on their legs and over their feet. Their tracks are very distinctive in fresh snow; they seem to have been made by three-pointed feather dusters. Finally I was able to get within eight feet of them. I left the mountain at three-ten, when the wind came up, reaching the Jeep at five.

I had gone about twenty miles back toward Gunnison when a bull elk and cow crossed the road. I stopped and two minutes later I heard a young bull bugle. This means the tension level is already high among the elk as mating season approaches. I responded with a bugle of my own and was rewarded by an immediate answer. I got my camera out and started down the slope, bugling and being bugled at about every five minutes. The slope was covered with aspen but most of them had dropped their leaves, so there was very little cover. I was concerned that the elk would see me, so when I got to the bottom I hid in some willows and continued bugling. This brought a reaction I have observed before when attempting to call elk. As soon as I stopped moving after each bugle the elk became suspicious. There was a silence for about five minutes, then I heard a bugle quite some distance up the mountainside. I was disappointed but I waited another five minutes, then tried again. Before I had completed the bugle he was responding from very, very close by, so close I couldn't believe he wasn't in full view. It was getting dark, but he sounded very hostile, snorting and whistling, so I thought he might come out in sight. However, when I bugled the next time there was no answer. Apparently he had come down close, investigated, and perhaps smelled me in the shifting wind.

I went back to the Jeep and started on, but around the very next bend were a cow and young bull. As I was digging the camera from the case they moved out of sight, so I tried another bugle and the bull responded immediately. A few seconds later the bull I had just left responded across the mountainside. To bugle a bull elk is really an unexplainable thrill. And when you succeed in bringing the bull in close and he begins to become angry and to snort and whistle, it is scary enough to make your hair stand on end. When that elk bugled so close to me in the creek bottom I began to look around for an aspen I could climb. It is not unheard of for elk to charge people. They've even charged people on horseback and in Jeeps, especially during the rutting season. And bugling is a great stimulant to them. I chuckled to myself as I got back in the Jeep amid the bugling of these two bulls. I felt as if I had set up communication between them—introduced them, so to speak.

I got back to Gunnison about seven-thirty, had dinner, and then headed for Taylor Park. Three miles north of Gunnison a state patrolman stopped me. He said my taillights were not working. I knew they were somewhat unreliable; the Hermans had told me to jiggle them if they went out. So I told the patrolman there was no problem, all you have to do is jiggle them. Of course, as often happens at times like that, the trick didn't work. Then he asked me for my license and when I told him I didn't have it he completely forgot about the taillights. The reason I didn't have it was simple, at least to me: what would I do with a license at Brown's Cabin? Except perhaps lose it. This explanation fell on deaf ears and the patrolman said I could "tell it to the court." He actually set a hearing at Gunnison County court on October 26. I told him this was an inconvenient time for me, since I would be at Brown's Cabin, but he was adamant and would not change the summons.

Just a brief sociological note. There's no question in my mind but that my treatment by the state trooper, which was courteous enough but rather brusque and unrelenting, was caused by my appearance. The mountain boots, the beard, and the long hair unquestionably stiffened his resolve. I'm sure that if I had been in a business suit, clean-shaven, he would have responded otherwise. In any event, I plan to send my driver's license to the court with a note of explanation in hopes that this will be adequate; I don't want to have to leave Brown's Cabin again. I've been away too much.

I got to Taylor Park boathouse at ten. Joe Starbuck and his wife, two of the people who had been stranded on Cottonwood Pass, were visiting with the Hermans, so I joined them. This was so enjoyable I broke out a bottle of Scotch I had brought as a present for the Hermans, and we drank and talked until one in the morning.

October 9

This morning, the day my family is due to arrive, the Hermans let me sleep in until eight-thirty. Then Danny and I hurriedly ate breakfast, cleaned up some of our stuff, and left in the Jeep. We were waiting at the mouth of Denny Creek when Ross Moser showed up at eleven-fifteen. Ross is concerned about my getting snowed in at the cabin with the radio and weather station equipment, which belong to the Forest Service. The same thought has occurred to me, and I've decided to ask the Army to send the helicopter the first week in November. This is exactly what Ross had come to suggest, and he agreed to contact the Army.

At about eleven-thirty my family showed up, along with Charlie Combs. They had left the car in Buena Vista because we were concerned that it might be vandalized out here. It was certainly good to see them. I haven't seen Sharon since her graduation from Colorado State on June 4. We all hiked to the cabin, including Danny and Charlie, who helped carry the gear. We talked about the episode of the state trooper and his apparent reaction to my long hair and rough clothes; Carol made a good point about that. She told Danny that she thought every man should let his hair and beard grow for at least a year sometime in his life, that it would teach him humility and give him some understanding about what life is like for people who look or act a bit different. Danny has relatively long hair and is growing a beard this summer. His parents are strongly opposed to this, and he listened intently to what Carol was saying.

Although I intend to get a haircut and shave when the filming ends, I must admit there have been a few times, such as now, when I think about keeping the beard—better groomed, of course—and even keeping my hair longer than I used to wear it. This may seem silly, but I can't escape the observation that it has made it a good deal easier to communicate with the younger generation.

I had left the cabin in a terrible mess when I caught the helicopter—a dishpan full of undone dishes, an unmade bed, dirty floors—but Carol and Sharon cleaned up the house and made supper. I admit I was glad to be a "kept" man for one day, after taking care of these things alone for so long.

October 10

This morning Mark and I got some firewood in while Carol and Sharon worked inside. I packed water and heated it, and Carol did a large portion of my washing. This is something I hated to have her do, but she was insistent, and it *was* good to get out of that job.

At about one o'clock I hiked up to the pass with them; they were able to stay only one day. It was really hard to say goodbye, although I knew I would be home in a few more weeks. The experience of having them here was enough to show me that I don't want to be a hermit or a bachelor for the rest of my life. I have never felt homesick here, as I have mentioned before. But it was wonderful to have them with me again, and again I was reminded what a wonderful family I have. They filled me in on all the details of what they have been doing: Carol's classes and work with minority groups and elderly people; Sharon's part-time job at a nursing home; Mark's outstanding work at school (I relate rather boastfully that he makes top grades and has been elected editor of the school magazine).

October 11

The weather is so beautiful it was hard for my family to believe my tales of wind and snow. I have been pestered today by the gray jays. They were fun while the family was here; Mark and Sharon put leftover pancakes on their heads, on their stomachs, anywhere, and the jays would swoop in and snatch the pancakes. They fed them so much, in fact, that today the jays expect to be fed every time I go out the door. Several fly almost into my face to remind me. Finally I got some bread from the cabin and spent about fifteen minutes feeding them. I would stick a piece of bread in my ear, on my head, in my teeth, and the jays would try to land in my beard and grab the bread. One of them missed and hit my lip, bruising it a little. They seem to miss Sharon and Mark after having such a big day yesterday.

Most of the snow is gone from the south side of Brown's Pass, but at least 50 percent of the basin around the cabin is still blanketed. Where the snow has melted, most of the yellows and reds of a few weeks ago have faded to brown. There are tracks of weasel and marten, but no sign of the marmots. The pocket gopher in front of the cabin has put up a fresh mound, and the pikas are still making conversation and adding to their hay piles in the rocks.

October 12

I spent part of the day packing up additional equipment and writing letters and narrating. I have not been able to do any taping since October 4, so I had a week to catch up on. I don't like to do this, but on the trip to Taylor Park and Lake City I was coming in every night at ten or later, getting to bed after midnight, and usually leaving before daylight. I simply didn't have the energy.

October 13

Again I did no filming today. I had to go over the generator, which has run more than two hundred hours since my last maintenance check. Then I prepared for the impending visit by the Landsburg people: I swept the cabin from top to bottom, set up the cots and sleeping bags, and split wood. The weather forecast includes a cold front moving in, so maybe the fellows will get some real alpine weather.

October 14

The temperature continues to drop gradually, as does the barometer. I am not seeing any big-game animals in the area; the weather change may have something to do with it. After breakfast I went looking for elk in South Texas Creek drainage, but I saw only two elk tracks less than twenty-four hours old in the entire two- or three-mile walk.

Shortly after noon I was on a high ridge overlooking Brown's Pass when I saw the crew hiking in. I joined them and was sorry to discover that Larry was not coming this time. There were Don Ring, Herb Lightman, Joe Longo, and Paul Desatoff; only Paul was here in July. Charlie Combs and Danny Herman brought the camera equipment in on two horses Danny had rented out of Taylor Park. Danny had come over the previous day and is keeping the horses at a cabin near the mouth of Denny Creek.

After a late lunch, the Landsburg crew began filming—gray jays landing on my fingers, taking food out of my mouth, and Brown's Cabin in the snow.

October 15

The weather continues to get colder, but we had a clear day for filming. Danny came in with one horse this afternoon, bringing some items we had requested. This evening we enjoyed a few drinks and some conversation, and again I was impressed with the dedication of the people involved in this production. They share a surprising ability to get about in this high country. Paul, unfortunately, has another severe headache on his first night here. He is an uncomplaining person and I don't know just how bad he feels.

October 16

Another day of filming. The weather is decidedly colder. The wind blew hard last night and it snowed intermittently all day.

This has not been one of my best days, and I feel a bit disgusted with myself. Last evening I downed four scotches while visiting with the fellows and then had a restless night, featuring severe headache and nausea. As a matter of fact, I had vomited five times by noon. Don wanted to film me looking ruggedly uncomfortable this morning, standing around in my long johns, building the fire, breaking ice in the water bucket, and I think he got some authentic scenes. The silly part of it is that I have been warning people not to drink much at this altitude. Don and Joe were very solicitous, but I think I was able to do my share and we went right ahead with the filming.

This evening we again talked for a while, although the fellows went to bed a little early because they are leaving first thing in the morning. Herb Lightman, editor of *American Cinematographer* and here to write about high-altitude photography, gave us an example of high-altitude hypnotism. He hypnotized Paul, though I wasn't thoroughly convinced that Paul was really out, and I'm sure Paul himself was confused about exactly what happened. The goal was to stop Paul's headache, which has haunted him on and off since he arrived. Paul said his headache wasn't completely gone but he did feel better.

It is always interesting for me to visit with the professionals connected with this project. Sometimes I feel a bit like a country bumpkin, not knowing much about film making or certain "big" names in show business. So there are moments when I feel envious of their knowledge of bright lights and beautiful people. But in other ways I feel sorry for them. I pity them first for having to live in Los Angeles, which I cannot help but conclude is a lousy environment for human habitation. They live there only because, to use their language, they dig its life style (and make a good living). In my mind, the small town of Fort Collins and the Colorado Rocky Mountain area in general is a much superior place to live, both for its beauty and for its intellectual and cultural community, which, along the front range—the Colorado Springs–Boulder–Denver–Fort Collins area—I think compares very favorably with any along the California coast.

It has also been interesting to hear the crew, both in July and now,

discuss their social activities, their affairs, their divorces, and all the exciting things they do. I must admit to not being able to keep pace on these
topics, but here again I feel more pity than envy. While in no way exer-
cising a moral judgment, it makes me feel very fortunate to have married a
wonderful woman and to have remained married to her for over twenty-
seven years and to have raised four children, each of whom I honestly believe by any standards would be considered outstanding.

October 17

I think someplace along the way I lost a day, but today should be Sunday,
October 17. Life at Brown's Cabin has changed substantially; all of the
fellows are gone and my honest feeling is one of great relief at being alone
again. I did enjoy the visit by Don and Joe and Paul and Herb. They are
all fine people and I learned a good deal. However, even they noticed that
it bothers me to have the place disrupted and my things moved around. I
would guess that most people who have lived alone feel the same way. In
fact, it wasn't as much of a disruption this time as it was in July, because I
was prepared for it. It's just that with five people living in a small cabin,
each doing a variety of chores, the normal routine changes drastically. I
suppose I am a compulsive housekeeper, but when I came back after saying goodbye, it looked like a disaster area. The floors were dirty, equipment was strewn all over, and of course beds, bedrolls, and utensils had to
be cleaned.

I want to comment on the excellent support of local people for this
project. Charlie Combs left his house this morning about five, coming in
partly by flashlight in blowing snow. This certainly indicates what kind of
person Charlie is—a man sixty years old who hiked four and a half miles
in, helped pack up the horses, then hiked four and a half miles out. And
Danny has made three trips over the Cottonwood Pass on a snowy dirt
road with his Jeep, and has spent most of a week getting the horses over
here and back, plus three trips to the cabin and other activity I probably
don't even know about. I will dictate a proposed letter of thanks, which I
feel is a minimum courtesy that Landsburg and I should extend to Danny
and Charlie.

I had to change the charts at the weather station today, and it was
difficult because the wind was blowing hard and the snow coming down
heavily. We got about six inches of fresh snow, and it looks like a winter
wonderland again.

October 18

Yesterday the temperature only got up to 29 degrees, and last night it dropped to 4½. I have both fires going full blast now, at 9 p.m., and the cabin is just barely comfortable. I spent over an hour cleaning the stovepipe; the joints were badly rusted together, and the stove has been drawing poorly and giving off little heat.

I snowshoed up to the top of Brown's Pass today but I did not see a single animal track—not even a squirrel or a pika. On the way back I found the tracks of a marten on top of my own tracks and followed them to observe the hunting pattern. It was following chipmunks, or at least their trails. In two places the marten tracks intersected the end of a chipmunk trail, where a tiny hole indicated that the chipmunk had burrowed into the snow.

While the snows blow around me and things are quiet I think I'll finish off my life story. I'm sure I have been inserting a lot of myself in the daily narrative—apparently this is unavoidable when you are alone with your thoughts as much as I have been this summer—but I'll make an effort to organize it chronologically and be done with it.

As I remember, I had just finished talking about all the money I had earned with the Sears, Roebuck order blanks and through various farming jobs. In addition to these two sources of income I had a $600 profit from the potato crop of 1939, as well as a few hundred dollars saved up from logging. Since this would have easily financed two or three years of college you might think I would have relaxed and enjoyed my time at the University of Idaho. But for as long as I could remember, my parents were several thousand dollars in debt, and I felt I needed to make enough money to help out at home as well as earn my college expenses. So I had various jobs. I worked in the extension mail room, where I was paid thirty-five cents an hour. I also bought small pies for eight cents apiece at a local bakery and peddled them at the university in the evenings for ten cents.

Another feature of college life was the emotional turmoil of that prewar time. During the school year of 1940–41, just prior to our declaration of war, two students committed suicide in our dormitory alone. Apparently both of them were suffering the combined strain of the continuing Depression and the imminence of being drafted.

The strain got to me, too. I remember during the late fall I rashly proposed marriage to the girl with whom I had been going more or less steady. That was just before Pearl Harbor. I was twenty and she was nineteen. To her great credit, she declined. Of course, I was dramatically upset, both about being rejected and about the coming war, so one dreary afternoon I took my .22 rifle and drove out into the countryside, debating the most efficient and least painful way of shooting myself. After a couple of hours of this I remember sitting on a rock, alternately laughing and crying as I realized what a ridiculous plan it was. Whether I came to my senses or just didn't have the courage to shoot myself is not clear, but no matter how bad things have gotten I have been grateful I didn't pull the trigger.

The date of December 7, 1941, remains vivid even today. It was a Sunday; I had just gotten up and was reading the comics when the radio announcer told us about Pearl Harbor. I again proposed marriage to my girl, she again declined, and I left college a few weeks later to enlist in the Air Corps. I couldn't meet the 20-20 vision requirement, so I went to Seattle to train for a job with Boeing Aircraft. After two weeks I saw a notice in an employment office near the docks; a company was hiring laborers in Kodiak, Alaska, at 96 cents an hour. That was more than I had ever earned, so I went. (In all of this I never wrote my parents; fortunately my children have never been so inconsiderate.) I spent three weeks as a laborer and then saw a notice of exams for carpenter jobs. I knew very little about carpentering but a good deal about taking exams, so a few days later I was making $1.46 an hour as a third-year apprentice carpenter.

At that point I began to be bothered by the fact that I was clearing $100 a week constructing Army barracks for GI's making only $21 a month. So I went to the headquarters of the 37th Infantry Battalion and offered myself as a soldier. They were rather nonplussed. My face had not known a razor since leaving Seattle, and I looked about as military as I do now. Nor had they ever recruited anyone in Kodiak; they didn't know the procedure. They suggested that I go back to the barracks and think it over. I did, and was back the next morning.

After they finally decided to take me on, I had rather unusual treatment. Not only did the Army buy all my carpenter tools, but the battalion commander, a colonel, furnished me with his Jeep and driver while I completed my civilian affairs. Any notion that I was in tight with the power structure was dispelled, however, on my second day in service when I was stopped by a captain and reprimanded for not taking a cigarette out of my mouth while returning his salute.

During the first week I helped unload ships. Then I learned to fire an M-1 rifle—a weapon I had never handled before—and was proud to make the sixth-highest score in the battalion, which placed me on the rifle team. Then I was back to carpentering, making, of all things, twelve-hole latrines, six holes back to back. In fact, I have had so much experience with latrines and outhouses that while a member of Toastmasters the only speaking prize I ever won was for a speech titled "Outhouses I have Known, or Barefoot Boy with Cheek." This was so well received they asked me to tape it for submission to Toastmasters International. However, better judgment, in the form of my wife, prevailed and I declined. She said I was making an ass of myself, so to speak; and thus a speaking career was nipped in the bud.

I spent seven months on Kodiak Island, one month at Adak, and fourteen and a half months on Amchitka, recently well known as the place where the AEC set off several underground nuclear tests. It is interesting, at least to me, that during the two long, cold winters in the Aleutians I dreamed about nothing more than getting a cabin in the mountains where I would enjoy good literature, do a little trapping, photography, and writing. Well, here I am thirty years later alone in a mountain cabin, doing photography, but little reading, and no writing or trapping.

From Alaska I was sent to the mainland for six months, where I joined the 75th Infantry Regiment, which was getting ready to go to Europe. I spent two months in Wales, then went across the Channel to France on December 19, 1944. Our unit entered the Battle of the Bulge in Belgium on December 24. We were not a famous outfit, but we certainly suffered casualties. In two days our battalion of 1,045 men took 660 casualties, including dead and severely wounded. We were in the Bulge for about four weeks. After that we went to Holland for a few weeks, then to the Colmar pocket in southeastern France, then to the Ruhr Valley in Germany. On V-E Day we were in Westphalia Province; then back to France for a few months, expediting the return of soldiers home. We would take in their battle-worn equipment and reissue brand-new stuff—a ridiculous procedure, expensive and completely unnecessary. But that was the way of the Army.

Throughout my service, because of the unusual circumstances of my enlistment and my total lack of basic training, they kept me out of the front lines. It's probably just as well; I might have been of more assistance to the enemy than to our own troops. So I was generally confined to supply work, where I served as private, corporal, staff sergeant, battalion supply sergeant, warrant officer, and finally as a lieutenant with the job of battalion supply officer.

The most significant event of my forty-four months of duty occurred far from the war with the Germans. On April 17, 1944, I was in Medford, Oregon, for four days and had leave to go into town each night. On the first night I met a girl and made a date for the second night. On the second night I returned to find that she was drunk and maudlin. On my way to find a bus back to camp, I heard music coming from the community hall, where the citizens of Medford were putting on a local dance for the soldier boys. I wandered in and there was Carol, from Michigan, spending the summer with friends in Medford. We made a date for the next night, and for the second time in my life I proposed marriage. Again I was promptly rejected, but I did succeed in getting a date for my last night in Medford. That evening I pleaded my case further and won a compromise ruling: she agreed to write to me at my next duty spot, Camp Phillips, near Salina, Kansas.

Four months later we were indeed married, in a beautiful Catholic church at St. Vincents, Kentucky. It was not easy, however. The church was vigorously opposed to marrying a Catholic to a non-Catholic. I was too obstinate to say that I was Catholic when, in fact, I had a number of reservations about Catholicism. We talked to many priests and I became frustrated and angry many times before one finally agreed to marry us. The only concession I had to make was that our children would be raised in the church. This was agreeable to me, because I had no church affiliation and yet wanted my children to be raised as Christians.

It was after this that I was sent overseas and finally, after thirteen months, discharged on December 14, 1945. I headed straight to Michigan to get my bride. We spent Christmas with my parents in St. Maries, and by January 3 I had rented a room in Moscow, where the University of Idaho is, and had a job in construction, building a concrete block factory. I vividly recall that crew of about a dozen men, almost all of whom were ex-GI's. Only another ex-lieutenant and I had been officers, so we endured a good deal of ribbing about being soft. There was a rush to complete the job and we worked ten hours a day under a hard-driving foreman. By early February, when I returned to the university, it was a balm to my ego to realize that the other ex-officer and I were the only two men from the original crew still on the job.

My objective in re-entering the university was to get a degree in agriculture and a job teaching in high school. But after one semester I knew the indoor life was not for me and I transferred to the college of forestry. I got my bachelor's in 1949, then went for my master's. Stewart Brandborg, who is now executive director of the Wilderness Society in Washington,

D.C., and I took our final exams a month early and left in May for the Salmon River country in Idaho, where he did his master's research on mountain goats, and I did mine on bighorn sheep. Though neither Carol nor I recognized it at the time, the several years we spent studying bighorn were an unusually rich and romantic part of our lives. Stewart and I lived in a one-room log cabin for a month until Carol and the two children joined us. Then I pitched a 14-by-16-foot wall tent for us to sleep in, and we would all eat in the cabin. Late in November, with six inches of snow on the ground, we finally moved to a motel room in Hamilton, Montana, about seventy-five miles north. I would go to Hamilton about once every two weeks, stay three or four days, then return to the cabin.

I spent about four years working on the bighorn research. I'd say one of the high points was the next winter, when Carol and I and the two children, then aged five and three, lived at the Flying B Guest Ranch on the Middle Fork of the Salmon River, twenty-two miles from the end of the nearest dirt road, fifty miles from an open road when the snows came. Our lone link with the outside, besides a shortwave radio that sometimes worked, was a ski-equipped Piper Cub, which dropped in mail and supplies. It came a grand total of three times between the first big snow in the fall and April 8, when we left.

To travel any distance from the three-room cabin required snowshoes; putting them on got to be as familiar as putting on shoes. That winter was a marvelous time for me and, I have since learned, for the rest of the family. In some ways it was like being here at Brown's Cabin, particularly during the last few weeks. Every other week I made a fifty-mile round-trip on snowshoes to study the bighorn, their predators, and their feeding patterns. My routine would be to leave early one morning and snowshoe ten miles to a camp in a cave where I had stashed firewood. The next day I went fifteen miles to another cabin, then back to the cave on the third day, and finally returned to our cabin on the fourth day. It was cold and sometimes miserable, but it was also great to be alive and alone in that wild country. Carol and I even felt resentful on April 8 when the plane came in to pick us up. The place had become our own, and we resented intruders.

I have had much the same feeling here. On many days I have heard a sound and fervently hoped it would not be someone coming into the basin. The days without visitors have been the best ones. I count the days alone, and try to extend my string of visitor-less days. I always feel let down when someone comes in—even a packer bringing needed supplies.

On the Salmon River we also took care of some livestock, which in turn supplied us with food. Every other day I hitched a team of horses to a sleigh and hauled hay to the landing strip, where I fed twenty-three horses and ten cattle. Fifty chickens, which were in my wife's domain, supplied plenty of fresh country eggs all winter, and we also had all the milk and cream and butter we could use from the cows. There were four deer hanging in the shed that had been killed by hunters, and since the deep snow prevented the hunters fom retrieving them, we ate them. It was the first time I had ever let wild meat age long enough for the enzymes to work, and the meat was tender and delicious. It was a marvelous time, too, for the two children. They saw many bighorn sheep, elk, mountain goats, and mule deer at close hand. They were out every day in deep snow, often cold and wet, yet they never had the slightest illness. Modern Americans seldom understand the toughness of their children—and their need to be challenged.

That fall I returned to Moscow and lived in a house with my sister and her husband and wrote my thesis. Carol took the children to Milwaukee. After I finished we packed all our worldly goods into a homemade trailer and went to Salmon to live in a small ranch house, where I began work as a big-game biologist for the Idaho Fish and Game Department. I continued my bighorn research and in 1954 published it in a 154-page bulletin which was the first technical bulletin ever published by Idaho Fish and Game. In the fall of 1954 I entered Utah State University to start my Ph.D. program in wildlife ecology.

That year I had a heavy course load and was unable to work at a part-time job as usual. We felt that additional money was needed, and Carol took a job as a waitress from midnight to six in the morning, when she would come home and make breakfast for the rest of us and get our two oldest children off to school. This was a tremendous effort on her part. I am afraid that it has not been until this summer that I have really reflected on the magnitude of her contribution. When I finally got my Ph.D. last June, the dean of the college gave her a special certificate during the graduation ceremonies, describing how much Carol has helped me over the past twenty-five years to get an education.

In 1956 we moved to Fort Collins, where I worked for the U.S. Forest Service, and this marked the beginning of what I might call the blah years. I celebrated my thirty-fifth birthday in 1956, and by then I knew that I was not going to be the boy wonder I had imagined in earlier years. Some things had gone right for me and others had not. I always enjoyed my field work but I disliked writing up the results. So I have never published as many papers as I might have. Also during this period I began to miss all the hikes and camping and river trips I had enjoyed with the Fish and Game Department. I seemed to spend all my time in the office. For four and a half years I was a project leader in charge of range research and for four and a half more a project leader in charge of wildlife habitat research. I can recall only one true vacation during the entire period. That was a trip to the Grand Canyon, Disneyland, Marineland, and the coast with all the children.

In 1965 I left the Forest Service for Colorado State University and a job guiding graduate students in research, along with some teaching. There the pressure for completing my Ph.D. grew more intense. We took even fewer vacations and literally all my evenings and weekends and official vacation days were spent on the degree work. After two years of that heavy schedule I sank into a depression. I had had surgery on my spine, was not responding well to it, and felt I was not doing a very good job at the university, or as a husband and father either. I took a special leave and spent three months alone in a two-room cabin near Pike's Peak. This helped, but did not cure, my back or my depression. I got all my data analyzed and about a third of the dissertation written, but it took another four years to complete it and get the degree.

Now that the documentary is almost done I have already begun to think about my schedule when I return to Colorado State. In fact, I woke up in the middle of last night planning the work that lies ahead, and couldn't get back to sleep. I simply must not allow myself to be chained again to the all-work–no-play regimen that has been so unkind to us all. I plan to sit down with Carol and make a list of the jobs and goals that are really worthwhile, being sure to leave ample time for vacations and just relaxing with the family. This I simply must do.

October 19

We're still getting snow and it looks like winter is really settling in. The weather station shows another half inch, which brings the total on the ground to around eight inches. The high temperature today was 12 and the low last night 3½. Happily, I found the load of wood that had come in on the helicopter; I had forgotten about it in all the excitement.

I spent most of the day photographing snow scenes, particularly patches of "red snow," which I was pleased to find. The color is often attributed to windblown dust, but usually it is caused by algae which adapt to living in the austere environment of the snowbank. Sometimes the numbers of algae are so great that a red snowbank will smell and taste just like watermelon, and it is tempting to make a meal of it. But experienced mountaineers know better. The algae have a very strong laxative effect on many people.

The algae have lots of company, including cold-adapted bacteria, fungi, and protozoa. None of these are visible to the naked eye, but they appear readily under a microscope. Altogether, these cryophilic, or cold-loving, creatures make up a complete ecosystem. We can define an ecosystem as an area of nature composed of interacting living and nonliving components, fueled by an energy source. A snowbank ecosystem is simpler than, say, an alpine meadow or even a rotten log, but the basic components are there. The energy source is the sun, whose radiant energy is converted to chemical energy by photosynthesis. The algae themselves, which perform this chore, are known as primary producers. Then there are the protozoa, which prey on the algae and thereby absorb the energy harnessed by the primary producers. Finally there are the decomposers, bacteria and fungi, which take up the energy from the bodies of dead consumers and producers. A neat chain.

These cryophiles need water to grow and reproduce, as do all organisms. In a snowbank it happens that even on a subfreezing day numerous pockets and drops of water are melted by the sun, and this is where the algae bloom. But there is a potential problem: researchers at the University of Colorado's Institute of Arctic and Alpine Research have found that these cryophiles can grow only at a temperature of exactly 32 degrees. What happens when the sun continues to heat the water beyond 32 degrees, and what happens at night? Remarkably, the meltwater in a snowbank does not get any warmer than 32; additional energy serves not to raise the water temperature but to melt more snow. When the temperature drops at night, the organisms simply cease growing until the next day.

Food might seem to be another problem; nothing can live by sunlight alone. Nourishment for these snowbank creatures comes from a number of sources, and again illustrates the ingenuity of life forms to adapt to extreme conditions. Oxygen and carbon dioxide from the air dissolve in the meltwater, where they are easily absorbed. The snow itself contains minute amounts of nutrients, including nitrates, phosphates, sodium, and potassium. Some of these come from the adjacent soil or from windblown debris; others originate as atmospheric dust brought to earth by falling snow. Tiny amounts of sea salts may drift airborne from the Pacific Ocean; slight remnants of a dust storm in Utah may settle here a speck at a time.

These snowbank populations are so sensitive that they vary in color according to the exact location of their snowbank. Snowbanks at or below timberline are usually populated by green algae. Banks in parts of the alpine zone which receive full sun for at least half the day are populated by red algae. And banks in intermediate zones usually feature orange algae. The only explanation I have heard for this distribution is that the ultraviolet-rich sunlight at high altitudes is harmful to most living cells; the red pigments seem to offer the most protection from this sunlight. Orange pigments provide somewhat less protection, and green pigments are the most susceptible, flourishing only where screened or sheltered from heavy ultraviolet radiation. In evolutionary terms, these red algae may have evolved the ability to manufacture red pigment so as to survive in high-altitude snowbanks. A dubious achievement in our eyes, perhaps, but all-important to these algae.

The protozoa here are represented by four or five species, all in very small numbers compared to the algae they prey on. This is true in most predator-prey relationships; there are thousands of mice for every hawk, for example. I have heard there are about 100 protozoans in each milliliter of snow water, versus perhaps 500,000 algae in the same volume of water. At the university I saw a nice demonstration of who was eating whom. Melted snow water was placed on illuminated microscope slides, and through the microscope I could see the protozoa as opaque little forms. When the slides warmed up in the heat of the lamp, the protozoa would burst and out would come twenty or more little algae.

The last link in a snowbank food chain is the decomposers, the bacteria and fungi which break down the corpses of dead protozoans and algae. This step is essential to release the nutrients locked up in those corpses for use by new generations of snowbank organisms.

October 20

A busy and interesting day, though I spent nearly all of it working around the cabin. The temperature was only 9 this morning, but it soared to 43½ in the afternoon and I was able to do the wash wearing only a light cotton shirt. For the first time I made a careful inventory, figuring out exactly how much clothing I would need if I leave on November 2. Then I washed just that much. This may seem lazy, but I'm darn tired of washing clothes.

While heating the wash water, I made a brief tour of the basin to investigate a report from three hunters that a herd of elk had moved over the Continental Divide from Kroenke Basin and headed into the timber below my cabin. Sure enough, tracks indicated that about fifty elk had milled around and bedded in the snow about 300 yards below the cabin. They were so close, and I didn't know to photograph them!

What I regretted even more was that a cow and calf had been wounded. In the compacted spots where they had bedded, side by side, were pools of blood. Their tracks then drifted downhill through the timber towards Texas Creek. Every few yards they would lie down, leaving blood each time. The herd seemed to be moving out of the country, but I doubt that the cow and calf made it out of Texas Creek drainage.

This incident leads me to reflect about past hunting experiences and my present attitude toward hunting. It has been several years since I have killed either a deer or an elk. I suppose the reasons that I stopped entirely a sport I had pursued avidly for many years are complex. Most important, I think, is that just before my son Alan was killed I had purchased a new Winchester shotgun and customized a .30-06 rifle to add to our collection of guns. Alan bought fancy cases for each gun and we planned a lot of hunting together. When Alan died, I seemed to have no more heart for using either gun. As a matter of fact, I have never shot at a game animal with the rifle, which I have had now for seven years. But perhaps I would have quit hunting anyway. Over the years I have become increasingly aware of how few really good sportsmen there are and how difficult it is, even with the best intentions, to avoid leaving crippled animals.

Let me elaborate a little. As a biologist and ex-hunter, I do not subscribe to the idea that hunting is a dirty, cruel business. Nature also can be cruel in her treatment of old and sick—and sometimes healthy—wild animals. Starvation and disease on overpopulated ranges, severe weather conditions, the normal process of predation, all cause wild animals to die in ways not pleasing to human sensibilities. Man has evolved as a meat-eating predator, though technology has made him an exceedingly efficient one. Therefore, I shouldn't need to point out that the desire to hunt is not a recently acquired defect of character as some anti-hunters seem to imply. Further, I assume it is generally understood that it is loss of habitat due to man's activities rather than hunting that has most decimated wild-life populations in the past century. However, I'm not sure that most people know that properly harvested (hunted) big-game herds are often healthier than unhunted populations. That is, animals may be bigger, more fertile, more disease-free when hunted regularly, largely because they are kept within the "carrying capacity" of their habitat, and thus have more and better quality food to eat.

It is also important to recognize that predators, like coyotes or mountain lions, seldom "control" a population of large herbivores, like deer or elk. At their most efficient, they usually only "dampen" extreme fluctuations in population numbers. What generally happens when a healthy deer or elk herd is not hunted is that their numbers increase rapidly until they greatly damage food supplies; then, particularly during harsh Rocky Mountain winters, the animals may succumb in large numbers to starvation and diseases resulting from poor nutrition.

Although I agree that there are these positive results from hunting, I disagree with certain allegations often made by biologists and hunters. First, I do not agree that disastrous ecological consequences necessarily result from *not* hunting large, wild herbivores such as deer and elk. There is little question that suddenly to stop hunting a hunted herd would have deleterious effects on habitat and wildlife populations in the short-term, as I have described, and would change both in the long-term. The question turns on whether these changes must always be considered bad. I do not believe that they should.

After the initial die-offs, and now with fewer animals, the habitat would make some recovery, although it is likely that some of the more palatable plants might be eliminated and eventually be replaced by less nutritious plants. Ultimately the herd would become less productive; that is, not as many young would be produced or would survive. After a number of years of no hunting, other changes might take place, such as animals being smaller or males having smaller antlers. Such a circumstance certainly would not be desired by a game biologist managing a big-game herd for public hunting. However, many people interested in wildlife do not wish to hunt animals for meat or trophies; they may be more interested in viewing or photographing the animals in their natural habitats.

Perhaps the sharpest difference I have with those who aggressively promote hunting involves interpretation of quality of the hunting. It has been my privilege to know and hunt with some excellent sportsmen who not only observe wildlife laws but also know a lot about the animals and try to observe strict ethical codes in pursuing their sport. But my experience tells me that such hunters are the exception, not the rule. I would classify only a minority of hunters as truly high-quality sportsmen; conversely I would guess there is a small minority—perhaps 10 percent—that violates hunting laws and ethics consistently. I would split those in between into two roughly equal groups. Hunters in the "better" of these two groups have good intentions, although they may at times succumb to expediency, opportunity, inexperience, poor judgment, or greed. Shooting from a busy highway, going into a farmer's field without asking permission, leaving gates open, shooting when an animal is too far away or only partially seen are examples of misdemeanors that these hunters may commit. I can think of a hundred legal, ethical, and commonsense infractions that are apt to occur (and many will) on any major hunting trip and in the lifetime of every well-intentioned hunter. For hunters in the other half— often far from home and unknown in the neighborhood—the probability of violating legal and ethical constraints is limited only by opportunity.

Yet even these "opportunists" would probably respond with reasonable behavior if they knew what was expected, and hunter education is a possible answer. Already I see progress over the old Rod and Gun Club's almost exclusive emphasis on fishing and hunting which was so prevalent when I became a field biologist in the late 1940s. Now the management and biology of wildlife receives more attention. Much more could and should be done. Teaching neophyte hunters, whether young or old, too often still *begins* with instruction on the characteristics of the gun, how to handle it, take care of it, shoot it. When I challenge this training sequence, I have been told that people are interested in guns and shooting but that they become bored with the ecology, life history, or management of wildlife. Work I have done in the past few years with 4-H kids in wildlife management and habitat improvement projects has proved to me that this does not have to be so.

I would like to see every licensed hunter required to reach a reasonable level of understanding of management principles and ecological relationships *before* being taught the care and handling of guns. Both are important, but to emphasize guns over biology is wrong. In frontier times, the attitude that hunting was a right was understandable. Today, hunting is a privilege, not a right. It should not be given until earned—and should be denied when violated.

Of course, right now I am upset by seeing this cow and calf shot and wounded, knowing they will not even provide meat for some hunter's table. All I am trying to say is that I acknowledge hunting as a traditional, honorable sporting activity, although too often participants do not conduct themselves in honorable ways. I recognize that harvest of wildlife, particularly big game, is a useful management tool that helps to maintain healthy herds and habitats, but I disagree with biologists and hunters who project scenarios of permanent ecological disaster if game herds are not hunted. Finally, I believe that hunting will and should continue in this country except where nonhunting enjoyment of wildlife is an overriding consideration. At the same time, I strongly believe that new approaches and more intensive training of hunters are imperative; and that the penalty for proven unsportsmanlike conduct (not just illegal acts) should be denial of hunting privileges.

October 21

Another nice day, quite warm, practically no wind. This is the calmest period I've recorded since coming here.

I started to make a "heliport" for the helicopter, shuffling along on snowshoes, packing an area about twenty-five by forty feet, hoping to make it hard enough for landing. I also hauled two bottles of propane on the toboggan, one at a time, to the landing site.

I had just come in and was taking off my boots when I saw a weasel carrying something bulky in its mouth up the hill. I grabbed a camera and took off in slippers and shirt sleeves, up past the weather station. The weasel was carrying a pika. It kept just beyond camera range and I succeeded only in getting thoroughly chilled. This was disappointing because the weasel is now completely white except for a bit of dark down its back and a black tip on the tail. This white creature moving over the white snow with a dark pika in its mouth created an eerie visual effect. Much of the time I could see only the pika, suspended above the snow as though on an invisible wire.

October 22

I saw one of the elk hunters again; they were still trying to intercept a herd of about fifty elk down by Texas Creek. I went down there after they had gone and saw the tracks of two elk and three deer, but little else. Things are generally quiet now except for the gray jays around the cabin. I think there are six of them, probably the same ones who have been here all summer.

October 23

At seven twenty-five I left the cabin with pack and camera to hike down to Texas Creek, up to Magdalene Gulch, and farther on into Magdalene Basin. I had seen some tracks yesterday with the spotting scope that I thought were elk, but they turned out to be deer and coyote tracks. I had seen them from a distance of four and a half miles and was amazed that these small footprints could show up so distinctly. I was back at the cabin at five, exhilarated at having traveled alone through the country and at having seen no elk hunters.

October 24

Today I came close to getting good weasel footage. I was up at the rockslide filming pikas, and no more than two minutes after I left to change film a weasel moved right in. I was surprised at its bold move, but by the time I was ready to shoot it was moving through the upper end of the slide. Once again I seemed to be a day late and a dollar short.

This weasel was almost porpoiselike in its hunting technique. It would take long, slow, graceful bounds, then suddenly dive into the snow, where it tunneled feverishly, emerging just seconds later eight to twelve feet farther on. It would shoot straight upward out of the snow, turning and twisting, undoubtedly striving for altitude to get a better look around for prey and possible sources of danger.

I hadn't taken time to put on snowshoes, and the weasel lost me in the willows while I was puffing along waist-deep in the snow.

I had to spend a lot of time on the stovepipe again today. Apparently this is a result of burning wood that has a great deal of pitch in it. The first day after cleaning the pipe the fire drew like mad. The next day I had to close the lower draft a bit to keep the stove from smoking. This has worsened over the last four days until this morning it would hardly burn at all. I wish I had some Red Devil, which is what we use for the fireplace at home. You just sprinkle this into the fire and it keeps the stovepipe really clean. Here, I have to let the fire go out completely, which is easy; then disassemble the entire pipe, a piece at a time, clean it, and put it back together, which isn't easy. This involved seven (I counted them) trips to the roof and back. Where the pipe goes through the roof it is attached with metal screws, and a big problem is to get the pipe lined up so the screws will go back in again. And it took a crowbar to pry the carbon loose from the insides. It was coated so hard that it reminded me of the time I tried to bake brownies up here in a metal pan. By day's end I was covered with soot from head to foot, so this meant another bath and hair wash. But it was worth it: when I lit the fire this evening it leaped into life with a gratifying roar.

October 25

I forgot to mention that I have taken to filming the scenery while sitting in the outhouse. It was so beautiful from there just after our light snow, the mountains dusted with white, that I just sat on the seat and filmed away.

A winter phenomenon I now notice is the packing of snow around the stunted, high-altitude trees. One reason the Krummholz stands can survive up here, above normal timberline, is that this packed snow gives the lower part of the plants protection from the wind and severe temperature fluctuations. Equally important, the snow provides extra moisture when it melts in the spring, and soil temperature remains more stable. A number of flowering plants flourish in these sheltered pockets that could not otherwise endure the harsh conditions at this altitude: marsh marigolds, rose crown, the snow lilies with their yellow flowers, and, most typically, Jacob's ladder with its dainty leaves and sky-blue flowers.

In these distinctive Krummholz zones, the spruce, fir, pine, and other trees all have a "flagged" or "sheared" shape, with most of the branches extending downwind, away from the trunk. This pattern is created by the cold, hard prevailing wind, which tends to kill off new growth of needles and shoots, leaving the more vigorous growth on the leeward side.

Krummholz islands often create adjacent zones of unusually harsh conditions. This happens because wind diverted by the islands sweeps with extra fury along a path on either side of them. A distinctive community of plants has managed to survive in these zones, and they are different from the normal alpine species. The width of the zones is ten to thirty feet or so, and seems to depend on the size of each island. On warm days now we have some thawing around the islands, where the dark soil has been swept free of snow and absorbs sunlight. When the zones refreeze, however, the plants suffer doubly as the meltwater hardens to a crust of ice. So in addition to exposure to the harsh winds, each plant endures extreme temperature changes, fluctuating sharply from season to season and even from day to day.

Another cruel climatic trick up here is the way some plants are "cheated" out of their rainfall. I have called this area a desert, and it actually is, even though the annual precipitation at Brown's Cabin is thirty inches. (That's what you would find in the heart of America's grain belt—far more than the fourteen and a half inches we get in Fort Collins.)

Yet the soil here is probably drier than it is at Fort Collins and the plants must be as efficient at retaining water as desert plants. One reason is that the high wind evaporates the water faster. In addition, the steep slopes allow heavy rains to run off downhill rather than percolating through the soil. But equally important is the nature of the soil itself. Much of it consists mainly of sand, stones, and even large boulders, all of which have poor water-holding capacity. Where rain or snowmelt does sink into the soil, it drops fast past the root zone, beyond the reach of thirsty plants.

October 26

When I went to the weather station this morning I saw that the barometric pressure had been dropping, and today, sure enough, we've had a weather change. It began snowing this afternoon, and the temperature has gone down, reaching a high of only 24½, with the wind howling and gusting up to 45 miles per hour. I haven't been able to hold the camera steady, even on the tripod. I would say that this lightweight tripod is totally inadequate to the task up here.

Sometimes I wish the winds wouldn't blow so hard. During the last few days they blew a piece of roofing off. I didn't see it happen, but after the snow today I noticed water dripping on the floor near the stove. I ran upstairs and saw a patch of daylight through the roof. Once in a while I get uneasy when these terrific gusts hit the old cabin. It creaks and moans and I start wondering about the rest of the roof. Knowing that Charlie put it on, and knowing how stingy he is with nails, I can't help but wonder if it might not just become airborne.

October 27

The wind is up even higher. Charlie was coming in today with food, but since there is ten inches of snow on the level and twenty in drifts, I didn't want him to come in all the way. I know he doesn't like to use snowshoes, and it's tough going when the snow is up to your knees. Two or three days ago I told him I would meet him halfway, at the Hartenstein Lake turn-off. I repeated this twice and he came back with "Yes, I understand everything you say, okay."

This morning I headed down the mountain at exactly nine o'clock, as arranged. I was especially eager to see him, because he was bringing some Red Devil for the stovepipes, which are already clogged again. Well, we had another communication failure, and it wasn't electronic. We have both been traveling on what we call the switchback trail through the timber, but without any notice Charlie decided instead to go up through the meadow. As I was coming down through the timber, we would have missed each other cleanly except that I heard a sound from across the valley and whistled a few times and called loudly.

Sure enough, I heard Charlie call back—from the meadow, already a little nearer the cabin than I was. I went across the creek to join him, but he kept on toward the cabin. Finally I shouted, "Where in the hell are you going, Charlie?" He said, "Up to the cabin." When I finally caught up with him I asked if he hadn't understood that we were supposed to meet at the turnoff, and he said that yes, he understood, but he wanted to visit Brown's Cabin one more time. I'm completely at a loss in trying to make out the workings of Charlie's mind.

By the time we got back to the cabin it was nearly one o'clock. We built up the fires, heated some soup, and did some visiting, as there always seems to be a good deal for us to talk about. For some reason I'll never understand, he wanted to fix the two-wheeled cart, which hasn't been of any use to anyone. I think he simply needs to leave things in good condition so that other people can use them, and this is really an admirable quality.

I received a tape from Gus Swanson, my department head, who told me I would be teaching a newly approved course in basic ecology. I am looking forward to this. It will be nice to give a new course and develop it as I want. I also like the idea that I shall have students from the humanities and social sciences as well as the hard sciences.

I also learned in a letter from Carol today that we are invited to a coming-home party for the dean of the College of Forestry and Natural Resources, who has been in Norway. This will be on the evening of November 4, so with my present schedule I'll be shaving it pretty close.

October 28

I'm glad my weather instruments record the history of what's happening up here. It seems like every time I have visitors, whether it's Charlie or my family or the Landsburg people, the weather is serene. Again, it was a fairly nice day until Charlie left; in the late afternoon it really began to storm.

I didn't understand until this morning the real reason Charlie insisted on coming all the way in to the cabin. I must admit that yesterday I was a little disgusted to think I had made a five-mile walk for nothing, but now I realize that this was a sentimental journey for him. It was in the mid-1930s when he spent three years at Brown's Cabin. He's been in many times since, most frequently since 1966, when he filed the mining claims. In 1967 he did major repair work, even buying seven or eight burros, which he kept in the meadow at the bottom of Denny Creek trail, and hiring a man to watch them and work on the cabin. Apparently the fellow was much better at sleeping and drinking wine than at working, but Charlie paid out several hundred dollars in salary, plus the price of the burros and the cost of fixing the cabin. All of this activity apparently stemmed from a dream, which he had held since the 1930s, of returning to live in Colorado, someplace near enough to the cabin so that he and his family could spend the summers here. I've failed to appreciate fully how Charlie feels about the cabin.

Today Charlie and I cut some wood—a vital chore if the weather forecast is to be believed, and one thing I could do and still visit with him. We spent two hours at it, piling enough in the cabin to last until my departure, unless it gets really cold. I packed down the heliport again with snowshoes. Then, while we were having lunch, Charlie told me about a scheme he has been working on, and I was more than a little touched. He has gathered all the legal papers for the five mining claims and the cabin and he intends to turn them over to me. Even Charlie suspects that the Forest Service is not really interested in developing this as a historic site, so he talked quite seriously about wanting me to take over and work the claims.

I can't get Charlie off my mind. My heart really went out to the dear old guy today, and his reactions to leaving the cabin. He has put a lot of time and love into this place, and is resigned to leaving it all behind. He has finally accepted the fact that his wife is unalterably opposed not only to coming to Brown's Cabin but even to living in Colorado. She wants to return to the West Coast, to Tacoma, Washington, where they have a house. So, in what I'm sure has been an agonizing decision, Charlie has decided to go along, to leave for Tacoma just as soon as this project is completed.

I want to add, parenthetically, that the only reason Charlie is still in Colorado at all is his interest in the documentary. He insisted that they stay until it is all finished and I am out of here. Even in concrete terms, we owe Charlie a great deal. We paid him $400 to use the cabin, but I know that the value of the materials and equipment he brought to the cabin and made available for our use has come very close to that. This material was not to improve the cabin, because he knew all along that this was the last summer he would be here. He has also never been willing to write down the mileage he puts on his pickup for the project; but I would say that he has driven over a thousand miles for us. His cooperation has meant better service than we could have had through the Forest Service; in fact, I don't see how we possibly could have operated without him. He has arranged for packhorses, bought food, picked up mail, and altered his schedule to be at the radio at the appointed time every day, seven days a week, throughout the summer and fall.

Certainly some of these favors have resulted from a personal friendship that has developed between Charlie and me, and I will take responsibility for reciprocating. One thing I know he will enjoy is some color prints of the cabin and the surrounding country. He has never had any made, and I know he really does love pictures of these high mountains. But I am sure that the Landsburg staff will want to write Charlie a formal letter commending him for his work and friendship. This gesture will mean a great deal to him.

Anyway, after we had eaten lunch I snowshoed to the top of Brown's Pass with Charlie. I had sort of left him behind as I reached the top, and turned to find him. As I stood watching him I could see his head slowly turn as he swung his gaze all the way from the Three Apostles eastward to Mount Harvard, taking in the whole panorama. Still not realizing the emotions he was going through, I said jokingly, "Well, Charlie, I guess you'll have to soak up enough of this scenery to last you a long time." I was startled by his unnecessarily hearty laughter, and when he came closer I could see that his eyes were glistening with tears. It was then that it hit me what this trip was all about.

October 29

The temperature dropped to 2 below last night; I couldn't help thinking of the efforts of Don Ring and Joe Longo one morning to get some ice on the surface of the water bucket so they could film me breaking it. Don also wanted to show my breath in the cabin, but it wasn't cold enough. He should be here now. It only got up to 13½ this afternoon. But the wind is the big story; from nine twenty-five yesterday morning to ten-fifteen this morning the machine recorded 145 miles of wind—more than four times the average daily velocity during September. I woke up time and again last night to hear the wind howling and feel the cabin swaying.

And the snow is really coming down. I put a marker in a place I can watch from the window; about noon today the eighteen-inch mark disappeared, and now I estimate about twenty inches.

I saw no living creature all day; even the jays have left for shelter in the dense forest below. Recently the weasels and martens have been coming to the cabin. Twice lately I've heard a marten clambering on the roof, and I've seen tracks of the weasels all around the cabin and on the windowsills, from where I assume it peers inside. They also inspect the outhouse. I get a warm feeling knowing that other living creatures share this place with me and I would be quite lonely without them.

Since it was such a miserable day I, too, spent most of it in shelter—in my case, the cabin. I did make snowshoe trips to the weather station and to pack the heliport. Otherwise I pretty much tended the stoves and swept snow off the floor. New holes in the cabin have revealed themselves, thanks to this heavy wind, and snow is being forced into every room. At noon I discovered that even my bed was covered with a thin blanket of snow.

The snow also gave me a fright. Any time one of these blizzards hits the mountain my pulse quickens. This is not to say that a storm is unpleasant; I actually look forward to being enveloped by it. And I would say that my senses sharpen. I hear, smell, and feel things more clearly. My emotions seem to combine elation and dread. I'll usually stand looking out the glass in the door as the storm moves into the basin, then have an urge to get out and move around in it.

So about two o'clock I decided to go up to the weather station for a second time, mostly as an excuse to find out what the storm was like. The wind was blowing a constant 40 or 50 miles per hour, and I couldn't see too well. In fact, I couldn't even make out trees more than a hundred feet ahead. When I started to return, suddenly the storm worsened and all I could see was a white blanket of snow. After about three minutes of wandering along, I realized I no longer knew where I was and had no way of finding out. Fortunately just at the moment of that realization the wind let up for a few seconds and I could see. I discovered I was missing the cabin by at least a hundred yards, heading into the upper end of the rockslide. Another ten minutes in the wrong direction and it could have been my last walk.

Well, it was a short-lived incident, but it certainly added zest to the day. The walk was rather ridiculous and totally unnecessary, but it made me think a little about the need we have for challenges. I have thought about young people and their drug culture, which admittedly I don't understand, but it seems to have something to do with the lack of meaning-ful challenges offered by our affluent and protective society. I think this is why I was pleased when our oldest son, Alan, wanted to take up mountain climbing and avalanche work. For the same reason I gave approval when my daughter came to me with a release form required to go sky-diving (al-though I was grateful when she couldn't fit the activity into her busy schedule!). Gary, too, briefly took up parachute jumping, and once I took him at age fifteen to a wilderness area in Idaho and left him there totally alone for three months. My own challenges during this summer have meant a lot to me and caused me to think about the needs of other peo-ple, whose responses might be similar.

This brings me to something entirely different. It may seem strange, but I have been thinking about the time when I get so old and frail that I'm able to do very little for society. Perhaps living here alone, depending wholly on myself for my day-to-day needs, has made me more aware of how important it is to me to be self-sufficient. I've been thinking about men who have lived in cabins and various primitive situations in back-country, and the unfortunate results of their moving to a city. Both Sharon and Carol have met such people in their work and told me how unhappy these people become when they can no longer care for them-selves.

I guess I'm beating around the bush, but what I'm leading up to is that I have made a decision not to spend my last years in a rest home. I know that most of them have excellent facilities, with good medical care, good diets, and good recreation programs. But I have strong doubts whether this is the best solution for all the people there. My daughter Sharon agrees that a negative aspect of nursing homes where she has worked as an occupational therapist is that the elderly are deprived of the opportunity to make personal decisions about their lives. Even minute choices are taken out of their hands—what they're going to eat, when they're going to eat, when they're going to get up, when they're going out for a bit of exercise. I've talked with Carol about this and I think she agrees with me that we should somehow maintain our own home and in-dependence as long as we both live, no matter how inconvenient and painful it may be. As long as we can struggle to exist, we should make that struggle.

Maybe I'm overdramatizing the situation, but if I spend my last months or years as a widower, and if I am unable to be productive in so-ciety, I would like to move to a remote cabin in the mountains, perhaps even Brown's Cabin, where I would have to exert myself physically to survive. I firmly believe that if I do that my last years will be more rewarding than if I succumb to the confines of a rest home. This may be hard to do in our society; there are lots of agencies who are looking after our supposed welfare once we are unable to look after it ourselves. But somehow I am going to avoid that trap and get away to a place of independence for my last days. I vow that this is the way it's going to be, although of course that's an easy vow to make at age fifty when death still seems a long way away.

October 30

Winter has moved right down on top of us. Last night it was 11 below zero, and a lot of what I did today—and I was pretty busy—had to do with keeping warm. I had to pack the blankets up over the kitchen door again. So much wind was coming in that the stoves couldn't keep up. The water pails were frozen solid this morning and the inside temperature was 24. All I did outside was to pack down the heliport and chop some wood, which is disappearing as though it were going out of style.

I got word yesterday from Charlie that the helicopter is scheduled to arrive here at eight o'clock on Tuesday, November 2. So I've begun packing in earnest. It's amazing how much equipment is scattered around the cabin. I've begun to gather it all and tape it in boxes.

The jays have gone now for the second day in a row. I miss them, and somehow it bothers me that they are going to be left here in the cold of winter, although I suppose they have been left here for the last few thousand years without suffering. I guess I feel mostly that they'll miss me. I'm going to leave some food on stumps around the cabin so they'll at least be able to feast for a few days after I've gone.

I might mention that I have been plagued lately by chapped hands. This is surprising, because my skin has a good deal of natural oil, but even though I've been applying special salve and using hand lotion they have been getting steadily drier for the last month. One thumb and two of my fingers keep cracking to the point that they have gaping splits that bleed a little every day.

As long as I'm reduced to talking about my physical ailments I might as well admit that this bursitis, or whatever is plaguing my back, has been turning me every way but loose for the last three days. It seems to be associated with temperature changes, and in this cold it's difficult to concentrate on what I'm doing when a wave of pain hits.

October 31

The weather let up a bit last night; it only got down to 1½ degrees above zero. But it was a difficult day. I had looked forward to it because I was doing my final permanent photo points in both movies and stills. Everything is now covered with snow and the varying shades of white from before sunrise until after sunset are indescribably lovely. However, I had only a few moments of escape from high-level pain. I'm still optimistic that regular exercise and the sauna bath are going to cure it. My doctor has told me I am disposed toward arthritic-type pains and that I have this to look forward to in my old age. But I'm not convinced that it's going to be a major problem once I can get this particular siege under control.

At about three o'clock, after finishing the photos, I took some tools to the weather station and began dismantling it. It got really cold because the sun went down about three forty-five. A good deal of ice had formed around the precipitation gauge, but the dismantling went smoothly and I soon had the more delicate instruments loaded on the toboggan. I also brought down the weather shelter itself and the large precipitation gauge. If the helicopter pilot decides he's going to land on the bench by the weather station and not on my packed heliport near the cabin, I'm going to make him haul all the weather gear back up the hill.

November 1

A fantastic day to start a new month, mild most of the day, though I'm a bit concerned about forecasts of another cold front; the worst part is high winds for the mountain regions. As a matter of fact, Charlie told me during the radio check tonight that the Army has changed the helicopter arrival time from eight o'clock to nine tomorrow, and the Forest Service has asked me to turn on my radio at seven-thirty and leave it on for messages. Their original plan to bring two choppers has changed; now just one is coming.

I finished packing today, and it's taken me longer than I think it should have. I must have put in close to a full day. In addition to three large trunks—two of Landsburg's and one of my own—there are about twenty-five boxes and cartons and the Forest Service tools and equipment. I hauled out to the heliport everything that won't be harmed by snow and wind, and all in all I'm pretty proud of my planning. I am down to the last bottle of propane, so I ordered just the right amount. Well, it's probably more luck than planning.

There were a surprising number of details to take care of, like putting keys on wires and numbering them so they can be identified. I'm going to leave the cabin all locked but hang some keys outside. That way people will use them rather than break into the cabin. I talked this over with Charlie, and he feels that very likely there will be people in here this winter with snowmobiles, and certainly quite a lot next summer, if my experience is any indication.

In late afternoon there were some fantastic snow swirls, boiling and blowing up over the ridge between here and South Texas Creek. I took movies but had bad luck with the still camera. I was using that damned film loaded someplace in Los Angeles; sometimes the cassettes are not completely full, and most of the time they're packed so tight they rip out the perforations on the side of the film before I can get them going through the camera.

Until today, I'd been lucky—and had always detected quickly when film wasn't going through the camera. But this afternoon, just when I was getting spectacular backlighting and a sunset that was just out of this world, with colors changing by the minute, it happened. When I went to rewind I found that none of the film had gone through at all. I was really furious for a while, but of course nothing could be done by yelling. And I didn't even have the jays to yell at.

November 2

Well, here it is, the long-awaited November 2, my last day at Brown's Cabin. The hell it was; you'll notice that I'm still narrating. I got up at six-thirty this morning, had an early breakfast, tore up my bed, packed the bedding, and at seven-thirty called Charlie on the radio. He said the chopper still planned to be in between nine and nine-thirty and they wanted me to build a smoky fire. So I quickly got some pitch and green limbs out to the heliport. I was skeptical about starting a fire; the wind had blown hard all night and was still blowing, and I wondered if I'd want to be flying myself. Sure enough, about five past nine Charlie came back on and said that the helicopter couldn't get off the ground at Colorado Springs and that they would try again at the same time tomorrow.

Well, this was not so terribly disappointing. I had run out of some of the more palatable types of food, but I still have a lot of cans of meat and some vegetables and fruit. I have enough food to last more than a week, and my wood supply is in pretty good shape.

Actually it was sort of nice to feel that I had an extra day; I certainly could use it. I took more footage of some scenes I still needed, including a snow avalanche that has cut loose over on the ridge between here and East Texas Creek. That's the same slope where the avalanche buried Charlie Combs in the winter of 1936, until he dug himself out.

While I was wandering around the basin two ptarmigan flew across my view to some Krummholz cover and I was able to get perhaps twenty feet of them. They are now totally white, unlike the two-toned birds I photographed about three weeks ago near Lake City.

As I worry about the helicopter and move all the equipment around and think about leaving Brown's Cabin, I find myself with mixed emotions. In a way I dread leaving this quiet place and returning to the busy life that certainly awaits me, particularly as I face the job of developing a brand-new course at the university.

I suppose it might be a subconscious desire to stay that has led me in recent days to become much more affectionate toward the small creatures that have shared Brown's Cabin with me. I have found myself feeding the gray jays much more frequently and, in fact, have left the door open to let them come in and hop around the cabin. I never did this during the first months here. They have even fed at the table and around my feet. Then they would forget where the door was and fly into a window. I have been amazed by their reaction to hitting a windowpane. In town, when songbirds fly into the house, they will literally beat themselves to death against the glass if we don't catch them; then there is a flurry of feathers as we carry them squawking outdoors to a frantic escape.

The jays, on the other hand, would bump into the window two or three times, making distressed calls, then turn their heads toward me and coo sort of mournfully until I picked them up. I would hold them and stroke their feathers for a while, then carry them outside and release them. While in my hands they would stretch their beaks up toward my face, still cooing. I know this sounds ridiculous, but a couple of times I had tears in my eyes thinking that in only a few days I was going to leave these friends. One day I carried it so far as to start planning a container to take two of the jays back to Fort Collins with me. Of course I quickly came to my senses, realizing that they would be even more unhappy than I to leave this place.

The same sort of thing has been happening with the chipmunks. Throughout most of the summer I was pretty rough on them because they would vandalize my cookies, loaves of bread, soda crackers, and whatever else they could find. In the last few weeks, however, I have been purposely leaving the door open and letting them in to scamper around on the floor, up on the table, on the counter and shelves, and have really enjoyed their company. This enjoyment has been mixed with sadness in knowing I won't have it much longer.

This change in my behavior toward these furred and feathered friends was not deliberate. In fact, I've only today given any thought to the reasons behind my feelings for them. And I risk the ridicule of my colleagues by saying that the behavior of the animals has changed along with my own. During the summer the jays and chipmunks usually would not come into the cabin even when I left the door open. It was clear that my presence was a threat to them; they seemed to know that I grew angry when they nibbled my bread. Now, all I have to do is step out the door, and if the birds are around, one or more of them will soon be perched on my shoulder or the back of my hand, whether or not I have brought food. Likewise, the chipmunks will dart in the door as soon as I have opened it, nibble at my shoestrings, or crawl over my shoes, none of which they would do last summer.

What I'm saying, of course, is that I have the unscientific feeling that these animals know I'm leaving and are making friendly gestures during our last days together. Of course, any ecologist worth his salt would not accept that interpretation, and I suppose that deep down I would have to agree. Most likely the animals are reacting to the colder weather, the wind, and the snow cover we have had since October 17. Undoubtedly it is the warmth of my stoves rather than my personality that attracts these creatures into my presence.

Well, for once I can see that the tape is about to run out, so I will, too. I surely hope the chopper gets in tomorrow morning. A delay of one day was not bad at all, but if it becomes routine I certainly will be getting restless.

November 3

Well, this is as big a surprise to me as it may be to you. I'm narrating another day's activities from Brown's Cabin. This morning I got up at six-thirty, had breakfast, made our agreed-upon radio contact with Charlie, and learned that the chopper would be in about nine. I began shutting the boxes and hauling them out to the heliport on the toboggan. I left the radio on in case there were any further instructions, and when I came into the cabin at about nine Charlie was trying to get me. His message was that the Army was not going to send the chopper today and that he would let me know the next plan when we made contact at seven tonight.

After talking with Charlie I remembered a similar situation last spring. The Army was going to fly in the repeater station for the radio so that I could communicate with the outside world. First the delay was for one day, then another day, then a week, and finally three weeks. I strongly urged that they bring the repeater station in by packhorse, which is what they ultimately did. The Army never did make it, and needless to say, I'm beginning to be anxious about the present situation.

Nonetheless, today was a beautiful day, just fantastic, except for some wind in the afternoon. The only problem, really, is that food is dwindling. I've run out of bread and flour to make biscuits or pancakes, two of my staples. I had canned roast beef for lunch. For dinner tonight I plan canned roast beef. And for breakfast tomorrow it will also be canned roast beef.

Despite my impatience and the inconvenience of having to retrieve the gear from the heliport, I decided that life was worth living for at least another day. By ten o'clock I had my cameras unpacked and was headed into the upper part of the basin. I found where the two ptarmigan had roosted overnight—in neat little burrows they had made in the snow—and photographed them. After lunch I went into the timber below the cabin and followed a marten trail for several hundred yards. It was interesting that there were two sets of tracks. One set appeared to be a day or two old, the other only minutes. The two tracks indicated that this marten follows somewhat the same route each time it goes out hunting, checking the same trees on each circuit. Down in the trees I also saw a red squirrel and, for the first time in several weeks, a raven soaring overhead. It looks as though the wild creatures have not vanished after all.

As always, it was exhilarating to be out on the mountain. I have been aware of the beauty of this place daily since my arrival. But since the snow has piled deep and white I can't find the words to describe it. All I can say is that every time I turn my head I see something else that should be photographed.

Even the cold doesn't bother me when I'm outside. When it was this cold last spring I had to bundle up, but today I never wore a cap and only a light down parka, which I kept unzipped. Yet I was quite comfortable even when the wind was blowing 50 miles an hour. Around noon I caught a four-inch-square chunk of snow and ice on the side of the head, and even this did not spoil my enjoyment of the day. The wind kicked up clouds of snow that billowed on the skyline, and often I could see snow streaming in four or five different directions at once. Elsewhere the snow swirled and eddied like dust devils on the plains.

It's late afternoon now, almost time to contact Charlie again, and sort of a lonely time at Brown's Cabin. I was just wondering whether I completed taping my life story, and if so, why. I am almost positive that most of that information is of no interest or use to anyone other than myself, and even there I have my doubts. At the same time, it has been interesting to me, and may even have some bearing on how I lead what is left of my life.

I've been sitting here in the living room keeping up the fire and watching the blowing snow through the window. Although the skies are now gray I still seem to see the brightness of the earlier day and the billowing snow against the blue sky. I looked down at the tape recorder and at a few notes that I've made, and I'm unable to see them as the cabin grows dim. It's been a difficult thing, for some reason, to put all the details of my life on tape, but here at the end I find myself feeling much more relaxed about it than when I began. Certainly I have never before attempted such a thing.

Well, the wind is moving the snow around here and all over the mountains, so I'm going to put on the snowshoes and go out and give the heliport one final packing. If I don't have a solid place for them to land I might spend the remainder of the winter at Brown's Cabin after all.

POSTSCRIPT

Nearly a decade has passed since my time at Brown's Cabin. There have been many changes, both for me and for the cabin.

Charlie Combs did deed the mining claims to me, as he said he would, and I have done my best to maintain the cabin as a refuge of physical rest and spritual refreshment. During the early years I went back more or less regularly, year-round. I snowshoed in four times—twice with Mark and his friends, once with Mark and Gary, and once with just Mark, when we spent several wonderful days snowbound in the cabin. Carol and Mark and I hiked in several times during summer, and once we took a small group of people from our church.

In 1972 I decided to leave a message on a wall of the cabin, and a guest register. The message went in part:

From 1948 until 1966, Brown's Cabin suffered from lack of interest and care. The roof fell in. Passers-by broke up furniture and built fires on an old stove base like the one now under the kitchen range. Smoke drifted up through the caved-in roof.

In 1966, Charlie Combs, who mined with Brown during the mid-30's, staked five 20-acre mining claims. With nostalgia and dedication, Charlie worked hard to restore the cabin to livable conditions. He packed in materials and spent many hours making it possible for you and me to enjoy this historic place.

As a traveler in this spectacular country, you are most welcome to use these facilities. The cabin is beginning to show signs of old age, but I'm sure you appreciate the work of people who cared enough to keep it habitable for the past 87 years.

In its mountain solitude, this is a friendly place. Men and women who pause here can reward this friendship by leaving Brown's Cabin a lit-tle better than it was when they arrived.

These mountains, rough, harsh, and inexorable, have charms more potent than all the 'outside world' of luxury and ease. He on whom Brown's Cabin casts its magic will find no heart to dissolve the spell.

Thank you for your thoughtful care.

The response to this appeal was at first gratifying beyond words. Let me relay some of the early entries in the guest register:

Feb. 18, 1973: Beautiful sunset, dark at 5:30, snow powdery, hard to break trail. Moon rose at 7:30; cold, silent—arrived at 8:30, we love this place. It makes us feel closer, we sure appreciate everyone who made this cabin what it is.

July 8: We feel fortunate to have discovered Brown's cabin. We only re-gret that a cabin of sharing can exist only on a mountain top. Thanks for the experience.

July 25: It was like finding a treasure in the wilderness—so easy to treat like our own home—we love it and will take good care of it.

July 25–26: After two days in this magnificent cabin, I came to realize there are, indeed, honest people left in our world. Thank you for letting it happen.

July 28–29: Today we said our vows under the pines west of the cabin. There Rev. Kaspar pronounced us man and wife. The most beautiful wedding anyone could hope for.

August 5: We loved having hot chocolate . . . by the window . . . before sunset and now by candlelight! . . . The blade broke on the saw. Some of the counselors are returning in a few weeks. We'll bring a replacement. There are more things we'd like to bring. It's such a joy to contribute to an idea like this!

For the first few years, most of the entries in the register had this tone. People wrote inspired prose and cared for the cabin almost as if it were their own.

Then the backpacking craze began, and things began to change.

Hordes of people discovered the mountains. They came in all seasons, and for many reasons, some of which I'm sure I don't understand. They were surely not the same breed of people who visited Brown's Cabin in earlier years.

Disturbing reports began to filter out by way of cabin visitors who knew me. They reported inconsiderate acts, vandalism, ugliness, marijuana, liquor, quarrels, the cutting of *live* trees for wood. Ugly changes in our society seemed to be reaching all the way to timberline. Entries in the guest book degenerated to poor taste and even obscenity.

In the summer of 1974 our son Mark was killed when his car was hit by a drunken driver. After the funeral, Carol, Gary, Sharon, her husband Lou, and I went in to Brown's Cabin for a few days. I have never been back since. The trauma of the trip so soon after Mark's death and the memories of my trips to the cabin with him (Mark hiked in with me thirteen times altogether) have been too vivid.

A little over a year ago I deeded the mining claims to Charlie Comer of Buena Vista, a friend of Charlie Combs whom we both feel will take care of the cabin and who has a legitimate interest in mining the claims.

The Forest Service is still talking of proclaiming the cabin and the old mill a "historical site"; to my knowledge this is still just a plan.

The news about Charlie Combs is mostly good. The day after I left Brown's Cabin, Charlie and Lola returned to Tacoma. About a year later Lola died, and I went to her funeral in Salida, not far from Brown's Cabin. A year or so after that Charlie married a lovely widow of about his age named Opal. He had met her on a hike in the mountains.

Charlie and Opal have made annual treks to the cabin. His emotional visit at the end of my time there was not his last, after all. Charlie still scrambles over the mountains like a kid, despite his sixty-nine years. They have tried to keep the cabin in good repair, but even Charlie is despairing.

Danny Herman has married and moved to Alaska. J. D. and Rosie, his parents, write each Christmas from their home at Taylor Reservoir. Their most recent letter, written by Rosie, arrived about six weeks ago:

Winter has hit here in Taylor Park with lots of snow and wind. In fact we are snowed in except for the snow machines. . . . It would be great to see you again and to have a good visit. If you all ever get over here at Taylor or to Montrose, please stop and see us.

Winter, 1980

INDEX OF PLANTS
AND ANIMALS

A Note on the Type

This book was set in the film version of Electra, a typeface designed by W. A. Dwiggins. The Electra face is a simple and readable type suitable for printing books by present-day processes. It is not based on any historical model, and hence does not echo any particular time or fashion.

Composed, printed, and bound by American Book–Stratford Press, Saddlebrook, New Jersey. Color lithography by Alithochrome, Hauppauge, New York.

Typography and binding design by Virginia Tan

APR   1981